D1029703

International Review of

RESEARCH IN

MENTAL RETARDATION

VOLUME 3

Contributors to This Volume

ALFRED A. BAUMEISTER

SIDNEY W. BIJOU

J. P. DAS

IRMA R. GERJUOY

L. R. GOULET

SAMUEL L. GUSKIN

GEORGE KELLAS

KEITH G. SCOTT

MARCIA STRONG SCOTT

PAUL S. SIEGEL

HOWARD H. SPICKER

JOHN J. WINTERS, JR.

International Review of

RESEARCH IN

MENTAL RETARDATION

EDITED BY

NORMAN R. ELLIS

DEPARTMENT OF PSYCHOLOGY
UNIVERSITY OF ALABAMA
UNIVERSITY, ALABAMA

VOLUME 3

CONSULTING EDITORS FOR THIS VOLUME

Sidney W. Bijou
UNIVERSITY OF ILLINOIS
URBANA, ILLINOIS

Ivar Arnljot Björgen
UNIVERSITY OF OSLO
OSLO, NORWAY

Neil O'Connor
THE MAUDSLEY HOSPITAL
LONDON, ENGLAND

Edward Zigler
YALE UNIVERSITY
NEW HAVEN, CONNECTICUT

1968

ACADEMIC PRESS   New York and London

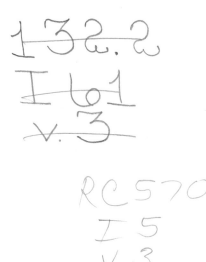

ACADEMIC PRESS INC.
111 Fifth Avenue, New York, New York 10003

United Kingdom Edition published by
ACADEMIC PRESS INC. (LONDON) LTD.
Berkeley Square House, London W.1

LIBRARY OF CONGRESS CATALOG CARD NUMBER: 65-28627

PRINTED IN THE UNITED STATES OF AMERICA

List of Contributors

Numbers in parentheses indicate the pages on which the authors' contributions begin.

ALFRED A. BAUMEISTER, *University of Alabama, University, Alabama* (163)

SIDNEY W. BIJOU, *University of Illinois, Urbana, Illinois* (65)

J. P. DAS, *Utkal University, Bhubaneswar, India* (195)*

IRMA R. GERJUOY, *Department of Psychology, Edward R. Johnstone Training and Research Center, Bordentown, New Jersey* (31)

L. R. GOULET, *Department of Psychology, West Virginia University, Morgantown, West Virginia* (97)

SAMUEL L. GUSKIN, *Department of Special Education, Indiana University, Bloomington, Indiana* (217)

GEORGE KELLAS, *University of Alabama, University, Alabama* (163)

KEITH G. SCOTT, *Children's Research Center, University of Illinois, Champaign, Illinois* (135)

MARCIA STRONG SCOTT, *Children's Research Center, University of Illinois, Champaign, Illinois* (135)

PAUL S. SIEGEL, *Department of Psychology, University of Alabama, University, Alabama* (1)

HOWARD H. SPICKER, *Department of Special Education, Indiana University, Bloomington, Indiana* (217)

JOHN J. WINTERS, JR., *Department of Psychology, Edward R. Johnstone Training and Research Center, Bordentown, New Jersey* (31)

*Present address: Centre for the Study of Mental Retardation, University of Alberta, Edmonton, Canada.

v

Preface

The appearance of three volumes of this serial publication within a three-year period attests to the increased interest of the scientific community in behavioral aspects of mental retardation. A decade ago it is doubtful that material for a single volume could have been gleaned, and its audience would have been diminutive as compared to the present one. Scholarly activities in mental retardation have grown from a few scattered efforts, mainly by-products of clinical functions, into an elaborate and concerted enterprise with footing in the academy as well as the clinic.

Though behavioral research in this field is far from mature, it shows signs of healthy growth. Generally, current investigations are characterized by sophisticated experimental designs, quantitative results, and occasionally by theoretical relevance. The study of the retardate promises to provide theoretically useful information about individual differences wherever they occur. On the other hand, there is a glimmer of application of laboratory findings to the training and care of the retardate. Treatment programs in institutions are beginning to exploit "operant procedures." Perhaps more aptly they have begun to use a common sense version of the empirical law of effect. Moreover, other concepts from the behavioral laboratory sometimes make their way into the clinic or classroom. In view of the paucity of sound methods of remediation in mental retardation more and more attempts to inveigle useful principles from basic research findings can be expected.

The purpose of this serial publication is to provide current accounts of scholarly efforts in the behavioral sciences as they bear on mental retardation. It is hoped that it reflects the state of scientific activities in a veridical manner.

University, Alabama
February, 1968

NORMAN R. ELLIS

Contents

Incentive Motivation in the Mental Retardate

PAUL S. SIEGEL

Development of Lateral and Choice-Sequence Preferences

IRMA R. GERJUOY AND JOHN J. WINTERS, JR.

Studies in the Experimental Development of Left-Right Concepts in Retarded Children Using Fading Techniques

SIDNEY W. BIJOU

Verbal Learning and Memory Research with Retardates: An Attempt to Assess Developmental Trends

L. R. GOULET

Research and Theory in Short-Term Memory

KEITH G. SCOTT AND MARCIA STRONG SCOTT

Reaction Time and Mental Retardation

ALFRED A. BAUMEISTER AND GEORGE KELLAS

Mental Retardation in India: A Review of Care, Training, Research, and Rehabilitation Programs

J. P. Das

Educational Research in Mental Retardation

SAMUEL L. GUSKIN AND HOWARD H. SPICKER

Contents of Previous Volumes

Incentive Motivation in the
Mental Retardate[1]

PAUL S. SIEGEL

DEPARTMENT OF PSYCHOLOGY, UNIVERSITY OF ALABAMA, UNIVERSITY, ALABAMA

I. INTRODUCTION

You'll get no argument from anyone, scientist or citizen, about the efficacy of rewards and punishments. Rewards encourage and facilitate, punishments deter and inhibit. But whereas this loose generalization is sufficient for the citizen, it is not for the scientist. The serious student of behavior has sought, and secured in part, answers to such questions as: Do larger rewards (in a quantitative sense) exert a greater influence? Do different rewards (in a qualitative sense) affect behavior differently? Is it learning that is influenced or just action at the moment? Can incentives be meaningfully scaled? What particular aspects of behavior respond to variation in the characteristics of the reward? In what manner do incentives relate to such "inner states" as wants, desires, and needs, social and biological? These questions, and others of a related sort, have been posed many times in the laboratory of the psychologist. And a substantial literature on both the human and the infrahuman subject has accumulated. It is the purpose of the present article to review that segment of the literature that bears directly on mental

[1] Preparation of this article was supported in part by U. S. Public Health Service Grant HD124.

1

retardation. Specifically, experimental studies will be critically reviewed that have manipulated the contingencies or consequences of action variously termed "rewards," "punishments," "incentives," "lures," "reinforcers," and "goal-objects," and have recorded some concomitantly varying aspect of behavior in one or more groups of subjects bearing the clinical diagnosis of mental retardation. This article will be concerned exclusively with questions relating to reward quality and quantity. Space limitations prohibit a consideration of the cognate issue of temporal delay of reward. At this writing (1967), it appears likely that the theoretical account of the latter will require additional assumptions (Spence, 1956). The role of success and failure experiences is also taken to be another story, one that has been told recently and well by Cromwell (1963).

Exhaustive coverage of the literature is intended,[2] but in this age of rapidly proliferating publication vehicles, this must remain a hope. Here and there, contact will be made with the broader literature on the normal child and the infrahuman. A final section will attempt synthesis and will examine the theoretical status of the issue.

Dismay will accompany the realization by some that the present article fails to recognize the often-made distinction between rewards and incentives; between reinforcement and incentive motivation. It seems to this writer that, to date, this distinction has been poorly drawn and quickly grows fuzzy. The argument here seems to be largely a matter of whether or not "incentive" sneaks "purpose" into the picture. It does. But the action of rewards must be conceptualized ultimately in just such terms. Whether one speaks of reinforcement, the action of rewards, or incentive motivation the basic problem remains that of accounting for the earlier "direction" lent behavior by events that occur later in time. Of necessity, "anticipation" or "purpose" must be wrestled with. Recent theorizing by Spence (1956, 1960) and by Mowrer (1960) indicates how this can be done without introducing teleology.

II. AN HISTORICAL ANTECEDENT

Perhaps the earliest systematic concern with the role of incentive variation in relation to the behavior of the mentally retarded should be credited to Aldrich and Doll (1931). These investigators posed modified Köhler-type box-stacking problems and utilized as overhead lures a ball, ball plus cookie, and a banana. By contemporary standards this study would be described as a loose one. Nevertheless, certain contribu-

[2]Through about August 1966.

tions were made and should be recognized. Their use of persistence at the task as a motivational measure is of methodological interest and their observations of occasional sudden solution (insight?) and the sometimes exaggeration of maladaptive effort with increased lure attraction invite notice.

III. THE BRITISH STUDIES

Utilizing either the Leg Persistence Test or the Nail Frame Task, a group of British investigators has been concerned with incentive motivation in the severely retarded for a number of years. The Leg Persistence Test requires of the subject that he persevere in holding his unsupported leg in suspension over a chair. The Nail Frame Task is a dexterity-speed test requiring the subject to insert escutcheon pins in holes arranged in columns in a metal sheet. The two tasks would seem to differ in intrinsic appeal with the latter affording more in the way of challenge and freedom from the quick onset of physical fatigue and boredom. These studies are clearly interrelated and can be treated as a unit.

Gordon, O'Connor, and Tizard (1954) found continuous verbal encouragement to exert a facilitating influence on the leg suspension task relative to controls simply instructed beforehand to do as well as possible. Even greater persistence at the task was observed with the presentation of a tangible goal (a progress "barometer"). The authors also report an interesting small positive correlation (.355) between IQ and initial performance on this task. When groups were shifted from one incentive condition to another, a "sequence" effect was observed: The shift to the less effective condition did not markedly weaken performance, and the shift to the more effective one failed to raise it to the level achieved by Ss started out under the stronger condition. After an 8-week layoff, Ss were reexamined under control conditions (told to do well). Performance related more strongly to that observed during the initial incentive condition than to performance seen under the switched condition, suggesting a kind of primacy effect. In what amounted to a better controlled partial replication of this study, Walton and Begg (1958) found competition and continuous verbal encouragement to be more effective than either the control condition (initial instructions to do well) or the tangible goal condition. They feel that this finding lends support to the argument of Loos and Tizard (1955) that "self-esteem" is a potent motivational variable in improving or sustaining the performance of the severely retarded. Over the course of 20 daily 1-hour trials, Walton and Begg noted, overall, a deterioration of performance and great variability between subjects and between trials.

A second experiment by Gordon, O'Connor, and Tizard (1955) utilized the Nail Frame Task and the four conditions—control, team competition, individual competition, and a tangible goal. This last was again found to be the most effective (highest pin-placing rate). And a shift from other conditions to this one served to improve performance. A later study by O'Connor and Claridge (1955) using the same subjects and the same task found remarkably good "recall" in the sense that the four groups exhibited an initial performance highly correlated with their records of a year earlier. Three groups, matched on the basis of this initial performance, were formed and run under the conditions: control (told to do well), tangible goal (performance goal displayed) with strong verbal encouragement, and tangible goal with indifference expressed by E. Over a series of daily 1-hour sessions, the verbally encouraged tangible goal group exhibited the strongest performance; the control, the weakest. The group experiencing tangible goal without verbal encouragement fell in between. The authors conclude that "self-competition" (tangible goal unsupported by verbal encouragement) is scarcely a potent motivator; goal-striving, per se, should not be taken to be a significant factor.

Again utilizing the Nail Frame Task, O'Connor and Claridge (1958) obtained a Crespi Effect (Crespi, 1942) with severely retarded Ss. After performing for 10 daily 1-hour trials under a weak incentive condition (instructed beforehand to do well), half of 20 Ss were shifted to a strong incentive condition (visual display of performance goal plus verbal encouragement); the other half continued under the weak condition. Half of 20 additional Ss were shifted from the initially strong incentive condition to the weak condition with the other 10 continuing under the strong condition. Within this factorial design, the weak-to-strong shift was accompanied by a performance surge that exceeded the level manifested by the strong-to-strong control (Crespi's "elation"). And the effect persisted for seven additional daily 1-hour sessions. Subjects shifted from the strong to the weak condition revealed very little deterioration in performance, continuing well above the weak-to-weak control for the full 8-day course. It is the feeling of the authors that the highly monotonous and fatiguing characteristics of the task exercised a potent role in generating "elation."

The British studies teach two lessons: First, the severely retarded retain considerable sensitivity to social influence. Whether or not conceptual clarity is enhanced by appeal to "self-esteem" remains to be explored. Second, there is methodological meat in the demonstration that the laboratory task is not free of influence from earlier experimental assignments (and, by implication, from the broader experiential history of the subject).

IV. THE PEABODY STUDIES

Several studies cluster by virtue of what might be termed the "Peabody influence." Almost all were actually conducted in the Peabody laboratories and almost all were conceived in the Hull-Spence tradition.

Cantor and Hottel (1955) assigned high and low IQ groups (medians about 57 and 36, respectively) to subgroups receiving one or four peanuts as reward in a two-choice discrimination task. In a noncorrection procedure, Ss were instructed to find the peanut(s) by lifting one of two boxes which presented either an upright or an inverted triangle as discriminanda. An analysis of error score over 48 trials revealed no differential reinforcement effect, an IQ effect, and, significantly, an experimenter effect (two were used). The last is readily taken to be an unwanted effect, possibly related to the social deprivation hypothesis of Zigler and Stevenson (treated in a later section).

Ellis and Pryer (1958) employed two groups of severely retarded Ss (mean IQ about 32) in a two-choice object-form discrimination task reinforcing one group with a jelly bean; the other with a 1-in. square of yellow drawing paper. It was the a priori conviction of these investigators that the two incentives differed strongly in value but they exhibited some uncertainty as to the proper conceptual specification of the paper square. It was variously described as a "secondary reward," "practically valueless," and providing "social reinforcement." Across successive blocks of learning trials, the two groups failed to separate in mean number of correct responses. Both manifested improvement, and with the establishment of extinction conditions, the performance of both deteriorated. The authors recognized a possible complication arising out of distraction attending the manipulation of the jelly bean. In a later study, Ellis and Distefano (1959) employed two matched IQ groups (mean about 52) on the pursuitmeter. One group was simply instructed beforehand to ". . . try to make as high a score as you can"; the other was continuously urged on and praised during task performance. Over successive trial blocks the two separated reliably and predictably in mean time-on-target. Still later Ellis (1962) varied reward quantity, engaging the mental retardate (average IQ about 46) in a plunger-pulling task (Lindsley manipulandum). Subjects, all smokers, were reinforced with either one cigarette or three within a fixed-ratio

(FR) requirement that started out at FR-1 (one response per reinforcement) and increased gradually to FR-128 (128 responses per reinforcement). With IQ partialed out, the low reward group exhibited a reliably higher mean response rate during conditioning and resisted extinction more strongly (but not reliably so). A second experiment permitted Ss to first declare a reinforcement option (cigarettes or penny candy). One group then worked for the single reward; the other for three. These Ss (mean IQ about 30) were taken through FR-1 to FR-64 and then extinguished. Again the low reward group yielded a higher mean response rate during conditioning but, this time, slightly less resistance to extinction. The latter is disappointing. The suggestive finding of quicker extinction of the high reward group in the first experiment fits quite neatly the frustration hypothesis of Amsel (1962), i.e., the experience of greater reward is the occasion for greater "disappointment" when it is withdrawn; hence more rapid extinction. The extent to which the IQ differential observed in the two experiments (mean of 30 versus mean of 46) can account for the contradiction in extinction findings may be pondered.

In offering the subject a reward option, Ellis made a modest methodological advance over earlier studies which leaned exclusively on the intuitive specification of incentive strength. Heber (1959) took a further stride. His subjects worked for prizes of their own choosing from among a wide variety which included such items as a pair of socks, a quarter, jelly beans, and a pack of cigarettes. In the ordering of choices, strong individual differences were expressed. Some stability over time was suggested by the finding that most Ss made the same initial selection 1 week later. On the basis of performance on the Sequin Form Board, two matched groups (IQ range from 41 to 68) were formed. The Minnesota Spatial Relations Test was elected as the criterion task. One group, the low reward group, was reinforced with the promise of their seventeenth prize choice; the other, the high reward group, with the promise of their first choice. Twelve trials were administered with marbles (one or three) given as token rewards at the end of each trial. Following the twelfth trial, the marbles were cashed for the agreed upon tangible prize. The two groups separated predictably and reliably in speed of responding (reciprocal of latency). They were then switched: the high to the low incentive condition; the low to the high. Six additional trials were administered. The high-to-low shift was accompanied by an immediate marked deterioration in performance, and this may be reasonably attributed to the motivational change. The low-to-high group exhibited further improvement. The experimental design does not permit a choice between learning and motivation in the interpretation of this last finding. The required low-to-low control was not conducted, and inspection of the curve suggests that an asymptote had not been reached at the time of the switch.

In examining the effect of certain incentive conditions on the reaction time of mental retardates (IQ range from 50 to 74), Wolfensberger (1960) made further application of Heber's preference technique. Subjects were permitted to order their choices among such prizes as candy, sunglasses, balls, rings, billfolds, combs, and jewelry. It was then requested of S that he work "well and fast" at the task of releasing a button in response to a buzzer. A ready signal (green light) cued S to depress the button. The interval between this signal and the buzzer was varied randomly in a series that consisted of five blocks of five trials each. Reinforcement was delivered by E at the end of each block. Variations in the last operation distinguished five groups. One was rewarded with a tangible prize of his choice which E dropped in a box before him. A second group was reinforced symbolically in the sense that pieces of black construction paper of little intrinsic value were deposited in the box with the understanding that they could be cashed in later for prizes of choice. Each S of a third group began the session with five prizes before him. He was told that he could keep these unless he "worked poorly" on the button; this being a condition that would prompt E to take away prizes. A fourth group worked under threat of loss of paper chips for poor performance. The conceptual distinction between the last two conditions is a bit murky. Wolfensberger used the descriptions "concrete punishment" and "symbolic punishment," respectively. A fifth group served as a control motivated only by the initial instructions to work fast. Reaction times increased significantly across the five trial blocks, but the various groups did not separate reliably. Wolfensberger recognized the possible overriding effect of social factors. The control group did exhibit the slowest reaction times over all, and inspection of Wolfensberger's data summary suggests that a statistical comparison with the other four (pooled) would probably turn up significant results.

The Peabody studies are certainly not without merit but at this stage of our knowledge certain conceptual and methodological flaws are readily discerned: (a) Time-independent measures such as error score are characteristically insensitive to wide variation in a given motivational condition (cf. Kimble, 1961; Pubols, 1960). (b) The between-groups design or absolute method, which permits the subject to experience but a single value of the incentive is a weak instrument for sensing differential incentive effects (Bower, 1961; Harlow & Meyer, 1952; Pubols, 1960; Schrier, 1958). (c) In the short-term or acute-type study, the novelty of the task may provide motivation potent enough to completely overshadow the relevant incentive condition. (d) It is not enough to assume that the social variable acts as a kind of neutral constant across conditions. Social effects can be powerful enough to override and totally obscure the contribution made by visible independent variables which, in final description, may turn out to be quite puny by contrast (Bijou & Sturges, 1959). (e) The experimenter-defined strength of a reinforcer may enjoy only weak correlation with the subject's preference. Intuitive specification of incentive variation can lead the investigator into the error of manipulating specious incentive differences.

V. EFFORTS AT SCALING INCENTIVES

Sophisticated solution to the problem of incentive effects upon performance and/or learning presupposes that the incentive is scaled in some meaningful sense. Minimum requirements demand that the scale possess definitional independence of the behavior that is predicted or explained and that it fulfill at least the criteria of ordinal measurement (connectedness, asymmetry, and transitivity). The ready availability of the physical scales of weight, amount, and number provides quick solution if it is incentive quantity that is of interest. Perhaps this is why almost every study of incentive motivation in the infrahuman has manipulated quantity. It does not follow, however, that the physical unit relates linearly to the behavior measure. The early work with monkeys of Harlow and Meyer (1952) and of Fay, Miller, and Harlow (1953) suggests strongly that, at least as far as food amounts are concerned, this assumption is untenable. It was log amount that was found to bear a linear relation to their behavior measure.

The scaling of incentive "quality" is a different matter. There exists no convenient physical scale to which quality can be immediately coordinated. By the very nature of things this dimension is subject-based and must be known in terms of some measure of preference. Significantly, preference occupies a level of abstraction sufficient to encompass quantity as well as quality; i.e., amount, weight, number, etc., can also be ordered in this fashion, and perhaps should be when used in a psychological context.

Harlow and Meyer (1952) and later Fay *et al.* (1953) seem to have pioneered the scaling of incentives utilizing the monkey and the psychophysical method of paired comparisons. Others have followed suit (cf. Cho & David, 1957; Warren, 1958). It was noted above that Heber (1959) and Wolfensberger (1960) in their studies of incentive effects in the mental retardate engaged in an elementary scaling procedure when they permitted their subjects to order their preferences among various tangible prizes. Witryol and his collaborators (Witryol & Fischer, 1960; Witryol, Tyrrell, & Lowden, 1964, 1965), in working with children, have given considerable attention to this issue. In their procedure each incentive is paired once with every other across successive trials and the subject permitted to either point to his choice (nonconsummation) or take possession of and cumulate his choices (consummation). They found the method to be reliable, and they have reported substantial agreement with preferences expressed in a five-choice discrimination task. They have also noted age, sex, and individual differences. A study by Tyrrell, Witryol, and Silverg (1963) found the preferences of mental retardates (MA range, 3 years 4 months to 4 years 6 months; CA range, 6 years 1 month to 17 years 10 months) among bubble gum, balloon, charm, marble, and paper clip to be in good agreement with preferences for the same prizes expressed by "normal" children (estimated mean MA, 4 years 11 months; mean CA, 3 years 11 months).

Siegel, Forman, and Williams (1967) gave opportunity to institutionalized mental retardates (IQ range from 38 to 69) to work for 10 minutes daily for the tangible incentives of a penny, miniature Tootsie Roll, Chiclet, candy corn, small lock washer, or nothing. These reinforcers were presented within a paired comparisons series with choice signaled by the operation of one of two associated Lindsley manipulanda. The first choice made daily and the proportion of total work output (work index) were utilized as scaling measures. Both indices rank-ordered the incentives from high to low: penny, Tootsie Roll, candy corn or Chiclet, washer, and nothing. A repetition of the test series with 19 Ss established satisfactory test—retest reliabilities. In a second and validating phase, Ss performed on a two-choice discrimination task in which the choice of one member of each of four pairs of junk objects was reinforced with a highly valued reinforcer, the Tootsie Roll; the other with a low valued reinforcer, the lock washer. Approximately half the Ss came to respond consistently to pair members associated with the Tootsie Roll; the other half expressed random choices. It was found that the preference for the Tootsie Roll over the washer, as reflected in the difference between the two work indexes, was reliably stronger for the learners.

Within an ambitious comprehensive research proposal designed to assess reinforcement functions in the retardate, Orlando (1966) described an ingenious method well suited to determine the preference value of various tangible (and possibly intangible) reinforcers. The subject is required to press one or more times a window (key) which gives access to a choice situation; four smaller windows (keys) light up

and each is distinctively identified with the picture of a particular reinforcer. The subject may then secure the reinforcer of choice by pressing
the appropriate window. The reinforcer is dispensed automatically, the
four-choice stimuli disappear, and the access stimulus comes on again,
permitting repetition of the sequence. When preferences have stabilized
over daily sessions, a controlled-choice procedure is instituted. The
most highly preferred reinforcer is removed and choice permitted
among the remaining three. The next preferred is then removed and
choice permitted between the remaining two. Each missing reinforcer
is then, in turn, put back into the array. The method seems a powerful
one for establishing individual preference hierarchies. In pilot studies
which afforded choice among a penny, M & M, a small trinket, and a
single Cheerio, Orlando found that his Ss expressed one of four preference patterns: one choice predominated to the near-total exclusion of
the others, one predominated but a second preference was exhibited
with a significant frequency, choices were ordered among all four, or
random responding obtained.

VI. SOCIAL REINFORCEMENT

This problem area has been extensively explored, largely by Harold
Stevenson, Edward Zigler, their students, and their associates. It has
become a story in itself. The recent comprehensive reviews by both
Stevenson (1965) and Zigler (1966) suggest that detailed treatment in the
article would prove redundant. However, the implications of this research are worth noting, and a summary of Zigler's most recent conclusions (1966) is given below, where the empirical account is also brought
up to date.

Zigler has suggested that, at this stage in the game, the following
hypotheses can be entertained, at least tentatively: (a) Institutionalized
retardates suffer relatively greater deprivation of adult approval and
affection, hence are more strongly motivated to secure both. (b) They
also possess stronger negative-reaction tendencies because of earlier
frequent punitive encounters with adults. (c) Pre-institution history and
the effects of institutionalization work jointly to shape the mental retardate's motivational system; the issue is complicated by the absence of
uniformity in institutional practices. (d) The position of reinforcers in
the retardate's hierarchy is determined largely by environmental events
occurring in the institutional setting. (e) Institutionalized retarded have
learned to expect and settle for less success than the normal child.
(f) The retardate, possessing little in the way of inner resources that he

can trust, is likely to be more strongly influenced by the immediate environmental situation.

— Butterfield and Zigler (1965) have quite recently examined the effect of differing institutional climates on the mental retardate's persistence at the task of sorting marbles. Subjects (mean IQ about 57) were drawn from two residential schools operated under quite different philosophies. Institution A provided a homelike environment, imposing few external controls and providing considerable personal freedom and opportunity for individual responsibility. Contrasting sharply, institution B placed emphasis upon external controls and provided very little personal freedom. A group of subjects from each institution sorted marbles into blue and yellow holes with social support from an experimenter who smiled and expressed verbal approval on every tenth response. Two other groups, one from each institution, performed under nonsupport conditions (E withheld approval). Interaction between institutional setting and reinforcement was predicted by the investigators who reasoned that social approval should exert a greater positive influence upon Ss drawn from the "more depriving" social milieu, institution B. Variance analysis of time spent at the task (actually a log transformation) yielded a statistically significant institution effect but nonsignificance in the instance of both reinforcement and interaction. A second study utilizing a larger sample (mean IQ about 52) was carried out under the support condition (only) with experimenters (two) naive with respect to both theoretical expectancy and institution differences. Mean log time at the task was found to relate reliably to institution but not to E. However, interaction between E and institution was statistically significant. —

Terrell and Stevenson (1965) studied the rate of marble dropping in normal and retarded male subjects as affected by verbal reinforcement delivered by normal or retarded social agents. The normal subjects (IQ range from 96 to 122) and the retarded (IQ range from 60 to 89) were recruited from elementary grades one through three. Each child first served as subject and then as reinforcing agent. To insure familiarity with each other's academic and classroom social status, subject and reinforcing agent were both drawn from the same class. Reinforcement consisted of verbalizing the encouraging statements: "fine," "good," "very good," and "that's good." No reliable effects upon the marble dropping rate were turned up. However, a second study of similar design was successful. Subjects were drawn from grades four through six (male and female this time); IQs ranged from 99 to 141 in normal Ss and from 53 to 86 in retarded Ss. Over all (main effect), the normal social reinforcer was found to exert greater influence upon the marble dropping rate of all Ss. This differential was shown to be stronger in the instance of the normal subject (interaction between type of S and type of reinforcing agent) and in the instance of the female subject (interaction between sex of S and type of reinforcing agent). The authors argued cogently that the data make a strong case for a prestige dimension to social reinforcement.

Fagot (1966) has shown that type of experimental task may interact with verbal (social) reinforcement. Verbal reinforcement was found to be effective in bringing about a change in initial position preference in both a two-hole marble dropping task and a gun-two-targets setup, but the two change scores failed to correlate reliably. Subjects were normal children.

Much, but not all, of the experimental work in this area has taken the form of assessing the interaction of various factors with praise statements in influencing the behavior of the subject in the marble dropping or marble sorting task. Certain features of the method, as practiced by some investigators, have drawn criticism from Parton and Ross (1965). Their strictures possess considerable generality and will bear summary here: Typically, the increase in traffic with an initially less preferred hole, now verbally (or by gesture) reinforced, is taken as evidence for the positive effect of social reinforcement. Reliance upon too brief a base period of observation (unreliable estimate of operant level) coupled with the failure to conduct a nonreinforced control can introduce a confounding of the reinforcing operation with the statistical artifact of regression to the mean, or with some time trend such as warm-up. Of more than passing interest in this connection, Bijou and Oblinger (1960) have related operant or base level to IQ, sex, age, and social history. They gave opportunity to their subjects to pick up and drop a ball repeatedly through a hole in the absence of identifiable reinforcement. The number of responses made by the subject before satiation (and cessation) set in was found to be greater in retardates than in normals, females than males, and older than younger. In their analysis this activity was sustained by reinforcing properties inherent in the fixed physical and social characteristics of the task situation. And they speculated on possible relations of their findings to social and educational histories. Parton and Ross suggested that developmental characteristics may interact with the dependent variable to vitiate conclusions about social reinforcement. For example, very young children are more prone to exhibit position preferences. This could base them at a lower level, providing more room for preference change. They also lament the absence of sensitivity to the adaptive significance of various reinforcement schedules and to the subject's interpretation of the demands of the task and the investigator.

Witryol and Alexander (1962) directly manipulated social influence in a study of normal preschool children's expressed preferences for certain tangible incentives. An initial paired-comparisons series established the high-to-low mean order of choice as small plastic charm, bubble gum, balloon, marble, and paper clip. Nine to 20 days later the series was repeated. This time whenever the paper clip was presented, E said: "All of the other children like the paper clip best. Which do you like best, _____ or paper clip?" In this condition, the mean rating of paper clip was found to be second only to the charm. The shift from last to second place is taken by the investigators as evidence for social enhancement—an interpretation that seems quite likely but is a bit weakened by the absence of control for "spontaneous" change during the interpolated interval.

Hollis (1965a) has attempted assessment of the reinforcement effectiveness of various well-defined forms of social interaction. He provided opportunity for institutionalized preadolescent and adolescent profoundly retarded male and female children to interact with an adult human experimenter (the "stimulus-person") in a "free field." When approached by the subject, the "stimulus-person" executed one of the following reactions: passive response (E essentially disregarded S), playful response (E tickled, pushed, pulled at S), petting (E held S and stroked his hands, arms, legs, or face), signaling (E gestured to S, called him by name, held and talked to him), and withdrawal (E turned away and crouched in a corner). The investigator states that social stimulation was made contingent upon the subject's approach response. How this arrangement was accomplished in the instance of the signaling condition is not apparent to this reader. In the description, this action would seem to be one initiated by E; hence, independent of S's behavior. The duration of S's physical contact with the stimulus-person was taken to be the principal measure of reinforcement effectiveness and was found to be greatest for the signaling action. Petting, play, passive reaction, and withdrawal followed in that order. During two of the social interactions, petting and signaling, E "held" the subject. This appears to be a contamination of the dependent variable serious enough to vitiate conclusions based upon the duration of S's voluntary contact with E.

VII. DISCRIMINATION LEARNING AND THE INCENTIVE

Three reviews of discrimination learning in the mental retardate have been published within the last few years (Denny, 1964; Ross, 1966; Stevenson, 1963). In general, the evidence supports the existence of a discrimination learning deficit in the retardate. More often than not, the mentally retarded have exhibited performance inferior to normal controls, and this is seen even in studies that have employed the MA match. Zeaman and House have devoted more than 10 years to the development of a theoretical account of discrimination learning that readily accommodates the MR deficit. The theory finds its fullest explication in a chapter in the *Handbook of Mental Deficiency* (1963). Theirs is a two-stage model. The subject must first learn to attend to the relevant dimension (a class of cues) and then, in a second stage, learn to associate the instrumental or approach response with a particular cue (one member of the class). It is in the first stage that Zeaman and House place the peculiar weakness of the mental retardate. Earlier, less complete versions of the theory have stimulated a good deal of research. Especially germane to the topic under review here are the studies of Shepp (1962, 1963, 1964) designed to explore the cue properties of incentives. In the 1962 study, the basic strategy was that of manipulating rewards in a two-choice discrimination task in such a way as to lend distinctiveness to position (right or left), a dimension rendered irrelevant to problem solution, hence defeating should the subject elect to respond to it. He showed that the use of distinctively different rewards on the two sides (chocolate candy kiss versus a small marshmallow) slowed the learning of a simultaneous junk-object discrimination relative to controls experiencing a conventional procedure that presented the same reward for a correct response to either side. A third group reinforced with a variety of candies on the two sides (inconsistent association of incentive with position) failed to achieve the expected superiority over the double-reward group.

In two-choice successive discrimination learning, a pair of identical cues can be presented on each trial. If one pair requires the subject to choose the left member and the other pair the right, positional accent should facilitate learning. In the same study Shepp found this to be so. Subjects enjoying the consistent association of a distinctive reward with each of the two positions learned the successive discrimination more rapidly than controls experiencing a random assortment of rewards.

The 1963 study employed as discriminanda distinctive candies (miniature marshmallow and an M & M). These were displayed atop the covers of two "foodwells" of a modified Wisconsin General Test Apparatus. The relation of the discriminanda to the reward actually obtained by lifting the "correct" cover distinguished three groups: Group P (positive transfer) was rewarded with a candy that matched the positive cue, Group N with a candy that matched the negative cue, Group C with a candy dissimilar to both cues (Hershey's Kiss). The three groups separated in performance in the order P, C, and N, from best to worst. In the final study (Shepp, 1964), four groups of mental retardates learned a two-choice simultaneous discrimination. For one group, discriminanda consisted of a pair of junk objects (multidimensional); for the other, the discriminanda combined only color and form (color — form discrimination). It was felt that the junk objects represented a richer source of relevant cues. Each of these two major groups was divided into two subgroups. In one subgroup a correct response was rewarded on one side with a candy kiss and on the other side with a miniature marshmallow. The other subgroup, essentially a control, was consistently rewarded with a single kind of candy (either the candy kiss or the marshmallow) for correct choices when made to either side. The learning series randomized the positional presentation of the correct stimulus. Shepp hypothesized that the learning of the two subgroups experiencing "distinctive incentive-position stimuli" (candy kiss when correct on the left; marshmallow when correct on the right) should be impaired because of undue attention given the irrelevant position cue. Further, this interfering effect should be stronger in the color — form task because of the lessened number of relevant cues. His results confirmed both predictions. Shepp's account puts the emphasis squarely on attention and cue-distinctiveness. Siegel and Forman (1967) have offered an alternative interpretation, one more strongly motivational in character. They suggested that the impaired learning of the double-incentive group may arise out of an imbalance in the "demandedness" of the two rewards. If the candy kiss is more strongly valued, the subject simply fails to yield solution to a problem that requires him to abandon the favored choice half the time. And it was noted that, if he should totally fixate the favored side, the partial reinforcement schedule involved assures him of the "better" reward fifty percent of the time. Utilizing 56 institutionalized retardates (mean IQ 46), this interpretation was examined in a two-choice simultaneous junk-object discrimination that replicated the Shepp procedure. Two groups were formed, distinguished by a difference in the degree of imbalance in the preference value of the two rewards. Group RE (rewards equal) was reinforced for correct choices on one side with a piece of candy corn and on the other side with a Chiclet. For the other group, group RU (rewards unequal), correct choices were reinforced on one side with a penny and on the other side with a small lock washer. An earlier scaling study of a related population had established the approximate equality in preference value of the candy corn and Chiclet and the marked preference dominance of the penny over the washer (Siegel et al., 1967a). In good agreement with the motivational or conflict interpretation, fewer members of group RU mastered the problem, their errors piled up disproportionately on the penny side, and more subjects fixated (the penny side).

VIII. POTPOURRI

There remains a handful of studies not readily encompassed by the topical organization of this article. Inclusion within the present section is dictated solely by this consideration and should not be taken to be evaluative or as denying the systematic value of these experiments.

Hunt and Patterson (1957) have suggested that verbal urging plus candy improves performance on the Goodenough Draw-a-Man Test.

Stevenson and Knights (1961) hypothesized that the number of stimulus elements necessary to produce a response is negatively correlated with intellectual ability. They introduced bright normal children and retardates to a "television game" in which presentation on the screen of a line drawing was made contingent upon the pressing of a button(s). The subject was told to press the button to see an animal picture and left to his own devices for 10 minutes. The picture was presented on an average of once every 10 responses (VR-10), and the experimental design varied the duration of exposure (½ vs 2 seconds), the number of differing visual stimuli (one vs five), and the number of response alternatives (one vs five buttons). Over all, the response rate of the MR was initially lower than the normal and it declined more slowly. No main effects were found to be statistically reliable, but the interactions were. Contrary to theoretical expectation, more responses were made in the condition of longer exposure duration. The experiment was a short-term one and it is possible that visual reinforcement effects were partially obscured by task novelty.

Hollis (1965b) first allowed 12 severely retarded girls (mean CA about 121 months) to solve bent-wire problems utilizing candy or Coca Cola as incentives. Half the group was shifted to social reinforcement (*E* stroked the head of the subject lightly and expressed verbal approbation) and half to a condition of no reinforcement. Both were later shifted back to the candy–Coca Cola reward. Reliable differences in starting time, problem-completion time, and number of correct solutions were seen only in the no reinforcement condition. All subjects entered this experiment well-rehearsed and this may have imposed a ceiling on performance, thus permitting change only in the downward direction.

McManis (1965) examined young retardates (IQ range 58–85) and normal fifth- and sixth-grade children (IQ range 85–115) for accuracy on the pursuit-rotor under the following verbal-incentive conditions: neutral ("Do your best"), reproof (during rest periods S reproved for "poor" performance), praise (during rest periods S praised for his performance), and competition (two Ss alternated at the task with E urging each to best the other). A persistence score was obtained in a final session that afforded opportunity for S to continue voluntary trials. For both groups, the accuracy rank order of treatments was found to be competition, praise, reproof, and neutral—from high to low. The retardates performed less accurately under all four conditions, but this difference was also seen prior to treatment. McManis reported the additional trends: stronger effect of treatment on both accuracy and persistence in the male, stronger relation of IQ to accuracy in the female, and less persistence at the task for all Ss under the reproof treatment.

In an exploratory study of plunger-pulling for edibles, Spradlin, Girardeau, and Corte (1965) found no variation in response rate accompanying the presentation of six differing reinforcers: M & M's, grapes, corn chips, cheese sticks, maraschino cherries, and mints. Two of their 15 profoundly or severely retarded subjects did respond with a rate increase when mildly food-deprived (17-hour overnight fast).

Baumeister and Ward (1967) gave institutionalized retardates (mean IQ 62; mean CA 18.9) 20 reaction time trials under instructions to react quickly (key release) to a tone. Each S then competed with his base record for 20 additional trials under one of the following four motivational treatments: bell signal for success, E's verbalized "good" for success, bell plus two pennies for success, or a control condition in which success went unrecognized. With the exception of the control, all groups exhibited improvement with bell plus pennies showing the strongest effect. In a second experiment, improved reaction time was shown to accompany the introduction of the condition bell plus penny for success, and further improvement with the condition bell plus five cents, and performance deterioration with incentive removal.

Siegel, Williams, and Forman (1967b) demonstrated a reliable relation between incentive or reward "quality" and response rate in a marble dropping task. For each 10 responses (FR-10), the retardate (IQ 35 – 59) was rewarded with either a small washer (low in preference value) or a penny (high in preference value). The shift from the low to the high incentive condition yielded a rate increase, whereas the shift from high to low produced little change. Extinction accompanied the withdrawal of these tangible reinforcers.

Giles and Wolf (1966) have reported wide individual differences in the effectiveness of various positive reinforcers in the management of toilet habits in institutionalized severely retarded Ss. Reinforcing operations effective with one S were sometimes found to be neutral or even aversive to another. Several of the reinforcing operations they devised were quite ingenious (a ride in a wheelchair, a warm shower, etc.).

Perry and Stotsky (1965) failed to turn up significant differences among mentally retarded (IQ 52−89; CA 16−42 years), physically handicapped, and graduate student groups all performing on a bolt-assembly task while rewarded materially (nickels given) or nonmaterially (rating or grade assigned). However, retardates achieved asymptotic performance more rapidly under material reward conditions than did controls.

IX. SOME GENERAL METHODOLOGICAL CONSIDERATIONS

The study of incentive motivation in the mentally retarded is plagued with problems of experimental control more than most other areas of psychological inquiry. One of the richest sources of confounding resides in the social interaction that so often takes place between the experimenter and the subject. Bijou and Sturges (1959) have been particularly articulate on this issue.

Typically, E issues verbal instructions and, quite frequently, is physically present during the observation of crucial behaviors. It is sometimes true that social interaction is permitted prior to the conduct of the experiment. The experimenter's social influence, often obvious, sometimes subtle, is quite likely to be considerable−possibly overriding. This is particularly true when the criterion task possesses an absolute character, i.e., when the recorded behavior of S is restricted to a single response. Few investigators have performed the operations necessary to separate extraneous social factors (conduct of an extinction phase or presentation of differential response possibilities, i.e., choice).

The discovery that within the same study, two different "standardized" experimenters have come up with reliably different outcomes (the E effect) is becoming commonplace. To choose an example almost at random, Cantor and Hottel (1955), in their study of the effect of reward magnitude (one vs four peanuts) on discrimination learning in the MR, turned up no incentive effect but a reliable difference relating to the two Es involved. Denny (1964, p. 112) reports that institutionalized retardates master certain discrimination tasks more readily vis-a-vis an experimenter than when essentially unattended in an objectively structured experimental setup. Whereas investigators are fast becoming sensitive to the E effect as it holds within a given study, little awareness is exhibited of the implication that the generality of their findings may be impugned, i.e., that conclusions may be experimenter-specific.

Closely related is the instruction issue. Like the weather, instructions provide the occasion for much talk but little is done about it. Headrick (1963) has shown that the knob-pulling behavior of the mental retardate is strongly influenced by the degree of ambiguity built into preliminary instructions. Evans and Spradlin (1966), in what some would take to be a demonstration of the obvious, have shown that negative instructions given the mental retardate exercise an almost totally inhibiting effect on knob pulling for money. Skinner (1966) doubts the "qualitative" similarity of behaviors emitted with and without prior instruction.

Although fully cognizant of the powerful control exerted by instructions some investigators still settle for a brief general description of how they instructed the subject. (The zeal with which editors guard space may be contributory here.) In some studies it seems quite likely that considerable variation in actual wording was permitted among subjects. At the very least, E should make effort to standardize and report his instructions verbatim. If the psychologist is to meet any final standard of rigorous control and reporting, phonetic description will be required. Syllabic accent could be influential.

Most behavior theorists recognize that performance is determined jointly by cognition (know-how, habit, or what has been learned) and motivation. Failure at the performance level, then, can result from a weakness of cognition, motivation, or a combination thereof. Studies turning up a performance difference between the mentally retarded and normals must take on the burden of eliminating motivation as causal before positing some cognitive inadequacy. A particularly clear illustration of this point is found in a recent study by Jeffrey and Skager (1962). They questioned the conclusion of earlier investigators that 7-year-old children generalize more strongly along a spatial dimension than 11-year-old children because of developmental differences, or age as such. They succeeded in weakening this "age difference" simply by enhancing the incentive motivation of the 7-year-old. Investigators have not always weighed the contribution of motivation before positing a cognitive inadequacy in the retardate. A common source of error here is seen in the assumption that some particular incentive or reward is valued equally by normal and retardate, i.e., that equality of motivation is assured by presentation of the same (as physically described) reinforcer. This is probably rarely true. Stevenson (1963, p. 436) has said this earlier: "It is likely that a particular type of incentive may have quite a different effect in motivating retarded Ss and normal Ss."

The converse of this argument is equally compelling. Valid inference about the effect of incentive motivation assumes that the cognitive factor has been controlled. If variation in the incentive is introduced before learning is complete, the incentive contribution becomes confounded with further learning (cf. Spence, 1956, pp. 130−132). Proper controls (groups continuing unchanged) are required to separate the two factors. There is, incidentally, no convincing a priori reason why the shift from high-to-low incentive should exercise an effect upon performance that is strictly the inverse of the low-to-high effect. At least two studies of incentive motivation in the mental retardate (O'Connor and Claridge, 1958; Siegel *et al.*, 1967b) report facilitation with the change from low to high but little or no deterioration with a shift from high to low. Gordon *et al.* (1954) and Stevenson and Snyder (1960) have both noted what the former investigators refer to as a "sequence effect." When the incentive condition (verbal or social in both studies) is changed, performance relates in part to the earlier condition, i.e., interaction is the rule. To illustrate, Stevenson and Snyder have shown that the marble dropping rate of institutionalized retardates experiencing verbal reproof (punishment) is considerably higher if preceded by earlier verbal approval (reward) than if preceded by the punishing condition.

Another kind of complication is seen when incentive variation is introduced after performance has leveled off. Meyer (1951) has argued cogently that final performance in a differential reward situation is relative to the range of available rewards (for a detailed development of this argument, see Bevan, 1963). And Meyer points out that asymptotic performance may be realized when the reward, in absolute description, is quite weak. To take this one step further, the late introduction of a stronger reward may find the criterion measure insensitive because performance can improve no further (ceiling effect).

Unhappily it is also true that interaction between incentive and task (behavior context) is quite likely the rule. This has been noted by Meyer (1951) in the rhesus monkey and recently by Fagot (1966) in normal children. This may place severe restrictions on the generality of a given set of incentive findings.

An incentive can introduce into the experimental situation responses antagonistic to the criterion behavior. To illustrate, Ellis and Preyer (1958) have suggested that the jelly bean used by them as a reinforcer in the discrimination learning of severely retarded Ss may have been distracting, hence disruptive of learning. In a study of the discrimination learning of 9-year-old normal boys, L. B. Miller and Estes (1961) found knowledge of results to be a more effective reinforcer (accompanied by fewer errors) than either one penny or fifty cents. This somewhat paradoxical outcome was explained in part as resulting from preoccupation with the money.

A final note: it sometimes happens that stimuli intended by the investigator to serve exclusively as cues or as information turn out to possess unwanted reinforcement properties. To illustrate, Ross (1966, p. 50) describes a study conducted in his laboratory by Yaeger in which light-on and light-off were introduced as discriminative cues in a go—no go learning task. Unexpectedly, retardates exhibited a strong light preference, responding to light-on at such high initial rates as to render impossible the planned analysis. This kind of extraneous motivation, oftentimes idiosyncratic, is not always detected within the experimental design followed by the investigator of incentive motivation.

X. A THEORETICAL ACCOUNT

In the past 20 years or so, incentive motivation in its general theoretical development has occupied stage center in the theorizing of the psychologist. And a great deal has been written. Up-to-date reviews may be found in Cofer and Appley (1964), Hall (1966), and Kimble (1961). Bolles' (1967) very recent critical treatment is particularly stimulating.

It is apparent that a comprehensive theory of incentive motivation must accommodate the following primary phenomena: (a) The likelihood, vigor, and persistence of behavior is in substantial measure governed by the characteristics of rewards, reinforcers, or broadly, events occurring at the terminus of a chain of behavior. (b) In exercising influence upon behavior, the capacity of the reward (its "strength") relates to both its magnitude and its "quality." At the moment, exclusively physical or objective specification quickly breaks down as a predictor. Something akin to preference value seems recommended as a measure. (c) Preference value, in turn, relates to needs, learned and unlearned, temporary and more or less permanent. (d) Needs may be highly idiosyncratic. (This last makes difficult the establishment of incentive norms that hold uniformly across a given population even when related variables such as sex, chronological age, developmental stage, and social and educational accomplishment are taken into account.) (e) Since behaviors antecedent in time come under the influence of the reinforcement experience, some kind of expectancy or anticipatory mechanism must be recognized. Here lies the crux of the issue: How does the reinforcing event come to exercise control over instrumental responses occurring earlier in time?

It is well to take a moment and spell out the distinction observed here between instrumental and consummatory behaviors. By and large this definitional issue has been handled poorly in psychology. Since many theorists believe that different sets of laws hold for the two, clear definition would seem to be essential. But it has not been given. Attesting

to the confusion is the frequently seen misspelling (and mispronuncia-
tion), *consumatory* (single *m*), implying the much too narrow meaning of
eating, drinking, or devouring, as opposed to behaviors that merely
bring some act to completion. In the present context, *instrumental
behavior* will be taken to mean all behaviors that lead up to, and serve
to bring the organism into perceptual contact with, the reinforcing
event. Interaction with the reinforcer, i.e., behaviors following upon
perceptual "grasp" of the reinforcer, will be deemed *consummatory*. It
seems to the present writer that such usage is not entirely unconventional, but is actually implicit in the writing of many behavior theorists.

The theoretical account of incentive motivation advanced by Hull
(1952) and by Spence (1956, 1960), while incomplete, still best accommodates the facts. This position enjoys the additional virtue of development within a comprehensive theory of adaptive behavior. Similar
accounts have been voiced by Crespi (1942, 1944), by Mowrer (1960),
and by Seward (1952, 1953). Since Spence is the more recent writer, his
argument will be given the most attention. Hull's differs in minor details.

Spence makes conceptual capital of the covert antedating fractional
goal response of Hull (1930, 1931). This construct, r_G, is taken to be the
vehicle of incentive effects. Its properties, vigor and cue value, are
essentially the same as those of the full goal (consummatory) response
and thus relate somewhat directly to the characteristics of the reinforcer
(amount and "quality"). In an instrumental chain, r_G is generalized
forward in degree proportionate to the similarity between cues occurring earlier and those to which it was conditioned at the terminus. When
elicited early in the chain, r_G is assumed to lend vigor to ongoing instrumental responses and, through its associated cue, s_G, direction. Just how
r_G develops the energizing capability is not conceptualized with any
finality. Spence has suggested two possibilities: through the contribution of s_G to the total stimulus dynamism and through "excitement"
arising from the conflict between r_G and the instrumental response.
Bolles (1967) questions the logical necessity of postulating this dimension. The associative dimension of the $r_G - s_G$ mechanism fares
better and there seems little reason to question its theoretical usefulness.

In accounting for the effects of variation in reward magnitude, Spence
(1956) leaves a conceptual void between r_G and instrumental behavior.
He assumes that, somehow, variation in the vigor of r_G gets translated
into differing degrees of drive induction and it is largely through this
medium that instrumental behavior is influenced. In other words, he
stresses energizing effects but never really gives full attention to just how
this comes about. Recently, Kendler and Kimm (1964, 1967) have
offered theoretical repair. They have filled the void with the following

argument. At a choice point behavior is controlled by a pattern of cues made up of a fixed total number of external (environmental) stimuli and internal (r_G generated) stimuli. Within this pattern the proportionate representation of internal cues is positively related to the magnitude of the reward. Larger rewards are assumed to generate more vigorous r_G's which, in turn, introduce more s_G's at the point of choice. Since the total number of stimulus elements comprising the pattern is assumed to be fixed, external stimuli must necessarily play a weaker controlling role.

Kendler and Kimm (1964, 1967) have examined this hypothesis in studies of reversal learning in the rat, reasoning that the extinction process (loss of r_G) takes out s_G as a source of stimulus control. It follows that the extinction of the original instrumental response should proceed more slowly with small rewards than with large because of control by proportionately more external cues. Thus, the learning of the competitive response demanded in the reversal learning situation suffers greater interference from the original response. Support for the hypothesis was found to be partial.

A somewhat different treatment is required to explain the control of instrumental behavior associated with variation in the "quality" of the reinforcer. Many years ago, in accounting for certain latent learning phenomena, Spence, Bergmann, and Lippitt (1950) suggested that different r_G's derive from differing consummatory responses (such as eating versus drinking). Conditioned to particular drive stimuli, it is a unique r_G that is generalized forward to, and finds representation at, the choice point. The associated distinctive s_G then provides, in part, the basis for discrimination and choice appropriate to the dominant drive or privation state. Thus, if a rat has experienced water in the left arm of a T maze and food in the right arm, he will subsequently come to choose the turn, left or right, appropriate to the momentarily dominant need, thirst or hunger. The $r_G - s_G$ construct becomes the counterpart of "expectancy" in cognitive theory (Tolman, 1959). To the extent that $r_G - s_G$ can be assumed to obey the laws governing observable stimuli and responses, it gains in theoretical substance over the somewhat vaguely defined "expectancy."

There is compelling face validity to the assumption that distinctive r_G's are associated with such topographically different consummatory responses as drinking and eating and that the resulting s_G's are sufficiently differentiated to mediate discrimination and choice behavior. However, there are those who take to be untenable the assumption that adequately differentiated r_G's accompany variation in consummatory responding within a single response mode. Estes (1966, p. 283), for example, finds it difficult to imagine that differing fractional goal responses attend the monkey's eating of four currants as opposed to one. The present writer feels that such a view is not unreasonable; it is even plausible. Since the monkey's *total* interaction with four currants is different from his *total* interaction with one currant, he has expressed two differing consummatory responses and associated antedating fractional components may be taken to be sufficiently differentiated to mediate subsequent discrimination. The criterion advocated here is simple and straightforward: If the behavior interaction of S with reward object A, considered *in toto*, is different (by observation or measurement) from the behavior that he exhibits in relation to reward object B, differing consummatory responses may be said to have occurred, differing fractional components (r_G's) become possible, and differentiated feedback (s_G's) result when these fractional response components are elicited early in the behavior chain.

Within the definition of consummatory responding adopted here, these fractional components need bear no "natural" relation to the final act as does salivation to eating. Many years ago N. E. Miller (1935) demonstrated that cues associated with unusual postures required of the animal in eating could, if later associated with punishment, reinstate responses antagonistic to food-oriented locomotion. Bolles (1967) toys with the thought that no stronger assumption is required than the elicitation of simple approach or avoidance tendencies. This, in a nutshell, is the position developed by Mowrer (1960).

A (the?) major issue confronting the incentive motivation theorist is that of relating choice behavior to the needs of the organism. In the Hull-Spence logic, choice behavior comes under the control of needs via the conditioning of their stimulus consequences to r_G at the point of reinforcement. When r_G is pulled forward through generalization it introduces an associated cue, s_G, at the choice point. This cue, in turn, becomes conditioned to instrumental behaviors providing the basis for predictable and adaptive choice behavior when the need is later activated. In the instance of hunger and thirst, this conceptual treatment seems plausible. This is true largely because stimuli associated with both of these need states have been "identified." Each of us knows subjectively that hunger (food deprivation) and thirst (water deprivation) generate characteristic signals in the alimentary tract and buccal region, respectively. A number of investigators have shown objectively that inarticulate organisms can discriminate between these two need states (for example, Bolles & Petronovich, 1954; Hull, 1933; Leeper, 1935). There is even experimental evidence supporting the assumption that degrees of hunger can be discriminated by rats (Bloomberg &

Webb, 1949; Jenkins & Hanratty, 1949). In the instance of more subtle needs, the case becomes less compelling (see Webb, 1955). Identifiable stimulus consequences or cues, seemingly, do not attend the want of an ice cream cone as opposed to a sour pickle, companionship as opposed to solitude, a quarter as opposed to a nickel, a new bicycle, social approval, bock beer, etc. Nevertheless, the human organism goes about his daily business apparently discriminating among these needs, talking about them, and, for the most part, suiting his actions to their diminution. It would appear that at this point the problem becomes unanalyzable: we must take it as given that the human usually knows his wants and needs and discriminates among them. And this implies the "existence" of correlated signals or cues. These cues, whatever their ultimate character, like those associated with hunger and thirst, are assumed to become conditioned to consummatory responses and their fractional components. And, continuing the analogy with hunger and thirst, in turn, through generalization they may reinstate at the point of choice, a particular $r_G - s_G$ to provide control of choice behavior.

Within this theoretical analysis, additional assumptions are needed to explain the control of choice associated with variation in reward "quality." Like the effect of quantity, it is required that the vigor of the consummatory response and its attendant r_G vary with "quality." But then how shall we give independent definition to "quality"? The search for its specification in the objective characteristics of the reinforcing event has met with very limited success. And, indeed, in the nature of things this seems a fruitless endeavor. During the great depression of the thirties, people jumped from high buildings when reduced in affluence from six to two million; meantime the bum counted his day a success upon discovering a substantial cigar butt in the gutter. "Quality" must ultimately find specification in relation to the need system of the organism. Stronger needs "endow" the reward with greater reinforcing strength than do weak needs, and it is in this sense that rewards must be thought of as possessing degrees of "quality."

All is not speculation in this area. Fortunately, the "quality" of a reinforcer can be known rather directly through preference scaling (see Section V). Within a two-stage procedure, once such values are established objectively, the effects of variation in this variable (now independently defined) upon various measures of learning and performance may be investigated quite readily. With the laboratory rat as subject, Young, his students, and associates (Young, 1941, 1948) have carried out such a program successfully for many years, utilizing various foodstuffs as reinforcers (see also Witryol et al., 1965).

The Kendler-Kimm hypothesis (Kendler & Kimm, 1964, 1967),

alluded to briefly above, asserts that larger rewards generate more vigorous r_G's resulting in greater "internal" choice point control through associated s_G's; i.e., the larger the reward, the stronger is r_G, and the greater the complement of s_G elements present at the point of choice. The assumption that the vigor of r_G also varies with the "quality" of the reward permits the extension of this hypothesis to accommodate "quality" as well as quantity. Currently, in this laboratory, some of the implications of this reasoning utilizing incentives of known preference value are being investigated. The mental retardate is often characterized as lacking foresight or planning ability, or as an organism largely governed by environmental (as opposed to inner) events. This kind of research would seem uniquely suited to assessing such notions, and it is hoped that our current effort will yield at least partial insight into the peculiarities of the anticipatory processes in the mental retardate.

REFERENCES

Aldrich, C. G., & Doll, E. A. Problem solving among idiots. *Journal of Comparative Psychology*, 1931, **12**, 137-169.

Amsel, A. Frustrative nonreward in partial reinforcement and discrimination learning. *Psychological Review*, 1962, **69**, 306-328.

Baumeister, A. A., & Ward, L. C., III. Effects of rewards upon the reaction times of mental defectives. *American Journal of Mental Deficiency*, 1967, **71**, 801-806.

Bevan, W. The pooling mechanism and the phenomena of reinforcement. In O. J. Harvey (Ed.), *Motivation and social interaction—Cognitive determinants*. New York: Ronald Press, 1963, Pp. 18-34.

Bijou, S. W. & Oblinger, B. Responses of normal and retarded children as a function of the experimental situation. *Psychological Reports*, 1960, **6**, 447-454.

Bijou, S. W., & Sturges, P. T. Positive reinforcers for experimental studies with children—consumables and manipulatables. *Child Development*, 1959, **30**, 151-170.

Bloomberg, R., & Webb, W. B. Various degrees within a single drive as cues for spatial response learning in the white rat. *Journal of Experimental Psychology*, 1949, **39**, 628-636.

Bolles, R., & Petronovich, L. A technique for obtaining rapid drive discrimination in the rat. *Journal of Comparative and Physiological Psychology*, 1954, **47**, 378-380.

Bolles, R. C. *Theory of motivation*. New York: Harper, 1967.

Bower, G. H. A contrast effect in differential conditioning. *Journal of Experimental Psychology*, 1961, **62**, 196-199.

Butterfield, E. C., & Zigler, E. The influence of differing institutional social climates on the effectiveness of social reinforcement in the mentally retarded. *American Journal of Mental Deficiency*, 1965, **70**, 48-56.

Cantor, G. N., & Hottel, J. V. Discrimination learning in mental defectives as a function of food reward and intelligence level. *American Journal of Mental Deficiency*, 1955, **60**, 380-384.

Cho, J. B., & David, R. T. Preferences of monkeys for objects other than food. *American Journal of Psychology*, 1957, **70**, 87-91.

Cofer, C. N., & Appley, M. H. *Motivation: Theory and research.* New York: Wiley, 1964.

Crespi, L. P. Quantitative variation of incentive and performance in the white rat. *American Journal of Psychology,* 1942, **55**, 467-517.

Crespi, L. P. Amount of reinforcement and level of performance. *Psychological Review,* 1944, **51**, 341-357.

Cromwell, R. L. A social learning approach to mental retardation. In N. R. Ellis (Ed.), *Handbook of mental deficiency.* New York: McGraw-Hill, 1963. Pp. 41-91.

Denny, M. R. Research in learning and performance. In H. A. Stevens & R. Heber (Eds.), *Mental retardation.* Chicago: University of Chicago Press, 1964. Pp. 100-142.

Ellis, N. R. Amount of reward and operant behavior in mental defectives. *American Journal of Mental Deficiency,* 1962, **66**, 595-599.

Ellis, N. R., & Distefano, M. K. Effects of verbal urging and praise upon rotary pursuit performance in mental defectives. *American Journal of Mental Deficiency,* 1959, **64**, 486-490.

Ellis, N. R., & Pryor, M. W. Primary versus secondary reinforcement in simple discrimination learning of mental defectives. *Psychological Reports,* 1958, **4**, 67-70.

Estes, W. K. Transfer of verbal discriminations based on differential reward magnitudes. *Journal of Experimental Psychology,* 1966, **72**, 276-283.

Evans, G. W., & Spradlin, J. E. Incentive and instructions as controlling variables of productivity. *American Journal of Mental Deficiency,* 1966, **71**, 129-132.

Fagot, B. I. Conditioning effects on two apparatus uses. *Psychonomic Science,* 1966, **4**, 349-350.

Fay, J. C., Miller, J. D., & Harlow, H. F. Incentive size, food deprivation, and food preference. *Journal of Comparative and Physiological Psychology,* 1953, **46**, 13-15.

Giles, D. K., & Wolf, M. M. Toilet training institutionalized, severe retardates: an application of operant behavior modification techniques. *American Journal of Mental Deficiency,* 1966, **70**, 766-780.

Gordon, S., O'Connor, N., & Tizard, J. Some effects of incentives on the performance of imbeciles. *British Journal of Psychology,* 1954, **45**, 277-287.

Gordon, S., O'Connor, N., & Tizard, J. Some effects of incentives on the performance of imbeciles on a repetitive task. *American Journal of Mental Deficiency,* 1955, **60**, 371-377.

Hall, J. F. *The psychology of learning.* Philadelphia: Lippincott, 1966.

Harlow, H. F., & Meyer, D. R. Paired comparisons scales for monkey rewards. *Journal of Comparative and Physiological Psychology,* 1952, **45**, 73-79.

Headrick, M. W. Effects of instructions and initial reinforcement on fixed-interval behavior in retardates. *American Journal of Mental Deficiency,* 1963, **68**, 425-432.

Heber, R. F. Motor task performance of high grade mentally retarded males as a function of the magnitude of the incentive. *American Journal of Mental Deficiency,* 1959, **63**, 667-671.

Hollis, J. H. Differential responses of profoundly retarded children to social stimulation. *Psychological Reports,* 1965, **16**, 977-984. (a)

Hollis, J. H. Effects of reinforcement shifts on bent-wire performance of severely retarded children. *American Journal of Mental Deficiency,* 1965, **69**, 531-535. (b)

Hull, C. L. Knowledge and purpose as habit mechanisms. *Psychological Review,* 1930, **37**, 511-525.

Hull, C. L. Goal attraction and directing ideas conceived as habit phenomena. *Psychological Review,* 1931, **38**, 487-506.

Hull, C. L. Differential habituation to internal stimuli in the albino rat. *Journal of Comparative Psychology,* 1933, **16**, 255-273.

Hull, C. L. *A behavior system.* New Haven: Yale University Press, 1952.

Hunt, B., & Patterson, R. M. Performance of familial mentally deficient children in response to motivation on the Goodenough Draw-a-Man test. *American Journal of Mental Deficiency*, 1957, **62**, 326-329.

Jeffrey, W. E., & Skager, R. W. Effect of incentive conditions on stimulus generalization in children. *Child Development*, 1962, **33**, 865-870.

Jenkins, J. J., & Hanratty, J. A. Drive intensity discrimination in the albino rat. *Journal of Comparative and Physiological Psychology*, 1949, **42**, 228-232.

Kendler, H. H., & Kimm, J. Reinforcement and cue factors in reversal learning. *Psychonomic Science*, 1964, **1**, 309-310.

Kendler, H. H. & Kimm, J. Reversal learning as a function of the size of the reward during acquisition and reversal. *Journal of Experimental Psychology*, 1967, **73**, 66-71.

Kimble, G. A. *Hilgard and Marquis' conditioning and learning.* (2nd ed.) New York: Appleton, 1961.

Leeper, R. The role of motivation in learning: A study of the phenomenon of differential motivational control of the utilization of habits. *Journal of Genetic Psychology*, 1935, **46**, 3-40.

Loos, F. M., & Tizard, J. The employment of adult imbeciles in a hospital workshop. *American Journal of Mental Deficiency*, 1955, **59**, 395-403.

McManis, D. L. Pursuit-rotor performance of normal and retarded children in four verbal-incentive conditions. *Child Development*, 1965, **36**, 667-683.

Meyer, D. R. The effects of differential rewards on discrimination reversal learning by monkeys. *Journal of Experimental Psychology*, 1951, **41**, 268-274.

Miller, L. B., & Estes, B. W. Monetary reward and motivation in discrimination learning. *Journal of Experimental Psychology*, 1961, **61**, 501-504.

Miller, N. E. A reply to "sign-gestalt or conditioned reflex." *Psychological Review*, 1935, **42**, 280-292.

Mowrer, O. H. *Learning theory and behavior.* New York: Wiley, 1960.

O'Connor, N., & Claridge, G. S. The effect of goal-setting and encouragement on the performance of imbecile men. *Quarterly Journal of Experimental Psychology*, 1955, **7**, 37-45.

O'Connor, N., & Claridge, G. S. A 'Crespi Effect' in male imbeciles. *British Journal of Psychology*, 1958, **49**, 42-48.

Orlando, R. Reinforcement functions in the mentally retarded. Summary Progress Report, June 1, 1966, Research Grant 11818, U. S. Public Health Service.

Partan, D. A., & Ross, A. O. Social reinforcement of children's motor behavior: a review. *Psychological Bulletin*, 1965, **64**, 65-73.

Perry, S. L., & Stotsky, B. A. Type of reward, incentive, and incentive sequence as factors in the motor performance of mentally retarded, physically handicapped, and college students. *Journal of Psychology*, 1965, **60**, 55-65.

Pubols, B. H. Incentive magnitude, learning, and performance in animals. *Psychological Bulletin*, 1960, **57**, 89-115.

Ross, L. E. Classical conditioning and discrimination learning research with the mentally retarded. In N. R. Ellis (Ed.), *International review of research in mental retardation.* Vol. 1. New York: Academic Press, 1966. Pp. 21-54.

Schrier, A. M. Comparison of two methods of investigating the effect of amount of reward on performance. *Journal of Comparative and Physiological Psychology*, 1958, **51**, 725-731.

Seward, J. P. Introduction to a theory of motivation in learning. *Psychological Review*, 1952, **59**, 405-413.

Seward, J. P. How are motives learned? *Psychological Review*, 1953, **60**, 99-110.

Shepp, B. E. Some cue properties of anticipated rewards in discrimination learning of retardates. *Journal of Comparative and Physiological Psychology*, 1962, **55**, 856-859.

Shepp, B. E. Some cue properties of incentives: Discrimination of distinct rewards by retardates. *Journal of Comparative and Physiological Psychology*, 1963, **56**, 1078-1080.

Shepp, B. E. Some cue properties of rewards in simultaneous object-discriminations of retardates. *Child Development*, 1964, **35**, 587-592.

Siegel, P. S., & Forman, G. E. The role of incentive strength in the discrimination learning of the retardate. *Journal of Comparative Physiological Psychology*, 1967, **63**, 552-554.

Siegel, P. S., Forman, G. E., & Williams, J. An exploratory study of incentive motivation in the retardate. *American Journal of Mental Deficiency*, 1967, **71**, 977-983. (a)

Siegel, P. S., Williams, J., & Forman, G. E. Instrumental behavior in relation to qualitative differences in the incentive. *American Journal of Mental Deficiency*, 1967, **72**, 450-454. (b)

Skinner, B. F. Operant behavior. In W. K. Honig (Ed.), *Operant behavior: Areas of research and application*. New York: Appleton, 1966, Pp. 12-32.

Spence, K. W. *Behavior theory and conditioning*. New Haven: Yale University Press, 1956.

Spence, K. W. *Behavior theory and learning: Selected papers of K. W. Spence*. Englewood Cliffs, N. J.: Prentice-Hall, 1960.

Spence, K. W., Bergmann, G., & Lippitt, R. A study of simple learning under irrelevant motivational-reward conditions. *Journal of Experimental Psychology*, 1950, **40**, 539-551.

Spradlin, J. E., Girardeau, F. L., & Corte, E. Fixed ratio and fixed interval behavior of severely and profoundly retarded subjects. *Journal of Experimental Child Psychology*, 1965, **2**, 340-353.

Stevenson, H. W. Discrimination learning. In N. R. Ellis (Ed.), *Handbook of mental deficiency*, New York: McGraw-Hill, 1963. Pp. 424-438.

Stevenson, H. W. Social reinforcement of children's behavior. In L. P. Lipsitt and C. C. Spiker (Eds.), *Advances in child development and behavior*. Vol. 2. New York: Academic Press, 1965. Pp. 97-126.

Stevenson, H. W., & Knights, R. M. Effect of visual reinforcement on the performance of normal and retarded children. *Perceptual and Motor Skills*, 1961, **13**, 119-126.

Stevenson, H. W., & Snyder, L. C. Performance as a function of the interaction of incentive conditions. *Journal of Personality*, 1960, **28**, 1-11.

Terrell, C. & Stevenson, H. W. The effectiveness of normal and retarded peers as reinforcing agents. *American Journal of Mental Deficiency*, 1965, **70**, 373-381.

Tolman, E. C. Principles of purposive behavior. In S. Koch (Ed.), *Psychology: A study of a science*. Vol. 2. New York: McGraw-Hill, 1959, Pp. 92-157.

Tyrrell, D. J., Witryol, S. L. & Silverg, E. Incentive scaling in mental retardates by the method of paired comparisons. *American Journal of Mental Deficiency*, 1963, **68**, 225-227.

Walton, D., & Begg, T. L. The effects of incentives on the performance of defective imbeciles. *British Journal of Psychology*, 1958, **49**, 49-55.

Warren, J. M. Effects of satiation on food preferences in monkeys. *Journal of Genetic Psychology*, 1958, **93**, 33-36.

Webb, W. B. Drive stimuli as cues. *Psychological Reports*, 1955, **1**, 287-298.

Witryol, S. L. & Alexander, A. A. Social manipulation of preschool children's paired comparisons incentive preferences. *Psychological Reports*, 1962, **10**, 615-618.

Witryol, S. L., & Fischer, W. F. Scaling children's incentives by the method of paired comparisons. *Psychological Reports*, 1960, **7**, 471-474.

Witryol, S. L., Tyrrell, D. J., & Lowden, L. M. Five-choice discrimination learning by children under simultaneous incentive conditions. *Child Development*, 1964, **35**, 233-243.

Witryol, S. L., Tyrrell, D. J., & Lowden, L. M. Development of incentive values in childhood. *Genetic Psychology Monographs*, 1965, **72**, 201-246.

Wolfensberger, W. Differential rewards as motivating factors in mental deficiency research. *American Journal of Mental Deficiency*, 1960, **64**, 902-906.

Young, P. T. The experimental analysis of appetite. *Psychological Bulletin*, 1941, **38**, 129-164.

Young, P. T. Appetite, palatability, and feeding habit: A critical review. *Psychological Bulletin*, 1948, **45**, 289-320.

Zeaman, D., & House, B. J. The role of attention in retardate discrimination learning. In N. R. Ellis (Ed.), *Handbook of mental deficiency*. New York: McGraw-Hill, 1963. Pp. 159-223.

Zigler, E. Research on personality structure in the retardate. In N. R. Ellis (Ed.), *International review of research in mental retardation*. Vol. 1. New York: Academic Press, 1966. Pp. 77-108.

Development of Lateral and Choice-Sequence Preferences

IRMA R. GERJUOY[1] and JOHN J. WINTERS, JR.

EDWARD R. JOHNSTONE TRAINING AND RESEARCH CENTER, BORDENTOWN, NEW JERSEY

I. INTRODUCTION

Much behavior that appears to be random, or unlawful, can be analyzed into lawful components. The relative importance of these components may vary from situation to situation, but recognition of their existence will aid in the prediction of future behavior. Even a comparatively simple situation, such as a series of binary-choice decisions, where no immediate feedback is given to the S, can be analyzed into at least the three major components of stimulus preferences, response preferences, and choice-sequence preferences. The available evidence suggests that these preferences and their relative importance develop and change over time. These changes may, however, be differentially affected by MA, CA, or IQ.

The purpose of this article is to summarize the findings of a number of studies where some of the factors that evoke nonrandom response in binary-choice decisions were investigated. Much of the nonrandom

[1] Deceased.

31

behavior referred to herein was elicited within the context of non-reinforcement or lack of knowledge of results. Further, it is intended to indicate the relationships among these nonrandom components of binary-choice decisions and MA, CA, and IQ. Therefore, data will be reported which was obtained from normal children, retarded children, adolescents, college students, and retarded adults.

A stimulus preference is inferred when a S or group of Ss responds more frequently to one stimulus of a stimulus array than to any other(s). Generally, but not necessarily, a stimulus preference results from a learned bias; e.g., in guessing the first toss of a coin, most Ss will respond "heads." Other biases include color preferences, form preferences, structural preferences, etc. Essentially, the stimulus preference is based upon the nature of the individual stimuli and is unrelated to the configuration of the stimulus display.

A response preference is demonstrated when a S or group of Ss responds to a stimulus on the basis of its location within a stimulus array or when the response is chosen without regard for the differential characteristics of the stimuli. The most common response preference is a position preference, i.e., a preference for the left or right stimulus in a two-choice decision. Response preferences may be perceptual, motor, or verbal. Examples of these preferences are visual displacement of an object to one side of the visual field, pressing a response key on the left rather than on the right, and the tendency to say "yes" more often than "no." Response preferences are determined, at least in part, by the response mode and may differ with the type of response required.

It should be noted that stimulus and response preferences are logically independent of one another. Under some experimental conditions these preferences may be additive, but under other conditions they may be competitive. If the preferred stimulus is in the preferred location, these preferences will correspond, and the likelihood of a response to the preferred stimulus will increase; when the stimulus and response preferences are discordant, on the other hand, the probability of a response to the preferred stimulus will decrease.

Choice-sequence preferences are exhibited by a pattern of responses over a series of trials. This pattern may be a repetitive one (e.g., perseveration, single alternation, or double alternation) or it may simply be a tendency to perseverate or alternate more than is expected by chance. Although a stimulus preference is dependent upon some characteristic of the stimulus, and a response preference is dependent upon the structure of the stimulus array, a choice-sequence preference is contingent upon the previous response(s). Factors that could influence the sequence of responses are time between trials, similarity of the stimuli, number of trials, and S- variables.

The manner in which stimulus and response preferences combine with the pattern preference to determine the response depends upon the type of preferred pattern and the stimulus configuration. When the stimulus and response preferences are in agreement (i.e., the stimulus S prefers is always in the location he prefers), these preferences will be additive with a perseveration preference and competitive with an alternation tendency (on half the trials). In the latter case, if the experimental variables are manipulated to increase stimulus or response preferences, then alternation must decrease; if the conditions favor alternation, then the influence of stimulus and response preferences will decrease. If the stimulus and response preferences are discordant, then, of course, the relationships among the three variables become more difficult to analyze.

In the above analysis we have been concerned with forced-choice tasks in which only one response was permitted on each trial. When the task requires that S respond to both stimuli, a choice-sequence preference over trials is usually disrupted, and S's order of response within a trial is mainly determined by his response preference when the stimuli are of the same type. If the task is made more complex by the requiring of responses to more than two stimuli on each trial, then the initial response is probably determined by a response preference, but the organization of the remaining responses in each trial is dependent upon S's "order of response" preference. As the stimulus array becomes more complex, the "order of response" preferences available to S become more numerous.

Because more research has been conducted with the binary-choice uni-response task than with the more complex, multiple-response situation, most of this article will be devoted to the former task, with only minor consideration given to the latter. Many of the studies to be cited will be discussed within more than one context.

II. STIMULUS PREFERENCES

Subjects enter most experimental situations with preferences for some stimuli, preferences that have developed through past experience. In a simple discrimination task Ss often prefer one color or one form and will respond to their preferred stimulus at the outset of training. Since the E rewards the S for responding to the stimulus of E's choice, S's initial preference is increased by reinforcement if it coincides with E's choice or it is extinguished if it differs from E's choice. Thus, stimulus preferences change with the reinforcement schedule.

When the task is such that E has no control over changes in S's preferences in the course of the experiment, i.e., he neither reinforces S nor gives him any feedback about the correctness of his responses, any changes in stimulus preference that do occur must be internally mediated. If large changes occur, it must be assumed that the bias was strong for the preferred stimulus only for the initial choice in the series or that the stimulus preference was diluted by other possible preferences in the task, such as a response preference or a choice-sequence preference.

Two types of paper and pencil tasks have been utilized in the investigations of stimulus preferences. Both consist of 20 trials to which S responds by encircling one of each pair of stimuli. In the first type, the same pair of stimuli occurs on each trial; in the other type, the pairs of stimuli differ from trial to trial.

In the first two experiments of the former type (I. R. Gerjuoy & Gerjuoy, 1965), the S chose either the letter A or the letter B on each of the 20 trials; B was always presented to the right of A. Some Ss were instructed to produce a random sequence of responses, whereas others were instructed to produce a simple pattern of responses. Subjects were normal fourth- and fifth-grade children, adolescent educable retardates, and college students. All groups regardless of age, intelligence, or instructions exhibited a preference for A over B on the first trial. These preferences ranged from 66% to 84%. Under instructions to produce a pattern, this preference was significantly greater among college students than among retarded adolescents or normal children. The proportion of A responses on the first trial was larger under pattern-set than under random-set for all groups, although only in the college group was this difference significant. For all 20 choices combined, however, the A preference was negligible except for retardates, who chose stimulus A 53% of the time. This group, alone, maintained at least a slight preference throughout the 20 trials.

Gerjuoy and Gerjuoy interpreted their results as an indication of a preference for A. It should be noted, however, that since A was always on the left, these results might as easily be interpreted as a preference to respond on the left in this task. In order to separate a possible stimulus preference from a possible response preference, a second study was conducted by the present authors (in collaboration with H. Gerjuoy) with 3192 college students. The format was the same as in the earlier study: There were 20 trials with identical pairs of stimuli. But there were 16 treatment combinations: Each of four types of stimulus pairs was combined with one of four kinds of instructions. The stimulus pairs were AA, AB, BA, or BB; the instructions included a pattern-set or a random-set, together with the request to respond either the way S thought was correct (self-instructions) or the way he thought most people would respond (others' instructions). The present discussion will be concerned primarily with the *AB* and *BA* treatment groups, since there must be at least two different stimuli to elicit a stimulus preference.

For all instructional combinations the percentage of left responses was significantly greater with the stimulus pair *AB* than with the stimulus pair *BA* on the first trial. Combined over groups, these percentages were 81.2% vs 61.2%, respectively. It seems clear that the difference in left responses between the two stimulus conditions results from the differential placement of the letter *A*, in the first case on the left and in the second case on the right. When *A* is on the left, the preference for *A* combines with the preference for responding on the left; when *A* is on the right, the two preferences are in conflict.

It should be added, that the difference in left responding between the two stimulus configurations was greater under pattern-set instructions than under random-set instructions. This result suggests that randomness connotes unpredictability and that under random-set instructions *S*s avoid responses that they regard as obvious or popular even when they are trying to respond in the way they think others would respond.

Over all 20 responses the tendency to respond on the left decreases markedly. In comparing the left responses under *AB* with those under *BA*, it was found that the difference was considerably smaller. There was still some difference, however, with 51.5% lefts under *AB* for trials 2–20 vs 49.4% lefts under *BA*. It would appear that the left response preference was completely counterbalanced by the *A* preference in the *BA* configuration. Very slight left-responding and *A* preferences increased the number of left responses in the *AB* configuration to produce this difference between the left responses in the two configurations.

After it had been established that both a stimulus preference and a response preference exist in this task with college *S*s, the *AB* and *BA* configurations were administered under random-set instructions to 92 additional adolescent educable retardates. In the analysis the data from the *S*s in the *AB* condition were combined with those from the *S*s in the same condition in the first *AB* study (a total of 143 *S*s). Under the *AB* condition 69% of the *S*s responded on the left in the first trial, whereas under the *BA* condition only 45% responded on the left. For trials 2-20 these percentages were 54% and 50%.

These results indicate that, although college *S*s had a somewhat greater initial left preference than the retardates, the difference between the two conditions was similar for the two populations (see Table I). The overall left responses were similar for the two populations under each stimulus condition. In this situation it appears that after the first trial both college students and adolescent educable retardates had the same stimulus preference and in the same relative amount. A comparison of the initial left preferences of the two populations under the two conditions suggests that the college students had a greater initial response preference than the retardates but that their stimulus preferences were equivalent.

TABLE I

PERCENT OF LEFT SIDE RESPONSES TO TRIAL 1 AND TO TRIALS 2 – 20

Group	Condition	N	Trial 1	Trials 2 – 20
College Ss	AB	831	81.2	51.5
	BA	814	61.2	49.4
Retardates	AB	74	68.9	53.8
	BA	69	44.9	50.3

In an experiment in which the stimuli changed from trial to trial (I. R. Gerjuoy & Winters, 1965), the S was presented with 20 triads consisting of one English word and two Japanese characters. His task was to circle the Japanese character that he believed meant the same as the English word above. Neither normal children nor retarded Ss (children, adolescents, and adults) tended to select one stimulus over another on the basis of the stimulus characteristics. College students, however, did respond to the salient features of the stimuli; they exhibited some strong stimulus preferences. These preferences were exhibited more often when the choice lay between two dissimilar stimuli than when the choice lay between two similar stimuli. It would seem that although the other subject groups tended to respond more automatically, with perseveration or increased alternation, the college students attempted to follow the instructions and to select Japanese characters that they were able to associate in some way with the English words. They did not readily adopt the guessing-game, response-dependent strategies of the lower MA groups. In this situation, stimulus preferences occurred only in higher MA Ss. They were able to respond differentially to new and unfamiliar stimuli, whereas the other groups seemed to ignore the differences between the stimuli in each pair regardless of their similarity or dissimilarity.

These studies suggest that both normal and retarded Ss have initial preexperimental sets or stimulus preferences that substantially dissipate when the same stimulus pairs are repeated in the same configuration over many trials. Only college students respond to structural differences in unfamiliar stimuli. The different populations responded similarly when the preferences were based upon old, repetitious experiences. College students, however, unlike normal children and retardates, were able to extract from past experiences in a novel situation.

III. RESPONSE PREFERENCES

In this discussion the term "response preference" is synonymous with the term "position preference"; i.e., it reflects the tendency of Ss to select one side in a two-choice decision more frequently than the other when the two stimuli or the two response manipulanda are placed side by side. As with stimulus preferences, response preferences may be strong initially and dissipate to varying degrees over the course of an experiment, or they may be maintained at the same strength throughout an experiment. Both diminishing and constant preferences will be discussed. Unlike stimulus preferences, response preferences are usually independent of the particular stimuli.

A. Probability Learning Studies

Probability learning tasks are those in which the probability of reinforcement for alternative responses is preset by the E. The subject is given a guessing-game set. On each trial he must guess which response E will reinforce. After many trials his responses to the alternatives usually match the probabilities of reinforcement. In a probability learning study (I. R. Gerjuoy, Gerjuoy, & Mathias, 1964) 80 college students were required to press one of two keys on each of 180 trials. One key was reinforced twice as often as the other in a random sequence. Subjects for whom the right-hand key was more frequently reinforced overmatched the probability of reinforcement; Ss for whom the left-hand key was more frequently reinforced undermatched the probability of reinforcement. Collapsing over Ss it was found that 52.24% of all responses were to the right-hand key. The overall right side preference was small but consistent over blocks of trials. In addition, 64% of the Ss chose the right-hand key on the first trial before any reinforcements had been given. Results of this study suggested the importance of position preferences in binary-choice tasks. In a replication and extension of this study, Miller (1966) found a right side preference both when S moved a lever to the right or left with his preferred hand and when S pressed one of two keys. The same degree of preference was observed for both response methods.

Rosenhan (1966) used 64 first-grade children in a probability learning study in which the left hand of two response keys was reinforced 70%

of the time. Contrary to some findings with children, he found that his *S*s significantly undermatched the probability of reinforcement. Because Rosenhan did not counterbalance the more frequently reinforced side, no conclusive interpretation of this finding can be made; it is possible, however, that the undermatching of his *S*s may have resulted from a right side preference.

In the studies just cited, response preferences were maintained throughout in spite of reinforcement schedules controlled by the *E*. Clearly, if one response were reinforced 100% of the time, the pre-experimental response preference would vanish. The effect of a partial reinforcement schedule upon preferences is not so clearcut. It may be better evaluated by comparing these studies with others in which no reinforcement or feedback is given.

B.   Paper and Pencil Tasks

The tasks to be discussed in this section have one common property: The stimulus elements for the entire task are available to *S* from the start. In addition, he has access to all his previous responses before he makes each new response. These tasks are not only self-paced but also provide the opportunity, if *S* chooses, to review and even change his previous responses. All *S*'s responses are made within the context of the complete stimulus display. No reinforcement is given.

It has been mentioned in the section on stimulus preferences that more *A* responses than *B* responses occurred in a pencil and paper task with the format AB throughout the 20 trials of the task, and that this preference might be interpreted either as a stimulus preference for the letter *A* or as a response preference for encircling the letter on the left (I. R. Gerjuoy & Gerjuoy, 1965). The follow-up study, with college students only, included two conditions in which a stimulus preference was not possible: the stimuli were pairs of *A*'s throughout or pairs of *B*'s throughout. Under both of these conditions about 75% of the *S*s responded on the left on the first trial. This strong response bias largely dissipated after the first trial; nevertheless, 51.9% of all responses after the first trial were to the left-hand stimulus. Thus, the initial left preference was evident throughout but at lower strength than during the first trial.

Although the studies just cited demonstrated a left side preference, the *S* groups in the Japanese symbol study mentioned previously (I. R. Gerjuoy & Winters, 1965) exhibited, with one exception, an initial right side preference. Except for the normal second-grade children, all the normal and retarded children and normal and retarded adults had a preference for the right-hand stimulus on the first trial. The second-grade children had a significant left side preference. Since these children were still beginning readers, it may be that their left side bias was a consequence of the emphasis given by their teachers to starting each line of reading on the left. Over the course of the 20 trials, the initial preference dissipated for all the pre-adult groups. College students and retarded adults, however, maintained a slight right side preference.

Another study conducted by I. R. Gerjuoy and Winters (1967) revealed a left side preference. Twenty-eight adolescent educable retardates and 263 fourth- through eighth-grade normal children were presented five numerical tasks. In each task a number was centered at the top of the paper and was followed by pairs of two- or three-digit numbers. For each task S was instructed to encircle the number in each pair that bore the greater relationship to the top number. Tasks 1, 2, 4, and 5 had 10 trials, whereas Task 3, the most difficult, included 20 trials. Subjects who followed any consistent pattern, such as always encircling the larger number or the smaller number or encircling the number that the Es considered the correct solution, were counted as solvers of that problem.

The left and right responses for the Ss with no solution were analyzed. It was found that the number of Ss in both populations whose left responses were above the median was significantly greater than the number of Ss whose left responses were below the median. In other words, when Ss found no solution they tended to encircle the left-hand number more frequently than the right-hand number. Contrary to the findings of other studies in this area, the initial response reflected no preference for the retardates and a strong (79.6%) but opposite (right) preference for the normal children.

In summary, an analysis of the performance of disparate groups reveals that a number of different types of variables affect initial and overall response preferences in the paper and pencil task. Three variables seem to affect initial response: population, material, and structure. Adult normals usually have the strongest initial preferences. Normal children's preferences generally follow those of adults, but they are weaker. The one exception to this generalization was the initial response preference of second-grade children in the Japanese symbol study. This preference was for the left rather than for the right. Retardates exhibited the least amount of initial response preferences. They revealed an initial response preference only in the AB studies under the AB condition.

The side of the initial preference seems to be related to the type of material. If the material is alphabetic, the preference is for the left-hand stimulus; if the material is nonalphabetic (i.e., numerical or nonsense figures), the initial preference is on the right. In two of the studies cited, there may have been an interaction between the type of material and the physical structure of the task. When the material was non-alphabetic the two stimuli were preceded by another, centrally located element, for the first trial. Consequently, Ss may have shifted their eyes from the central element to the right and encircled the right-hand stimulus without attending to the left-hand stimulus on that trial.

This hypothesis seems plausible, since the overall preference of normal children was for the left-hand stimulus when a central element no longer appeared in the structure after the first trial, as in the number study. In other words, for this group of normal children only, the initial preference was at variance with the overall preference. In other studies preferences decreased, but they never switched from one side to the other. This task was the only one in which a structural change in the stimulus configuration occurred after the first trial.

In addition to the variables mentioned, two other variables can affect overall preferences. The first is access to previous responses. Subjects may, if they look back at their previous responses, notice that they have responded inequitably to one side or the other and try to balance their responses. Second, particularly with younger or lower MA Ss, there may be such strong choice-sequence preferences, such as alternation, that these preferences may override any response or position preference. See Table II for side of initial and overall preferences for the studies cited.

TABLE II
SIDE OF INITIAL AND OVERALL RESPONSE PREFERENCES
FOR VARIOUS SUBJECT POPULATIONS

Task	Population	Initial side preference	Overall side preference
AB	Fourth- and fifth-grade children	L	None
	Adolescent educable retardates	L	L
	College students	L	L
BA	Adolescent educable retardates	R	None
	College students	L	None
Number	Fourth- through eighth-grade children	R	L
	Adolescent educable retardates	None	L
Japanese	Second-grade children	L	None
	Third- through sixth-grade children	R	None
	Adolescent educable retardates	None	None
	Adult retardates	R	R
	College students	R	R

Evidence that stimulus and response preferences exist adds weight to the importance of counterbalancing in psychological research. Particularly when several S groups, whose preferences may differ, are tested, meaningful comparisons can be made only when positional and stimulus preferences are counterbalanced to control for these variables. Although counterbalancing procedures are commonly used, it sometimes becomes necessary to add additional groups to a study in order to control for variables of this type that were not of primary concern to the researcher. He may find, of course, that these variables interact with his primary variables.

C. Perceptual Tasks with Verbal or Motor Responses

Position preferences were found in another series of studies, which employed geometric forms as the stimulus materials. In a study of gamma movement, the apparent expansion and contraction of tachistoscopically exposed figures (Winters & Gerjuoy, 1965), two circles of the same or varied sizes were successively presented side by side with an overlap of exposure. Sixty high school normals were quite consistent in their judgments. Comparison circles, equal to or slightly smaller than the standard, were judged "larger" significantly more often than chance. Of particular interest to this discussion is the finding that a comparison circle tends to be judged larger more often if it is presented on the right side. In this case Ss were not engaged in a guessing-game task; they seemed actually to perceive the form on the right as larger. This occurred in spite of the fact that any comparison figure of the same size as the standard, whether on the left or the right, tended to be seen as the larger more often than chance. Another process, in addition to gamma movement, seems to influence the perceived size of the right-hand figure.

In order to determine the applicability of these results to geometric forms in general, two experiments were performed. The first (I. R. Gerjuoy & Winters, 1966; Winters & Gerjuoy, 1966) used pairs of simple geometric forms and involved 96 adolescent educable retardates and 96 equal CA normals (college students).

In one task pairs of equal-sized forms (squares, circles, triangles, diamonds, and semicircles) were exposed tachistoscopically for .8 second with either a 10-second or a 30-second intertrial interval. Some Ss were instructed to press the key on the side of the larger figure; the remaining Ss were instructed to press the key on the side of the smaller figure. Subjects responded by pressing either a right-hand or a left-hand telegraph key.

In the second task pairs of identical squares, circles, triangles, and hexagons were presented on 4 x 6 in. white cards with unlimited exposure time to 60 adolescent educable retardates and 10 equal CA normals. For the retardates *E* pointed randomly to one figure in each pair, and *S* said "yes" if it appeared to be the larger one and "no" if it appeared to be the smaller one. The normals' task was to point to the larger figure in each pair. In both studies each card was presented rightside up and also inverted in order to counterbalance any possible objective differences in the sizes of the figures.

With the tachistoscopic exposure, retardates had no initial or overall response preference. Throughout the 10 presentations college students, however, responded as if the right-hand stimulus were larger. Of those college students who were instructed to indicate which stimulus was larger, 67% chose the right-hand stimulus on the first trial. This percentage decreased slightly after the first trial. The two college groups who were given 10-second and 30-second intertrial intervals did not differ significantly from each other in preference under these "larger" instructions. The results were somewhat different when the college *S*s were required to respond to the "smaller" stimulus; there was no significant side preference on the first trial. Over all, under the more distributed trials (30 seconds) the *left* side was judged to be the *smaller* significantly more often, about 58% of the time. Under "larger" instruction the perceptual preference and the motor preference were additive, but it would seem that under "smaller" instructions the *S* experienced a conflict between the judgment of the left side as the smaller and the preference, found previously, to respond with the right hand. When the trials were more massed (10 seconds), these two tendencies had equal strength and canceled one another; when the trials were distributed, the perceptual preference appeared to be stronger and to take precedence over the hand preference.

Different results were obtained when *S* was given a self-paced task with the stimuli drawn on cards. In this task both retardates and equal CA normals perceived the right-hand stimulus as the larger significantly more often than the left-hand stimulus. Although both populations had the same overall preference, neither group exhibited an initial side preference.

Subsequently, 40 fifth-grade normal children were tested in this task, the procedure being the same as that with retardates. The results with this group were similar. Under "larger" instructions they perceived the right-hand stimulus as larger significantly more often than the left. Under "smaller" instructions they perceived the left-hand stimulus as smaller significantly more often than the right. Neither first or second half of the task nor order of instructions produced a significant effect. In this task there were no differences among the three populations of adolescent retardates, equal MA normals, and equal CA normals. If there is a learned tendency to see a stimulus on the right as being larger than an identical stimulus on the left, this tendency has been established by age 10.

Tests of handedness and eyedness were given to the Ss in all three of these perceptual experiments. In no case was the side preference related to either the handedness or the eyedness of the Ss.

Regardless of instructions, the normal Ss who received tachistoscopic presentations of equal-sized stimuli perceived the right-side stimulus as being larger. It might be argued that under these two experimental conditions two separate intrasubject tendencies are operating: a learned or experiential right-hand motor preference and a purely perceptual process that makes one side appear larger. If such is the case, one might expect most people in our right-handed world to exhibit a right-hand motor preference, independently of the percept of one side as larger than the other. If there is, in addition, a right-side perceptual enlargement, there should be an additive tendency when Ss are instructed to respond to the larger stimulus. On the other hand, when Ss are instructed to respond to the smaller figure, the experiential tendency to respond with the right hand should be subtractive. Since the data did *not* show a symmetry for the two instructional conditions, i.e., since there was a greater tendency to judge the right side stimulus as larger under "larger" instructions than to judge the left side stimulus as smaller under "smaller" instructions, the data support the two-process hypothesis. It may be further hypothesized that these two separate processes may differ in relative strength with different experimental conditions. The results suggest that under a shorter intertrial interval the motor preference is predominant, whereas under a longer intertrial interval the perceptual component takes precedence.

In this study the two processes—a preference to respond with the right hand and a tendency to see the right-hand figure of two equal-sized stimuli as the larger—were confounded. They can be separated if S is required to make a nonmotor response. In an attempt to accomplish this separation an experiment (I. R. Gerjuoy, Winters, Alvarez, & Pullen, 1967) was run in which some Ss were required to make a motor response while other Ss were required to give a verbal response in the same task; the two conditions might be called perceptual and motor. For both conditions a vertical line was presented in the center of a rectangle. For the perceptual task a circle was placed outside the rectangle on one side and a square was placed symmetrically on the other side. The side of each figure was varied randomly over trials. The subject's task was to name the figure he thought the line was closer to. For the motor task no figures (other than the center vertical line) were in the visual field; instead, S was given two response keys. His task was to press the key on the side he thought the line was closer to. The same card, right side up or inverted, was used on all 20 trials in a random order. The figures were exposed for 3 seconds with a 17-second intertrial interval.

Sixty adolescent educable retardates, 60 equal MA normals, and 60 equal CA normals participated in equal numbers in each of the two conditions. The results indicate that different preferences were found under the two conditions. No initial preference occurred in the perceptual task, but a right side preference was found for both the retardates and the equal CAs in the motor task. No overall preference was found in the motor task, but in the perceptual task 73% of the equal MAs chose the left side more often, 70% of the retardates chose the right side more often, and 63% of the CAs chose the right side more often.

Both retardates and equal CA normals had a response preference to the right-hand key on the first trial; this result suggests that such a preference may be related to age. Seventy percent of each group responded on the right on the first trial, but this preference dissipated after the first response, as was the case in many of the studies cited earlier. Since there was no overall preference by any group in the motor condition (when the geometric forms were not in the field) there may have been no perceptual displacement in the nonmotor condition. One possible hypothesis is some differential interaction between the line and the geometric forms for equal MAs and the older groups. A second possibility is that the equal MAs attended more to the left half of the visual field, whereas the retardates and equal CAs attended more to the right side of the field and reported the geometric form on that side.

SUMMARY OF PERCEPTUAL TASKS

Equal CA normals had some right side preference in all these tasks. Except for the motor condition of the "line" experiment, they maintained this preference throughout the task. These results confirm those of Iwahara (1959), who found that in a guessing-game task in which S pressed one of two keys on each trial, both adults and young children had an initial right preference which decreased markedly after the first response in each block of trials. Adults' preferences were much stronger than children's preferences.

Other variables enter into the response preferences of retardates. Since the retarded Ss had a response preference under unlimited exposure but not under tachistoscopic exposure, such a preference cannot be simply a function of either MA or CA. The difference in the results of the two studies may, however, be related to slower processing of information in the retardate than in the normal; under short exposures retardates are unable to process the incoming information as completely as normals. This view is consistent with Spitz's speculation (1963) that cortical changes take place more slowly in the retardate, i.e., that there are physiological differences between normals and retardates of the same age. The fact that retardates do not differ from normals under unlimited exposure time, but do differ under short tachistoscopic exposure, lends support to the hypothesis that the primary process underlying the right side enlargement with short exposures is physiological rather than experiential. Retardates of the same age as normals should have had equivalent experience in a "right-handed" world. Therefore, they should not differ from normals in tasks in which experience is of primary importance. Thus, it is likely that the primary process underlying the right-side enlargement with unlimited exposure is experiential, since the extended exposure time allows elicitation of past experiences which foster these subjective responses, whereas the tachistoscopic exposure allows time for only a purely perceptual process.

Finally, it should be noted that perceptual preferences are stronger and more persistent than motor preferences even for normal adults. As indicated in previous studies, when a motor choice was predominant or was the only choice available to S, this preference was less pronounced. Although retardates were found to have a strong perceptual preference, they never exhibited more than a slight right side *motor preference* under any experimental conditions.

D. Multiple Responses in Tachistoscopic Recognition

In tachistoscopic recognition tasks, S must report as many stimuli as possible each time the material is flashed on. Investigators in this area have been concerned with which half of the visual field has the lower threshold for recognition under various conditions. Because Ss can give more than one response, the data in these studies are analyzed for order of responses.

Winters, Gerjuoy, Crown, and Gorrell (1967) presented pairs of both alphabetic and nonalphabetic stimuli for 1 second to adolescent educable retardates, equal MA normals, and equal CA normals. Two Os recorded the direction of S's eye movements and the order of his verbal reports. The normal groups' eye movements and order of verbal reports were from left to right significantly more often than were the retardates; all group responses were from left to right significantly more often than from right to left. The correlations between eye movement and verbal

report were significantly higher for normals than for retardates. Retardates who were more consistent in their organization of eye movements and verbal reports gave significantly more correct responses in
the experimental task and scored higher on a word recognition reading
test than did retardates who were less consistent. Of special importance
here is the fact that, although there was no side preference because
*S*s had enough time to perceive and report both stimuli, the retardates
reported from right to left more often than did the normal groups.

   Another study using samples from the same population was conducted to determine whether there would be differential recall in the
two visual fields under two different exposure times (Winters & Gerjuoy,
1967). Subjects were presented groups of four consonants in a rectangular display, one consonant in each of the four corners of the rectangle, first with a .01-second exposure and then with a .3-second
exposure. Under the shorter exposure the retardates and equal CA
normals correctly reported letters from the right visual field more often
than letters from the left visual field. Equal MAs had no greater accuracy
in one field than in the other. When *S*s were able to report two letters
correctly, the MAs generally reported from left to right in the top half
of the visual field. The older *S*s, retardates, and equal CAs, on the other
hand, tended to report either from upper left to upper right or from
upper right to lower right. Some equal CAs had other response orders.
The three populations did not differ in amount of recognition. Under
the longer exposure no group had better accuracy in one visual field
than in the other; the groups did differ, however, in numbers of correct
recognitions. Retardates recognized fewer letters than did equal MAs;
MAs recognized fewer letters than did equal CAs. The difference in
accuracy seemed to be related to the consistency of order of report.

   These studies indicate that when the exposure time is long enough
for reading scanning behavior to occur, it will occur and the *S*s will
choose a left stimulus first. Normal *S*s, whose reading experience is
greater than retardates', adopt this strategy more consistently. With a
very brief exposure time that inhibits the reading scanning pattern, the
older *S*s have more accurate recognition in the right visual field; the
equal MAs have no differential accuracy in the two visual fields.

IV. CHOICE-SEQUENCE PREFERENCES AND RESPONSE STRATEGIES

   When a *S* is instructed to choose between two stimuli, his responses to
the two stimuli are not random even when he is instructed to guess or
when he has difficulty in perceiving differences between the two stimuli.

As indicated earlier, he may have a stimulus or response preference. In addition, he may have a choice-sequence preference or a response strategy that is independent of the particular stimuli. Each response is dependent upon the previous response. Observations of this phenomenon date back to the psychophysical studies of the twenties. Fernberger (1920), for example, found that Ss avoided repetitions of the preceding judgment in a weightlifting experiment in which unequal weights were used. Later experimenters, such as Arons and Irwin (1932) and Preston (1936), found the same result for judgments in which equal weights were presented; i.e., they found that Ss tended to alternate judgments above chance when they received no feedback.

Response strategies are also used in learning tasks with reinforcement. Although these strategies can be analyzed, when one response is always reinforced and the other response is never reinforced (100−0), S may change a hypothesis that does not lead to 100% reinforcement before E is aware that S has such a hypothesis. To illustrate, S might start a binary-choice task with the hypothesis that the solution is the pattern AABB; but if B proved to be the correct response for the second trial, his hypothesis would become untenable and would probably be abandoned before he could fully exhibit even one cycle. This difficulty in analyzing response sequences is eliminated in the tasks in which both alternatives are always reinforced (100−100). If a hypothesis is abandoned, it must be for some reason other than nonreinforcement. Since nonreinforcement cannot occur, the primary hypothesis is likely to be maintained. When both responses are always reinforced, the extent to which S maintains the strategy is determined by S and not by E's behavior. Therefore, the 100−100 reinforcement situation provides the purest method for determining S's strategy.

A. 100% − 100% Reinforcement

Schusterman (1964) found that normal 3-year-old children perseverated after each of five binary-choice pretraining trials in which they were positively reinforced on every trial regardless of their response choices. Their task was to pick up one of two bottle caps. Under the same conditions 5-year-old children tended to alternate five times in a row while 10-year-old normals had no significant response tendency. Some of his retarded children (CA = 10 and MA = 5) perseverated five times in a row, some alternated five times in a row, and the rest were inconsistent in their choices. The switch from the strategy of perseveration to the strategy of alternation occurred at about MA 5 or 6 for Schusterman's Ss. Older Ss had no consistent strategy.

Jeffrey and Cohen (1965) presented 3-year-old and 4½-year-old children with two identical blocks. For some of the Ss a token was placed under each block on all trials, but S was allowed to pick up only one block to find a token. Over a period of 60 trials the 3-year-old Ss perseverated almost completely, whereas the 4½-year-old Ss exhibited strong alternation behavior. A third group, whose average age was 4 years, included some perseverators and some alternators. Thus, Jeffrey and Cohen's results are consistent with those of Schusterman. Their 3-year-olds perseverated and their 4½-year-olds alternated. Those in an intermediate age group (4-year-olds), however, exhibited neither tendency to the exclusion of the other; thus, Jeffrey and Cohen found the mean age for the shift from perseveration to alternation for normal children.

A study covering a wider age range was conducted by Gratch (1964). Subjects from 2 to 8 years of age were given 10 trials on each of which they were to guess in which hand E held a marble. Children 2 to 3 years old perseverated; at 3½ years old there was an abrupt shift to alternation, and at 5½ years old there was a reduction in the number of Ss who alternated consistently. Most Ss after this age had no consistent pattern of response. Gratch found a shift to alternation at a slightly earlier age than did Jeffrey and Cohen, 3½ rather than 4 years. Gratch included S groups between Schusterman's 5- and 10-year-olds. He therefore found a shift away from alternation to more random responding in a younger age group than did Schusterman.

Rieber (1966) used 7- to 9-year-old children in a test situation similar to the one employed by Jeffrey and Cohen. He found that his Ss alternated 72.7% of the time. Rieber concluded that alternation persists through age 8, and drops out by age 10 (cf. Schusterman). Rieber's findings may at first glance appear to be in conflict with those of Gratch. However, a reanalysis of the data from Gratch's Ss who were 5½ years old and older reveals that the average amount of alternation for these children was 70.37%. It appears, then, that although children above age 5½ rarely alternate persistently throughout a task, their alternations are well above chance.

In any analysis of alternation behavior, we must make the distinction between invariant alternation and alternation above chance, since they are, undoubtedly, two separate processes. Invariant alternation is a single strategy that is used throughout a task, whereas "above chance" alternation (i.e., alternation on more than half the trials in the binary-choice task) may be a form of behavior that masks a number of strategies that may or may not change during a task. For example, a strategy such as *ABB* will yield above chance alternation on a task of sufficient length. A change from this strategy to *AAB* or some more complex patterns of this type will also yield above chance alternations. In the case of Rieber's Ss and Gratch's older Ss, only a small number used invariant alternation, but most of them still alternated above chance.

A binary-choice guessing-game task was given to 9- and 10-year-old normals, to high-grade (IQ 66−79) and middle-grade (IQ 46−61) adolescent institutionalized retardates, and to college students by H. Gerjuoy and Gerjuoy (1964, 1965). Although a group from each population was given 100% reinforcement of both alternatives, this study differed from those just cited in that S was required to make not a motor but rather a verbal response ("beep" or "buzz"), and he was reinforced by the tone of the same name. Training was stopped if S gave the same pattern on five consecutive blocks of four trials or, if he did not maintain a pattern, after 200 trials.

All populations exhibited mean percentages of alternations above chance. Inspection of Table III reveals that these percentages decreased from middle-grade retardates to high-grade retardates to 9- and 10-year-old normals and to college students. Thus, overall alternations decrease with increasing MA. Part of this difference results from the decrease in the number of invariant alternators in the more intelligent groups.

TABLE III

A Comparison of Alternation Tendencies under 100% − 100% Reinforcement

Studies	Alternation by all Ss (mean %)	Invariant alternators (%)	Alternation excluding invariant alternators (mean %)
Schusterman			
5-year-olds	77.4	50.0	54.8
Retardates (MA = 5)	55.6	37.5	29.0
10-year-olds	46.5	3.0	44.8
Gratch			
3½ − 5-year-olds	80.8	51.1	60.1
5½ − 8-year-olds	70.4	26	59.8
Rieber			
7 − 9-year-olds	72.7		
Gerjuoy and Gerjuoy			
Middle-grade retardates	94.9	74.0	81.0
High-grade retardates	78.6	54.0	54.0
9 − 10-year-olds	72.9	33.0	59.4
College	57.3	19.0	47.2

Although there is some variability in the data cited, it seems to be rather consistent on the whole. The stronger alternation tendency of Gerjuoy and Gerjuoy's Ss' may result from the difference between their task and others' tasks. Both the responses S could make ("beep" or "buzz") and the reinforcements he received (one of two tones) were more distinctive than the stimuli and responses in other studies. In addition, this experiment gave only feedback, whereas the other experimenters gave some type of tangible reward. Schultz (1964) has pointed out that alternation is facilitated by dissimilarity between the stimuli. Iwahara (1959) found evidence to support this statement.

Schusterman's retardates alternated less than would be expected. His group, however, included a great many Ss who perseverated on all trials. In fact, the responses of his retardates appeared to have been a combination of those of his three normal groups; i.e., about one-third behaved as the 3-year-olds, one-third as the 5-year-olds, and the remainder as the 10-year-olds.

In sum, when both alternatives are reinforced 100% of the time, the youngest Ss, up to age $3\frac{1}{2}$ or 4, choose one alternative and repeat the same choice on each succeeding trial. From then until about age 6, invariant alternation is the most popular choice-sequence preference. Retardates, over a rather wide age range from early adolescence to adulthood, also prefer this mode of response. Normal children above age 6, even when they do not alternate consistently, will still alternate well above chance. This tendency decreases over age so that by late adolescence it has been reduced to chance.

B. 100%—0% Reinforcement

The usual learning task is not a 100−100 reinforcement task but rather a 100−0 task, in which one stimulus or one stimulus position is always rewarded while any other stimuli or stimulus positions are never rewarded. We have chosen only two of the many examples of this type of task to point out how differences in strategy can affect rate of learning.

After Schusterman (1963, 1964) gave his Ss their five 100−100 pretraining trials, he gave them a simple positional discrimination learning task to their nonpreferred side to a criterion of 15 consecutive errorless responses. Ten-year-old retardates and equal MA normals did not differ in the number of trials (11) to reach criterion. Equal CA normals, on the other hand, took significantly more trials (25) to reach criterion. If we assume that alternation was the strategy with which the lower MA groups began this phase of the task, which is true for the 5-year-olds and for some of the retardates, after the first nonreinforcements, they probably tried another strategy, the one next highest on their response hierarchy. We have seen that perseveration is a strong tendency for somewhat younger subjects, and it is likely that they tried that strategy next. In this case it was the winning strategy, and they learned the task rather easily. Since 10-year-old normals have had experience with many more response strategies than the lower MA groups, it is reasonable that perseveration, particularly to a position, is much lower on their response hierarchies. If this is true, then they would have had to have tried intermediate strategies and have received non-reinforcement for them before having tried perseveration, the winning strategy.

Baumeister (1966) has made an extensive analysis of errors in a three-choice size discrimination problem. Fourteen of 26 adolescent educable retardates and fifteen of eighteen 7-year-old normals reached the criterion of five consecutive errorless trials within 60 trials. Since almost all the normals but only half the retardates learned the task, Baumeister was interested in determining whether differences in strategies discriminated the learners from the nonlearners. He enumerated five types of errors and found the percentages of each type committed by retarded learners, retarded nonlearners, and normal learners. He called the first type of error "differential cue"; i.e., S responds to the rewarded position rather than to the rewarded object. This might be renamed win—stay to the immediately rewarded position. The second type of error was called "stimulus perseveration." This is a lose—stay strategy to a nonrewarded object and reflects a strong stimulus preference. The third type of error was designated "position habit." Errors of this type reflect Ss' responses to the same position; i.e., it is a response preference. It might also be called win—stay, lose—stay to position. Baumeister called the fourth type of error "+ response shift." This error describes the tendency to win—shift to a different object and a different position. Finally, he described "− response shift," the strategy of lose—shift to a different object and position.

Retardates and normals who learned the task did not differ in the amounts of each of the five types of errors that they made. The percentages of both groups, however, differed from those of the retarded nonlearners. On only one type of error, differential cue, were the proportions of errors similar for learners and nonlearners. Learners tended to have large numbers of + response shift and − response shift errors. In contrast, nonlearners made predominantly stimulus perseveration and position habit errors.

In order for learning to occur, S must switch his responses. A stimulus perseveration error is the least efficient strategy, since S never receives a reinforcement in this task. With a position habit he is reinforced one-third of the time. This schedule may be high enough to maintain this behavior for some Ss. Clearly, in a task in which the rewarded stimulus can occur in more than one position, no learning can occur while S persists with a position habit. Some type of alternation behavior must occur so that eventually S separates the reinforcement of the stimulus from the reinforcement of a position. Until S "knows" the solution and can perseverate his responses to the correct stimulus, he must use some form of alternation behavior. Thus, at least two strategies, first alternation and then perseveration, are needed in the solution of a stimulus discrimination task.

It can be seen from these studies that neither the age nor the intelligence of the Ss is the only variable that predicts ease of learning. A coincidence between the highest strategy in S's hierarchy and the strategy needed to solve the problem will result in the fastest learning. Varying of the nature of even simple discrimination tasks (e.g., positional vs stimulus discrimination) can change the order in which various S groups can solve the problem.

C. Partial Reinforcement

Other tactics have been utilized by researchers in the investigation of the response strategies of different subject populations. One popular method has been to vary the schedule of reinforcement. The binary-choice format has been used most frequently, but occasional studies have been designed with a ternary-choice format.

Variations in the schedule of reinforcement have ranged from equal amounts of reinforcement of each response, a 50:50 schedule, to almost total reinforcement of one response and only slight reinforcement of the other, such as a 90:10 schedule. Another variation is the partial reinforcement of one response together with no reinforcement of the alternative response. The present concern is with the response strategies of normal and retarded individuals regardless of the particular schedule of reinforcement.

Using a 50:50 and a 70:30 schedule, Kessen and Kessen (1961) gave 3-year-old and 4-year-old children a task in which they had to guess the color of cards (red or black) in a deck. The younger children were likely to perseverate even when their previous response was wrong. Older children alternated more than younger children, and they alternated even more when their previous prediction was wrong. They exhibited a strong lose—shift strategy, whereas the younger children adopted a win—stay, lose—stay strategy. The response strategies did not differ under the two reinforcement schedules.

Similar results were found by Jeffrey and Cohen (1965) with their

3-year-old children in both a 50:50 and a 33:33 ratio. Their 4½-year-old Ss, however, did not alternate or perseverate above chance under either of these schedules, although their 4½-year-old Ss under 100:100 had alternated significantly above chance.

Rieber (1966) replicated Jeffrey and Cohen's procedure with 7-year-old to 9-year-old children under 50:50 and 67:67 schedules. His Ss had a tendency to alternate following a nonreward; i.e., they adopted a lose–shift strategy. With his procedure both stimuli were baited on the same trials. Under 50:50 some of the Ss were rewarded and nonrewarded on alternate trials; others received rewards 50% of the time on a random schedule. This variable did not affect his Ss' behavior.

A 70:30 binary-choice task was given to first-grade children by Rosenhan (1966). He analyzed the children's responses for perseveration, single alternation, and double alternation. In order for a response to qualify as belonging to one of these patterns, it had to be preceded by four similar responses, a very strict criterion. These three strategies accounted for most of the data; i.e., there was little random responding or other patterns of responding. His figure and text indicate that 15% – 18% of the responses were perseverations, 45% were single alternations, and 27% were double alternations. Single alternation was the most popular strategy of these 6-year-old children.

A wider age range was investigated by Craig and Myers (1963). Kindergartners, fourth graders and eighth graders were given a binary-choice task with both a 60:40 and an 80:20 ratio. Regardless of the schedule the 5-year-olds alternated following both reward and nonreward, and they undermatched throughout. Their strategy was win–shift, lose–shift. Older children alternated less, usually following nonreward. Theirs was a win–stay, lose–shift strategy.

Following pretraining and initial training Schusterman's Ss (1963, 1964) were given a 50:50 probability series. The 10-year-old retardates and equal MA normals (CA = 5) tended either to alternate without much regard to outcome or to show a strong position preference; the equal CA normals, however, had a win–shift, lose–stay strategy. Low MA Ss persisted less after an unsuccessful choice than after a successful choice; i.e., they had a tendency to a win–stay, lose–shift strategy.

A developmental trend is evident in the studies just cited. The youngest children perseverate without regard to outcome. Between ages 4 and 5 there is a shift to alternation, again without regard to outcome. Ten-year-old retardates exhibit this alternation behavior. After age 7, normal Ss' strategies are related to reward and nonreward: They may adopt a win–stay, lose–shift or a win–shift, lose–stay strategy depending upon the relative probabilities of the response events. In either case, they are responding differentially to a previous reward or non-reward. It may be assumed that verbal mediation accompanies adoption of one of these higher order strategies.

Weir (1964) used a more complicated ternary-choice task in a developmental study of strategies with Ss ranging in age from 3 to 20. Subjects saw three knobs in a horizontal array. In this task two manipulanda were never reinforced; the third was reinforced either 33% or 66% of the time. The youngest and oldest Ss, 3-year-olds, 5-year-olds, and college students, tended to maximize; i.e., they responded persistently to the partially reinforced knob. The younger Ss adopted this strategy quickly; for the college students this strategy developed over trials. For the intermediate ages an alternation pattern, LMR or RML (where L stands for left, M for middle, and R for right) was very common. Up to age 9, Ss use a win–stay strategy. At age 11 this reverses to a win–shift, lose–shift. Eleven-year-olds alternate the most. Peak alternation occurs later in the ternary-choice task than in the binary-choice task.

Choice-sequence patterns of adolescent retardates, 9 - and 10-year-old normals, and college students were investigated in two studies by H. Gerjuoy and Gerjuoy (1964, 1965). Their task differed from those mentioned previously in that their purpose was to pit pairs of common strategies — perseveration, single alternation, and double alternation — against one another by the reinforcement schedule. On certain trials only one of the two responses was reinforced, whereas on other trials either response received reinforcement. For one treatment group, for example, the pattern of reinforcement was AEAE. This means that S's response on the first trial, whichever it was, was reinforced, either (E) response was reinforced on the second trial, his first response was reinforced on the third trial, and either response on the fourth trial. This pattern was repeated until S reached criterion or 200 trials. It can be seen that either invariant perseveration or single alternation will lead to 100% reinforcement, as will some other less common patterns, but that double alternation will yield only 75% reinforcement. Other treatments yielded other combinations of patterns that were reinforced either 100% or 75% of the time.

We shall consider two of the treatments together, that in which perseveration is pitted against single alternation and that in which single alternation is pitted against double alternation. Of those Ss who reached criterion, 25/29 middle-grade retardates, 21/26 high-grade retardates, 14/22 normal children, and 16/48 college students chose single alternation. Retardates in the IQ range 46-79 had an overwhelming preference for alternation, more than half the normal children chose this pattern, but only one-third of the college students alternated. The latter group's response sequences were quite varied, reflecting their flexibility and use of many hypotheses.

D. Nonreinforcement

Experimenters have investigated choice-sequence patterns in another class of studies, that in which Ss receive neither reinforcement nor feedback. Their responses are less influenced by any interaction with E than in any other type of task. Patterns elicited through this technique demonstrate the effects of stimulus preferences, response preferences, choice-sequence preferences, and their interactions. Researchers have varied experimental conditions in order to determine the effects of certain variables upon the amount of perseveration or alternation displayed by the S. Schultz (1964) has mentioned four conditions that facilitate the elicitation of alternation behavior. They are (a) neither reinforcement nor knowledge of results, (b) dissimilarity between the stimuli, (c) a short intertrial interval, and (d) prior exercise on one alternative. The last condition will not be discussed, since it has been used primarily with rats that do tend to choose the alternate response.

In the following group of studies, alternation behavior should be enhanced because S received no reinforcement. Also to be considered is the similarity between the stimuli as well as various intertrial intervals. Two variables that Schultz did not mention—the age and intelligence of the Ss—must be emphasized.

An experiment in binary guessing (Berenbaum & Aderman, 1964) was performed with a group of 9- to 13-year-old normal children and a group of 10- to 15-year-old retardates. Without receiving any feedback, Ss were required to guess 100 successive tosses of a coin. Although both groups alternated significantly above chance, the retardates alternated significantly more than did the normal children.

Ellis and Arnoult (1965) gave 4- and 5-year-old children 20 trials on a T-maze tracing task. For half the Ss the color of the T mazes, the background color, and the color of their tracing implements were always the same from trial to trial; for the remaining Ss these colors changed from trial to trial. Subjects alternated their responses above chance in the constant condition but below chance in the varied condition. Peters and Penney (1966) replicated this study with fifth- and sixth-grade children who had been divided into high and low reactively curious on the basis of the Reactive Curiosity Scale. They found that the high and low reactively curious groups differed in the constant condition; the high reactives alternated above chance, whereas the low reactives alternated below chance. In the varied condition, however, both groups alternated above chance.

Because Ellis and Arnoult did not give a pretest to separate their Ss, the data from Peters and Penney's two S groups must be collapsed if one is to compare the results of these two studies. In the previous discussion of choice-sequence behavior, it was established that perseveration is the earliest pattern. Ellis and Arnoult's young Ss tended to perseverate under the varied condition and to alternate under the constant condition. Peters and Penney's older Ss went one step higher on the hierarchy under both conditions; i.e., they alternated under the varied condition and responded randomly under the constant condition. It appears that each age group found the varied condition more confusing or difficult and therefore resorted to a lower form of response; i.e., they regressed.

Iwahara (1959) investigated spontaneous alternation in a key-pressing guessing-game task with third- and fourth-grade children and college women. The children alternated consistently more than did the adults. Spontaneous choice alternation decreased slightly from 0- to 30-second intertrial intervals for the children but not for the adults. Greater intertrial intervals reduced alternation for both groups. In a second experiment, Iwahara found that the tendency to alternate was greater when the two choice objects were differently colored than when they were similarly colored. At least part of the difference in alternation of the two S groups results from the stronger right side preference of the adult Ss.

The intertrial interval was included in studies using tachistosopic presentation of geometric forms (I. R. Gerjuoy & Winters, 1966; Winters & Gerjuoy, 1966) in order to determine whether this variable affects the alternation tendencies of retardates. With a 10-second intertrial interval, retardates alternated above chance, but with a 30-second interval they did not (I. R. Gerjuoy & Winters, 1966). Thus, spacing of trials affects retardates as well as normal children. Retardates' alternation was considerably less, under more massed trials, than that in other studies in which trials were even more massed. It may be that the inaccessibility of previous responses, as well as the variability of the stimuli from trial to trial and the relatively long intertrial interval, reduced the alternation tendency. Failure of the college Ss to alternate above chance under these experimental conditions was, of course, owing to their very strong position preferences.

A number of investigators have observed that college students give binary-choice sequences rich in alternations. It was suggested by Reichenbach (1949, p. 153) that this might be a consequence of preconceptions they might have about the nature of random sequences. The results of the *AB* study mentioned previously (I. R. Gerjuoy &

Gerjuoy, 1965) in which S received 20 trials with an AB configuration, indicate that instructions to respond with a simple pattern produce as much alternation as do instructions to respond randomly. In fact, the normal children alternated more under the pattern-set instructions. Instructions to respond randomly may actually reduce the amount of alternation by discouraging Ss from persisting with the simple, regular pattern of single alternation. The tendency to alternate in this task decreased with increased mental age. Both adolescent educable retardates and equal MA normal children alternated significantly more than did college students.

The AB random condition of this study was used as a control condition in the more extensive, second AB study that included the stimulus pairs BA, AA, and BB with college students. The overall percentage of alternations for the AB random condition was 61.0% in the first study and 60.96% in the second study. In order to compare the amount of alternation with dissimilar stimuli with the amount of alternation with similar stimuli, the data from the AB and BA conditions were combined, as were those from the AA and BB conditions. The percentage of alternations for dissimilar stimuli was 61.36%; the percentage of alternations for the similar stimuli was 57.83%. These percentages differ significantly from one another; thus, alternation was greater with dissimilar than with similar (identical) stimuli, as previously indicated.

Similar results were obtained in the Japanese symbol study (I. R. Gerjuoy & Winters, 1965). With respect to frequency of alternation (from least to most), the subject populations ranked in the following order: college students, normal children, retarded children, and adolescents. Another S group was included in this study, viz., adult retardates. This group, whose members had lower MAs than did the younger retardates, had a strong perseveration tendency: 28.6% perseverated invariantly. Within this group there was a significant negative correlation between perseveration and IQ.

In this condition similarity between the stimuli did not prove to be an important variable. This may of course have been because of the Ss' lack of familiarity with Japanese symbols. For all groups, the amount of alternation in the Japanese symbol study was less than the amount in the AB study. In the Japanese symbol study the stimulus pairs varied from trial to trial; no pair of stimuli was ever repeated. Reduced alternation may have been a function of the stimulus variety from trial to trial. An alternative hypothesis is that alternation of position was the only type of alternation possible in this task whereas position alternation, stimulus alternation, or both were possible in the AB study.

Alternation is a preferred response strategy of all S groups except very low MA groups (very young children and low-grade retardates). Above this low MA range, alternation is strongest in retardates and normal children of 5 years old or more, decreasing in its strength as Ss become older. Even bright adults, however, do tend to alternate above chance in many diverse tasks.

The studies cited seem to indicate that age and intelligence variables are the most powerful in determining the amount of alternation in a task. Task variables such as instructions, similarity of the stimuli, and intertrial interval also affect the amount of alternation but to a lesser extent. Finally, it does not appear that even reinforcement is crucial, since alternation behavior occurs both without reinforcement and over a wide variety of reinforcement schedules.

E. Regression to Alternation

Alternation is a favored sequential response mode in binary-choice guessing-game tasks and in binary-choice learning tasks. Normal children and educable retarded adolescents have a greater tendency to alternate in these tasks than do normal adults. Even under 100%-100% reinforcement, alternation is higher in the response-sequence hierarchy of low MA populations than is any other response sequence. Even when alternation no longer leads to 100% reinforcement and when some other response pattern would result in reinforcement on each trial, retardates will persist in alternating. Further, when retardates try other patterns in binary-choice learning tasks and encounter nonreinforcement on some trials, they will fall back on alternation as their solution, regardless of subsequent reinforcement.

Put another way, it is suggested that retardates and possibly normal children may "regress" to alternation; i.e., they may choose this more primitive form of behavior in an objectively soluble binary-choice task that is too difficult for them to solve. To test this hypothesis, first-through fifth-grade normal children and educable retarded adolescents were administered a spatial orientation task (I. R. Gerjuoy, Winters, & Hoats, 1966) in which they were required to respond "left" or "right" at each choice point of the Road Map Test (Money, 1965). It was expected that the task would be too difficult for most of the younger children and retardates and that they would tend to make more errors and to alternate their responses more than the older children.

Only the fourth and fifth graders and the retardates had significantly fewer errors than chance. All groups alternated significantly above chance, with retardates giving the most alternations. The younger normals tended to alternate more than the older normals.

When faced with a task that can in no way be interpreted as a guessing game, these Ss tended to employ a more primitive form of behavior (alternation) in their method of solution. Such behavior, it would appear, is related to level of development of the S. That this is not a simple relationship with either MA or CA is illustrated by the performance of the various S populations in the present task. The retardates, who were of higher MA than the first through third graders, tended to alternate more, but in terms of errors they were superior to these young normals. On the other hand, retardates made more errors than their MA equivalents in grade 5.

A frequency count of Ss who alternated throughout the task sheds more light on the use of alternation by retardates. Although only 4/220 normal Ss (from the first through third grades) exhibited this invariant alternation behavior, 8/36 retardates did so.

These results led to the inference that in a soluble task with several levels of difficulty, more Ss will exhibit alternation as the task becomes more difficult; if the task then becomes easier, fewer Ss will alternate above chance. In order to test this hypothesis, I. R. Gerjuoy and Winters (1967) conducted the five-task number study described earlier. Since the data from the fourth through eighth grades did not differ reliably, they were combined and compared with those of the retardates. The percentages of no acceptable solution for each population are presented in Table IV.

TABLE IV
PERCENTAGES OF Ss WITH NO ACCEPTABLE SOLUTION ON EACH OF FIVE TASKS

Population	Task 1	Task 2	Task 3	Task 4	Task 5
Normals	4	16	28	11	3
Retardates	54	71	71	57	39

Inspection of Table IV reveals that Task 3 was indeed the most difficult task. Fewer retardates than normals found solutions for any of the tasks. Alternations were computed for those Ss who did not find an acceptable solution for a particular task. Over all five tasks, alternation was found to be significantly above chance for each population. Retardates, however, alternated significantly more than did normal children. In addition, some retardates displayed invariant alternation, a strategy that was not used by normals. The gradient of difficulty of the tasks was also related to the amount of alternation. Normals alternated significantly more on Task 3 than on the other tasks. The difference in alternation between Task 3 and the other tasks just failed to reach significance for the retardates since their overall alternation was extremely high on all tasks. As the task became more difficult, alternation increased among the nonsolvers; as it became easier again, alternation decreased. This suggests the possibility that amount of alternation could be used as an index of task difficulty for these populations.

V. CONCLUDING COMMENTS

An overview of the research cited provides conclusive evidence that the responses of subjects change as a function of increasing MA (see Table V). The youngest and dullest Ss choose a response and continue with that response throughout the task. They may start with a particular stimulus or response preference, or their initial response may be random. The preference to perseverate to the same position or to the same stimulus seems to be the overriding strategy. It is affected little, if at all, by the amount of reinforcement or by any reinforcement schedule. Whether or not a position habit has a physiological basis, however, cannot be determined at this time since the experimenters in this area have not mentioned the side of the perseveration. If early perseveration usually occurs on the same side, it may be innate.

The second most common response sequence is invariant alternation. This strategy eliminates any stimulus or response preferences with which a S begins a task. Here, again, the sequence of responses is more influential than stimulus or position preferences in determining S's behavior. Reinforcement schedules do little to alter this strong response tendency in Ss with an MA of about 5.

As Ss become older, they shift away from the strategy of invariant alternation because they become more affected by task variables and schedules of reinforcement. When two stimuli are differentially reinforced, these Ss' strategies are based upon the reward or nonreward of the previous response. In contrast to the youngest Ss who "stay" invariantly and the somewhat older Ss who "shift" invariantly, these Ss will adopt either a win–stay, lose–shift or a win–shift, lose–stay strategy, depending upon the particular reinforcement schedule.

When these older Ss receive no feedback or reinforcement, changes in behavior occur with changes in task variables, such as stimulus similarity, intertrial interval, accessibility of previous responses, and type of response required. Since the Ss no longer adopt an invariant strategy, the choice-sequence preferences are less powerful than the stimulus or response preferences that they bring into the situation. If, for example, alphabetic material is used, S's reading experience will play an important role in his responses; i.e., he will respond on the left or report from left to right. With other material, and particularly when a motor response is required, S's experience in a right-hand world will produce a right side response preference. That previous experience is effective in determining the responses of retardates is clear when we see that they have the same preferences as do normals of the same age when familiar material is used and no overall preference when unfamiliar material is used.

TABLE V

The Development of Strategies of Normal and Retarded Children under 100% — 100% and Partial Reinforcement

100% — 100% Reinforcement

(1) Normal children perseverate invariantly up to age 3½ in a binary-choice task.

Gratch (1964), Jeffrey and Cohen (1965), Schusterman (1964)

(2) Invariant alternation is the next higher strategy. It is employed by normal children up to age 5½, and retarded children and adolescents of the same mental age.

H. Gerjuoy and Gerjuoy (1964, 1965), Gratch (1964)
Jeffrey and Cohen (1965), Schusterman (1964)

(3) Response strategies become less consistent hereafter. Alternation is still above chance even in adulthood, but it decreases with age.

H. Gerjuoy and Gerjuoy (1964, 1965), Gratch (1964), Rieber (1966)

Partial Reinforcement

(1) Normal children up to age 4 adopt a win—stay, lose—stay strategy (perseveration without regard to outcome) under several reinforcement schedules.

Jeffrey and Cohen (1965), Kessen and Kessen (1961)

(2) A win—shift, lose—shift strategy (alternation without regard to outcome) is adopted by most normal 5- and 6-year old children and 10-year-old retardates.

Craig and Myers (1963), Rosenhan (1966), Schusterman (1963, 1964)

(3) After age 7, the strategies of normal children are related to reward and non-reward. They will adopt either a win—stay, lose—shift or a win—shift, lose—stay strategy depending upon the reinforcement schedule.

Craig and Myers (1963), Rieber (1966), Schusterman (1963)

Although this developmental sequence applies to retardates as well as to normal *S*s, at some ages the behavior of retardates is more variable from *S* to *S* than is that of normals. At the point at which most normal *S*s are affected by task variables and reinforcement schedules, some retardates are also affected by these variables; others, however, still maintain invariant strategies. Although retardates operate at a lower stratum than do normals of the same age, their range of behavior at some points on the developmental scale is wider than that of normals.

ACKNOWLEDGMENTS

The authors wish to express their deep appreciation to Peter L. Carlton, Sydell T. Carlton, Robert J. Greene, David L. Hoats, Edward A. Holden, Jr., and Herman H. Spitz for their critical readings of the manuscript.

REFERENCES

Arons, L., & Irwin, F. W. Equal weights and psychological judgments. *Journal of Experimental Psychology,* 1932, **15,** 733-756.

Baumeister, A. A. Analysis of errors in the discrimination learning of normal and retarded children. *Psychonomic Science,* 1966, **6,** 515-516.

Berenbaum, H. L., & Aderman, M. Comparison of binary guessing response tendencies of normal and retarded children. *American Psychologist,* 1964, **19,** 466. (Abstract)

Craig, G. J., & Myers, J. L. A developmental study of sequential two-choice decision making. *Child Development,* 1963, **34,** 483-493.

Ellis, N. C., & Arnoult, M. D. Novelty as a determinant of spontaneous alternation in children. *Psychonomic Science,* 1965, **2,** 163-164.

Fernberger, S. W. Interdependence of judgments with the series for the method of constant stimuli. *Journal of Experimental Psychology,* 1920, **3,** 126-150.

Gerjuoy, H., & Gerjuoy, I. R. Choice-sequence patterns in binary-choice "learning" by retardates. *American Journal of Mental Deficiency,* 1964, **69,** 425-431.

Gerjuoy, H., & Gerjuoy, I. R. Binary-choice hypothesis hierarchies in retardates, normal children and college students. Paper read at the *American Psychological Association,* Chicago, September 1965.

Gerjuoy, I. R., & Gerjuoy, H. Binary-choice sequences of retardates, normal children, and college students under random- and pattern-set instructions. *American Journal of Mental Deficiency,* 1965, **69,** 854-859.

Gerjuoy, I. R., Gerjuoy, H., & Mathias, R. Probability learning: Left-right variables and response latency. *Journal of Experimental Psychology,* 1964, **68,** 344-350.

Gerjuoy, I. R., & Winters, J. J., Jr. Binary-choice responses of retardates, normal children and college students to similar or dissimilar stimuli. *American Journal of Mental Deficiency,* 1965, **70,** 474-477.

Gerjuoy, I. R. & Winters, J. J., Jr. Lateral preference for identical geometric forms: II. Retardates. *Perception & Psychophysics,* 1966, **1,** 104-106.

Gerjuoy, I. R., & Winters, J. J., Jr. Response preferences and choice-sequence preferences: I. Regression to alternation. *Psychonomic Science,* 1967, **7,** 413-414.

Gerjuoy, I. R., Winters, J. J., Jr., Alvarez, J. M., & Pullen, M. M. Response preferences and choice-sequence preferences: II. Perceptual and motor conditions. *Psychonomic Science,* 1967, **8,** 75-76.

Gerjuoy, I. R., Winters, J. J., Jr., & Hoats, D. L. Alternation in a spatial orientation task. *Psychonomic Science*, 1966, **5**, 83-84.

Gratch, G. Response alternation in children: A developmental study of orientations to uncertainty. *Vita Humana*, 1964, **7**, 49-60.

Iwahara, S. Studies in spontaneous alternation in human subjects. III. A developmental study. *Japanese Psychological Research*, 1959, **1**, 1-8.

Jeffrey, W. E., & Cohen, L. B. Response tendencies of children in a two-choice situation. *Journal of Experimental Child Psychology*, 1965, **2**, 248-254.

Kessen, W., & Kessen, M. D. Behavior of young children in a two-choice guessing problem. *Child Development*, 1961, **32**, 779-788.

Miller, M. E. Right-response preference in probability learning and reversal. *Journal of Experimental Psychology*, 1966, **71**, 776-778.

Money, J. *A standardized road-map test of direction sense*. Baltimore, Md.: Johns Hopkins Press, 1965.

Peters, R. D., & Penney, R. K. Spontaneous alternation of high and low reactively curious children. *Psychonomic Science*, 1966, **4**, 139-140.

Preston, M. G. Contrast effects and psychophysical judgments. *American Journal of Psychology*, 1936, **48**, 389-402.

Reichenbach, H. *The theory of probability: An inquiry into the logical and mathematical foundations of the calculus of probability*. (2nd ed.) Berkeley: University of California Press, 1949.

Rieber, M. Response alternation in children under different schedules of reinforcement. *Psychonomic Science*, 1966, **4**, 149-150.

Rosenhan, D. Double alternation in children's binary choice responses. *Psychonomic Science*, 1966, **4**, 431-432.

Schultz, D. P. Spontaneous alternation behavior in humans: Implications for psychological research. *Psychological Bulletin*, 1964, **62**, 394-400.

Schusterman, R. J. The use of strategies in two-choice behavior of children and chimpanzees. *Journal of Comparative and Physiological Psychology*, 1963, **56**, 96-100.

Schusterman, R. J. Strategies of normal and mentally retarded children under conditions of uncertain outcome. *American Journal of Mental Deficiency*, 1964, **69**, 66-75.

Spitz, H. H. Field theory in mental deficiency. In N. R. Ellis (Ed.), *Handbook of mental deficiency: Psychological theory and research*. New York: McGraw-Hill, 1963, Pp. 11-40.

Weir, M. W. Developmental changes in problem-solving strategies. *Psychological Review*, 1964, **71**, 473-490.

Winters, J. J., Jr., & Gerjuoy, I. R. Gamma movement: Field brightness, series, and side of the standard. *Psychonomic Science*, 1965, **2**, 273-274.

Winters, J. J., Jr., & Gerjuoy, I. R. Lateral preference for identical geometric forms: I. Normals. *Perception & Psychophysics*, 1966, **1**, 101-103.

Winters, J. J., Jr., & Gerjuoy, I. R. Recognition of tachistoscopically exposed letters by normals and retardates. Paper read at the *American Association on Mental Deficiency*, Denver, May 1967.

Winters, J. J., Jr., Gerjuoy, I. R. Crown, P., & Gorrell, R. Eye movements and verbal reports in tachistoscopic recognition by normals and retardates. *Child Development*, 1967, in press.

Studies in the Experimental Development of Left – Right Concepts in Retarded Children Using Fading Techniques[1]

SIDNEY W. BIJOU

UNIVERSITY OF ILLINOIS, URBANA, ILLINOIS

[1] The first part of this research was accomplished while the investigator was on a Special Senior Fellowship from the National Institutes of Health (1961 – 62) at Harvard University. Subsequent research was supported by grants M-2232 and MH-12067 from the National Institute of Mental Health, U. S. Public Health Service.

I. INTRODUCTION

Retarded development results from limited opportunities to acquire and maintain essential behavioral equipment. The greater the restrictions, the greater the retardation. Three interrelated conditions singly or in combination, which impose limitations on development, result from restricted opportunities stemming from (a) physiological deficiencies and malfunctioning, (b) the absence of stimulating physical and social events, and (c) acquired behavioral mechanisms that mitigate against further learning and adjustment (Bijou, 1966).

It follows that one cannot be certain whether a retarded child can learn a specific task until he is given an opportunity to try. If he does not learn even under the guidance of a fine teacher using the most advanced techniques, one cannot justly conclude that the child is incapable of learning. One can conclude only that under those particular conditions (materials and procedures), he has not learned. He may do extremely well under another set of conditions derived from the application of new principles, or an improved application of old principles. It is therefore incumbent on those concerned with the technology of teaching to provide new know-how to the building of better and better learning histories in a child—a know-how built on the application of empirically demonstrated behavioral principles.

A research program which aims to provide a child—normal, retarded, or otherwise deviant—with an effective learning program presents numerous perplexing problems. For example: How can the material we want the child to learn be broken down into components to which he can readily respond? How can we motivate the child so that these easily managed, specific stimulus events will strengthen the desired responses? How can supporting behavior (such as attending to subject matter) be strengthened, and interfering behaviors (such as fighting with peers) be weakened? In short, how can one construct a segment of a child's history that will result in academic and social changes which will be both desirable and serviceable for that child's future behavior?

The aim of the research described here was to explore what is involved in constructing an experimental history which would enable a child to discriminate geometric forms differing in left—right orientation. More specifically, the question was: What materials and procedures must be developed so that a retarded child can demonstrate a left—right concept, or can make orientational discriminations on nonverbal material? To find a specific, objective answer to this problem is to have knowledge of at least *one way* of helping the retarded child to acquire behavior that is essential to learning a left—right concept, both nonverbal and verbal.

II. DEVELOPMENT OF METHOD AND PROCEDURE

A. Subjects

The normal group, used in developing and evaluating the program, consisted of 90 children from the preschool and primary grades of the Lesley-Ellis School, Cambridge, Massachusetts. Included were 52 boys, ranging in age from 3 years and 5 months to 6 years and 11 months; and 38 girls from 3 years and 3 months to 6 years and 8 months. Intelligence test scores were not available, but these children were presumed to be of at least average intelligence.

Fig. 1. Match-to-sample apparatus.

B. Apparatus

The apparatus, shown in Fig. 1, is a variation of a device used extensively in infrahuman research. It was originally conceived by Skinner and developed further by Holland and Long to study "inductive reasoning" in young children (J. G. Holland, 1960, 1963). A modification of the apparatus was used by Hively (1962) to study form discrimination in young normal children.

The device consists of a box with a panel of windows to display the stimuli and to register selections, a Bell and Howell 2 x 2 in. slide projector, an Esterline-Angus event recorder, and a circuitry rack. (In later versions, a Kodak Carousel Projector was used in place of the Bell and Howell projector and a Gerbrands event marker in place of the Esterline-Angus.) The subject was seated so that he faced the two horizontal, translucent, plastic windows. The upper window was a single unit; the lower one was divided into five equal parts. Geometric forms were projected on the windows from behind. One form, designated as the sample, appeared in the center of the large upper window; five forms, one in each of the row of lower windows, were the matches or foils. Presentations followed a temporal sequence. The sample was projected first; the matches appeared only after S pressed on the sample window. Temporal relationships between the sample and choices, order of slide presentations, and stimulus feedback (light and chime) were controlled by switching circuits.

The child indicated which one of the five forms presented in the row matched the sample by pressing on that particular window. If he made a correct selection, a red light glowed momentarily, a chime sounded, the sample and the five choices disappeared, and another sample appeared. The subject could then produce the next set of choices by pressing on the sample window, and proceed to make the next match. If he made an incorrect choice, neither the light nor chime operated, and the matches disappeared. (An audible and distinctive thud by the mechanism accompanied the blackout of the matches.) Pressure on the sample window removed the blocking screen and restored the choices providing a second opportunity for matching. If the second response was also incorrect, the choices blacked out once more. Again pressure on the upper window restored the matches. This four-component sequence (press on sample window to display choices, selection of an incorrect match, disappearance of choices, press on sample window to display choices) was continued until the correct response was made. The correct response removed both the sample and the matches and presented the next sample. Under this arrangement of contingencies the last response to a problem was always the correct response.

When one or more incorrect responses had been made to a given sample—say, on slide n—the slide following the correct response was slide $n-1$ rather than slide $n+1$. Given one or more errors on any slide n, the next three slides to be presented were $n-1$, n, and then $n+1$. Thus after making an error, a child could not move forward to the next task without responding a second time to both the preceding slide $n-1$, *and* slide n. It was therefore possible for a S to make "new" errors on slides previously matched without error, and to go backward rather than forward in the program.

C. Instructions

The subject was brought to the experimental room by a young, female experimenter. After inviting him to sit down and adjusting the height of the chair so that the child's eyes were approximately level with the strip separating the upper and lower windows, the experimenter sat beside him and said, "Put your finger on this (sample in upper window) and press it. Find one here (choices in lower window) just like it, and press it. Good."

After three correct consecutive selections, each followed by "good," the experimenter said, "Try to get it right the first time," and went to the rear of the room where she monitored the apparatus and observed the child's behavior through a mirror. Upon completion of each trayful of slides (usually 40), she said, "Very good. I have more for you." When the next slide tray was in operational position, she said, "Go ahead."

D. Stimulus Material

The stimuli consisted of 10 forms cut from 1½ in. squares of red, yellow, green, and blue paper.[2] (See the forms in the column designated "Original" in Fig. 2.) Each form was composed of five ½ in. squares; three formed a vertical staff, and two were horizontal members attached to the vertical staff at the top, middle, or bottom. In some forms, the two horizontal squares were attached to the same side of the staff, as in the shape of an L (second form from the top). In other forms, they appeared on opposite sides, as in a cross or inverted T. Three of the forms, winged L (fifth from the top), square Z (seventh from the top), and the flag (ninth from the top), could be rotated in the horizontal plane to make mirror-image forms. These rotations are shown in the sixth, eighth, and tenth positions in column one.

The sample and matches constituting a frame or a slide were photographed on 16-mm, color-sensitive film and developed into standard 2 × 2 in. slides. Two versions of the program were constructed: one with the forms all in one color in each slide (red, yellow, blue, or green), the other with the forms in four colors in each slide.

The program, consisting of 270 slides divided into elementary, intermediate, and advanced sets, was developed on a succession of small groups of Lesley-Ellis school children. The procedure involved setting up a trial series, testing it on a small group of children, contracting or expanding the sequence, testing it on another group of children, contracting or expanding the sequence again, etc.

[2]Commercially referred to as Color-aid paper, produced by the Color-aid Company, 329 East 29 Street, New York, New York. The yellow was designated No. 9, the red No. 57, the blue No. 130, and the green No. 170.

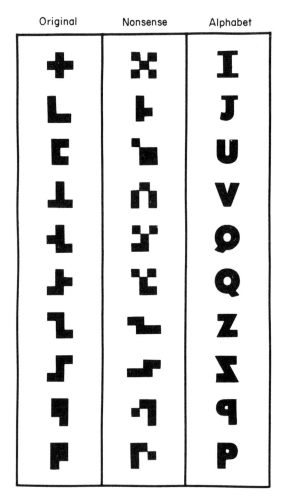

FIG. 2. Forms in mirror-image training and pre- and posttests. Reading from the top down, the first five figures in the column designated "Original" are referred to in the text as "cross," "L," "square C," "T," and "winged L," respectively. The eighth and last figures in the column are referred to as "square Z" and "flag," respectively.

1. ELEMENTARY AND INTERMEDIATE SETS

The elementary set, evolving from four such major revisions, first contained a solid colored circle, square, and triangle comparable in size to the experimental forms (see Fig. 3, slide 1-1). These simple forms served to ease the youngster into operating the apparatus. They were also effective in forcing the child to engage in the attending behavior necessary for making the matching response described in the next paragraph. Slides 1, 10, 13, 14, and 24, the last one in this series, are

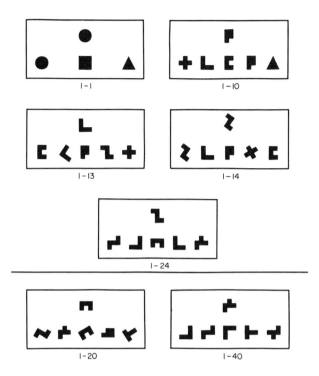

FIG. 3. Schematic drawings of five slides from the elementary set (above the horizontal line) and two from the intermediate set (below the horizontal line).

shown in the upper part of Fig. 3, designated as 1-1, 1-10, 1-13, 1-14, and 1-24. Except for slide 14, which was a probe to determine what effects, if any, would result from tilting the sample at 30 degrees, the sample always appeared in an upright position. However, the matches were presented in rotated positions, tilted to the right or left of vertical, first at 30 degrees, then 60 degrees, and finally at 90 degrees. Slide 1-24 in Fig. 3 shows a 90-degree discrepancy between match and sample.

The intermediate set, also produced after four major revisions, was designed to afford training in discriminations when *both* the samples and the matches are rotated in the vertical plane through 180 degrees and when *rotational discrepancies* between the sample and the matches vary as much as 180 degrees. In this series of 40 slides, the middle and last frames are shown in the lower part of Fig. 3, labeled 1-20 and 1-40.

2. ADVANCED SET

The advanced set, which underwent five major revisions, was designed to train the child to make discriminations between mirror images and nonmirror images of three forms presented with rotations in the vertical plane. Many abortive starts were made prior to the five revisions. The most promising and therefore the one incorporated into the program might be described as a "fading-in" technique, the procedure being similar in principle to that used by Terrace on infrahuman *Ss* (1966), and by Moore and Goldiamond on young children (1964).

In the advanced set, only the flag, square Z, and the winged L were samples. Half the time they were shown with orientational cues to the right, half the time to the left. In the early part of the program, foils or distractors were the seven other nonmirror-image forms, and partially developed mirror images of the sample; and in the later part, nonmirror-image forms and one or more complete mirror images of the sample. Because of its length (206 slides), the advanced set was subdivided into five units.

Unit 1 (slides 1-1 to 1-46) was constructed to give training in discriminating a mirror image from a nonmirror image by the fading-in technique mentioned above. This training required 15 specially prepared slides which contained one distractor made up of one of three (square C, winged L, and cross) altered to transform each, in gradual stages, into distractor mirror images of the flag, square Z, or winged L presented as the sample. More specifically when the flag oriented to the right was a sample, there was one distractor which was made by raising, in successive slides, the lower horizontal square of the square C (see Fig. 2, third from the top in column labeled Original) until it touched the upper square and formed a flag oriented to the left. By the same token the mirror-image form of square Z was formed gradually by raising the center horizontal square on winged L to the top of the vertical staff, and the mirror-image form of the winged L was made by gradually lowering one of the lateral squares of the cross until it reached the bottom of the vertical staff. Fading-in distractor mirror-image forms of the sample was achieved in six steps for each of the three forms. Figure 4 shows five of these partially constructed mirror-image distractors in slides designated as 1-1, 1-8, 1-14, 1-22, and 1-29. Slide 1-35, also shown, is the first presentation of a distractor which is a complete mirror image of the sample.

Unit 2 (slides 2-1 to 2-40) was designed to give further training in discriminating one mirror-image distractor and the correct match in the context of: (a) increased vertical plane rotations of both sample and matches; (b) increased discrepancies between sample and correct match; (c) increased discrepancies between sample and incorrect match, in the form of a mirror image of the sample; and (d) increased discrepancies between correct match and incorrect mirror-image match. Figure 4 shows two samples from Unit 2, marked 2-2 and 2-8.

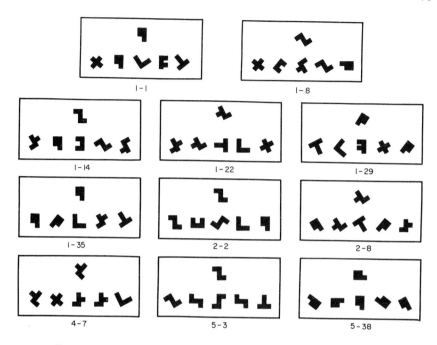

FIG. 4. Schematic drawings of eleven slides from the advanced set.

Unit 3 (slides 3-1 to 3-40) was designed to extend training in discrimination of the correct match from its mirror-image distractor by increasing the number of problems with discrepancies between sample and match at 30, 60, and 90 degrees. Because of the high error rate associated with 90-degree discrepancies, the step between 60 and 90 degrees was divided in half. This was accomplished by inserting six slides with 75-degree rotations. In this unit, samples, correct matches, and incorrect mirror-image matches were rotated zero, 30, 60, 75, 90, 105, and 135 degrees while the correct matches and the incorrect mirror-image matches were gradually separated in their window positions.

Unit 4 (slides 4-1 to 4-20) was designed to provide training to discriminate between the correct match and two mirror-image distractors starting with slide 4-7 (see Fig. 4). Rotational discrepancies between sample and correct match ranged from 0 to 90 degrees. In addition to introducing new rotational positions of mirror-image distractors in windows adjacent to correct matches, and gradually presenting them in the most widely separated windows, the two mirror-image distractors appeared initially in parallel vertical plane orientation; that is, both were shown at zero, 30, or 60 degrees. The two mirror-image distractors then appeared in different rotational positions with respect to each other, the correct match, and the sample.

Unit 5 (slides 5-1 to 5-40) was designed to provide training in matching problems having three and four distractor mirror images. Rotations appeared in gradual stages, and mirror-image distractors were displayed in parallel rotational deviations in the initial presentations, and then varied independently. In Fig. 4, slide 5-3 shows a problem with two mirror-image distractors at 90 degrees, and one at zero; slide 5-38 shows one with four mirror-image distractors with vertical plane rotations to 120 degrees.

E. Pretests and Posttests

Three tests, 20 slides in each, were prepared to evaluate discrimination before and after training in the program. The first test, designated "Original," was made up of four slides from the intermediate, and 16 from the advanced set. The second test, called the "New Nonsense," was composed of the same four slides from the intermediate set and 16 slides with new forms arranged to present equivalent problems to those in the first test. The third test, the "Alphabet," was also composed of the same four slides from the intermediate set and 16 slides with forms made from seven letters drawn at random. The latter, like the 16 slides in the New Nonsense test presented equivalent problems to those in the Original test. Hence all three tests were alike in length, in the initial four slides, and in problems presented. Only the forms differed in the last 16 slides of each test. Those in the Original were from the advanced set; those in the New Nonsense were the same in area and color but different in pattern (5 $\frac{1}{2}$-in. squares); and those in the Alphabet were also the same in area and color, but were letters rather than forms. All of these forms are in Fig. 2.

The tests were given prior to training as follows: (a) The experimenter gave the usual instructions and *S* proceeded to match the first 15 slides in the elementary set, to learn how to perform the task. (b) The instructions were repeated, and *S* was given the 60 slides in the three tests. Neither the light and chime following correct matches nor the slide back-up action of the projector following incorrect responses was used. (c) The instructions were given again, and *S* was started on slide 1-16 of the elementary set with light and chime following correct responses, and slide back-up action following incorrect responses. (To evaluate the influence of the pretests on performance in the program, the experimenter started some *S*s on the training series with slide 1-1.)

III. DATA AND INTERPRETATION ON TRAINING
OF RETARDED AND NORMAL CHILDREN

The retarded group was composed of 89 children in residence at the Walter E. Fernald School, Waverly, Massachusetts. There were 75 boys who ranged from 6 years 4 months to 16 years 11 months in chronological age; from 3 years 10 months to 8 years 10 months in mental age test scores; and from 32 to 65 in IQ scores. The 14 girls ranged from 12 years to 14 years 7 months in chronological age; from 4 years 11 months to 7 years 2 months in mental age test scores; and from 39 to 66 in IQ scores. All were educable.

The normal group consisted of the Lesley-Ellis children described in Section II. The ages and sex of the children used in this part of the study are given in Tables I, II, VI, and VII.

A. Sample Data from a Retarded Subject

To show the type of data obtained, the performance of a 14-year-old Fernald boy (S63) with a mental age score of 8 years 10 months will be presented in some detail. (see Fig. 5). Time is plotted in 20-second units on the abscissa and the order number of slides is on the ordinate. The cumulative curves were constructed from events marked on an Esterline-Angus recorder by representing a correct response as a step up to the next slide; duration of response time is represented by the length of the step-tread. The curves show a regression when slide order was reversed following an incorrect match. Errors are represented by vertical strokes or pips.

Figure 5 may be described as follows: In session one, S63 completed the elementary and intermediate sets at a fairly high rate making no errors on the elementary set and one first error on slide 4 of the intermediate sequence. In session two, his high rate was maintained on Unit 1 of the advanced set but he made six first errors. On Unit 2 of the same series, he made five errors—three first errors on the whole sequence and two repetitive errors on slide 2-35. His rate of matching decreased slightly after frame 2-20, the slide on which he made his second error. On Unit 3 he made a total of 14 errors. For the first time he made two errors before making the correct match (slide 3-13 shows two pips preceding a regression in the curve), and two errors previously passed on the first attempt (slides 3-19 and 3-39). In session three, he made 13 errors on Unit 4, and his rate of matching decreased further. In four instances (slides 4-7, 4-30, 4-35) he made two errors before making the correct selection. In one situation he alternated between slide 4-30 and

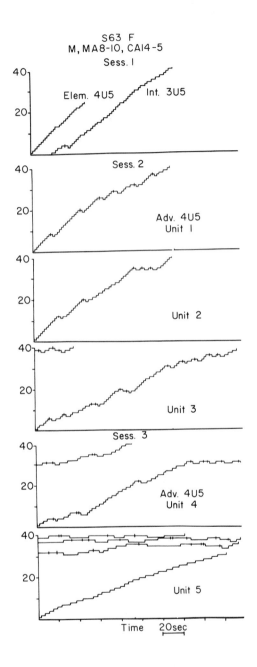

Fig. 5. Performance of a 14-year-old boy (S63) on the elementary, intermediate, and advanced sets.

slide 4-31 four times, repeating the same errors. On Unit 5 his rate of matching steadily decreased over the first 31 slides but he performed without error. After slide 5-31 he made 21 errors.

B. Performance of Retarded and Normal Children on Pretests and Posttests

The upper part of Table I shows the mean error frequencies for eight Fernald and five Lesley-Ellis children on the pretests. All errors

TABLE I

MEAN ERRORS OF FERNALD AND LESLEY-ELLIS CHILDREN ON ORIGINAL, NEW NONSENSE, AND ALPHABET PRE- AND POSTTESTS

Study	N	CA	MA	Interval (days)	Original (20 slides)	New Nonsense (20 slides)	Alphabet (20 slides)
			Pretests				
Fernald	8	11 years 10 months to 14 years 7 months	4 years 11 months to 7 years 2 months		10.3	10.6	8.9
Lesley-Ellis	5	4 years 9 months to 6 years 3 months			11.6	11.6	10.6
			Posttests				
Fernald	5	11 years 3 months	6 years	0 − 28	3.4	4.4	2.2
	5	16 years	8 years 10 months	30 − 59	3.6	7.0	2.0
Average					3.5	5.7	2.1
Lesley-Ellis	5	5 years 10 months		0 − 16	2.0	3.6	2.2
	1	7 years		37	3.0	8.0	1.0
Average					2.2	4.3	2.0

are first errors, since each response, correct or incorrect, moved the slide-tray forward. As will be noted, the mental age scores of Fernald children ranged about a year higher than the chronological age of Lesley-Ellis children. It is likely that the groups were roughly comparable in mental age scores since the Lesley-Ellis population is above average in all respects. Nevertheless, comparisons are restricted to relationships within groups. Both groups made errors on about fifty percent of the slides. The Fernald children, however, made somewhat fewer errors on the Alphabet series compared to their performances on the Original and the New-Nonsense series.

Mean error frequencies on the tests administered to 10 Fernald and six Lesley-Ellis children on the posttests are also shown in the lower section of Table I. Like the Ss listed in the pretest groups, the Fernald children had mental age scores ranging above the chronological ages of the Lesley-Ellis children.

The results on the 10 Fernald children are presented in two groups of five, each on the basis of the number of days between completion of the program and administration of the posttests. The first five Ss were tested within a period of 28 days following training, the second five Ss were tested within 30 to 59 days following training. The results on the six Lesley-Ellis children are also presented in two groups on the same basis. One group of five Ss were tested within 16 days after finishing the program, and one S was tested after 37 days had elapsed.

It is apparent that: first, Fernald and Lesley-Ellis children made fewer errors on the tests after training; second, both groups performed similarly on the posttests, with most errors on the New-Nonsense series and fewest on the Alphabet; and, third, aside from the slightly fewer errors by Fernald children on the Alphabet series before training, both groups made gains following training.

C. Performance of Retarded and Normal Children on Form Discrimination Training

Table II summarizes the first and subsequent errors for Fernald and Lesley-Ellis children on form discrimination training given with the elementary set (24 slides) and the intermediate set (40 slides). The Fernald Ss ranged in age from 6 years 10 months to 4 years 5 months

TABLE II

First and Repetitive Errors by Fernald and Lesley-Ellis Children on Form Discrimination Training, Elementary and Intermediate Sets

	N	Errors on elementary set (24 slides)			N	Errors on intermediate set (40 slides)		
		Total	Mean	S.D.		Total	Mean	S.D.
Fernald								
First	27	20[a]	.74	1.95	24	48[b]	2.0	3.78
Repetitive	27	11[a]	.41	2.12	24	32[c]	1.35	3.66
Lesley-Ellis								
First	9	5	.56	1.03	9	8	.89	.95
Repetitive	9	0	.00	.00	9	1	.11	.03

[a] One subject (S43) made 10 of the first errors, and all 11 of the repetitive errors.
[b] Subject S43 made 13 of the 48 first errors.
[c] A different subject (S45) made 17 of the 32 repetitive errors; four other Ss made the remaining 15 repetitive errors.

with mental age scores from four years four months to 8 years 10 months; the Lesley-Ellis children from 4 to 6 years in age.

The performances of Fernald and Lesley-Ellis children were similar on the elementary set, except for one Fernald child (S43) who made 10 first errors and 11 repetitive errors.

On the intermediate set, performance of the Fernald Ss differed measurably from that of the Lesley-Ellis Ss. Of the 24 Fernald Ss, 14 made first errors and five Ss made repetitive errors. Of the 14 children making first errors, 10 made two or more first errors. The five Fernald Ss making repetitive errors scored 2, 3, 5, 5, and 17 errors, respectively.

Of the nine Lesley-Ellis Ss, five made first errors and only one S made a repetitive error. Of the Ss making first errors, two made only one first error, and the other three made two each.

D. Performance of Retarded Children on Rotated Mirror-Image Discrimination Training

Data on mirror-image discrimination training for the Fernald children are shown in Table III. Comparable data for Lesley-Ellis children were not available.

Except for S43, ıl 24 boys who performed on the intermediate set (Table II) proceeded to the advanced sequences. Thirteen were given Unit 1 of the fourth revision of the series, in which there were five stages of change from nonmirror to mirror images of the sample; 10 boys were given Unit 1 of the fifth revision, in which the transition was in six stages.

TABLE III

MEAN ERRORS OF FERNALD BOYS ON MIRROR-IMAGE DISCRIMINATION
TRAINING, FIVE UNITS OF ADVANCED SET

Unit	Number Started	Number Finished	MA	CA	Mean Errors[a] First	Repetitive
1	10	10	4 years 4 months to 8 years 8 months	6 years 10 months to 15 years 11 months	5.8	2.0
2	10	9	4 years 4 months to 8 years 8 months	6 years 10 months to 15 years 11 months	5.6	3.9
3	9	5	6 years 10 months to 8 years 8 months	11 years 11 months to 15 years 11 months	8.4	3.6
4	5	5	7 years to 8 years 8 months	12 years 7 months to 15 years 5 months	6.0	1.8
5	5	5	7 years to 8 years 8 months	12 years 7 months to 15 years 5 months	8.4	5.4

[a]Does not include errors of Ss stopped before end of unit.

The same 10 boys were given Unit 2 of the advanced set, which contained forms with vertical plane rotations to 90 degrees. One S (S45) was stopped on the fourth slide of the series because of numerous errors and lack of progress. Another S (S72) made a disproportionate number of first—and repetitive errors—14 and 17, respectively, but was permitted to continue through the unit because his repetitive errors declined as he approached the end of the unit. The other Ss made fewer errors than S45 and S72, but more than they had made on previous sets and units. On Unit 3, which had vertical plane rotations to 135 degrees, nine Ss started, four were stopped, and five completed the unit. The five Ss who finished Unit 3 also finished Units 4 and 5. In addition to extreme vertical plane rotations, Unit 4 had two, then three, incorrect mirror images of the sample, and Unit 5 contained four. In Unit 5, all forms were the same in shape, all matches were mirror images of the sample, and forms were in one of 12 rotational positions. As is apparent in Table III, several Ss made many repetitive errors. With the exception of S72, a S was stopped in mid-unit if he made three first, or three repetitive errors.

E.   Relationship between Mental Age Scores of Retarded Subjects and Progress in the Training Program

The relationship between mental age scores and number of slides completed in the program was evaluated on 39 Fernald boys. For this analysis, the criterion for stopping a S was three consecutive first errors. The mean number of slides completed for each mental age group is given in Table IV.

TABLE IV
RELATIONSHIP BETWEEN MENTAL AGE SCORES AND SLIDES COMPLETED

Mental age scores	N	Mean No. slides completed
3 and 4	7	5.4
5	5	12.0
6	11	16.3
7	9	18.0
8	7	20.4

The differences between the means for the 3- and 4-year-old group and the 6-, 7-, and 8-year-old groups are statistically significant. The relevant figures are given in Table V. There is then a positive relationship between the mental age test scores of Fernald children and progress through the programs.

TABLE V
MEAN DIFFERENCE AND RELIABILITIES BETWEEN AGE GROUPS

Groups (years)	t-Values	Degrees of Freedom	Probability for 2-tailed
3−4 vs 5	2.70	10	<.05
3−4 vs 6	3.94	16	<.01
3−4 vs 7	3.98	14	<.01
3−4 vs 8	6.41	12	<.01
5 vs 6	3.44	14	<.01
5 vs 7	4.80	12	<.01
5 vs 8	2.69	10	<.05
6 vs 7	.52	18	>.05 (not significant)
6 vs 8	1.36	16	>.05 (not significant)
7 vs 8	.69	14	>.05 (not significant)

F. Influence of Color and Position of Forms

Data were analyzed on two characteristics of the stimulus situation: color of forms, and window position of the match with respect to the location of the sample.

1. PERFORMANCE ON SLIDES WITH FORMS IN FOUR COLORS VS SLIDES WITH FORMS IN ONE COLOR

The upper part of Table VI shows mean errors for 72 Fernald Ss; the lower part shows mean errors for 39 Lesley-Ellis Ss on the elementary and intermediate sets. The trend throughout is more errors on the multicolored slides. From these data and observations guiding the revisions of programs, it is apparent that similarity of color in sample and match is a compelling condition for selection of a match unless there is special training with a multicolored program.

2. PERFORMANCE ON THE BASIS OF WINDOW POSITION RELATIVE TO SAMPLE

These data were obtained by analyzing error frequencies in the pre- and posttests as a function of window position. It should be remembered that the windows are referred to by numbers one to five, from S's left to right, and that the sample always appeared in the center of the upper window above match window 3.

Table VII summarizes the findings. The upper section of the table shows the performances on the tests before training for eight Fernald and five Lesley-Ellis Ss in terms of mean errors for each window. The lower part of Table VII shows means errors on the tests, by window, for ten Fernald and six Lesley-Ellis children.

TABLE VI

Mean Errors of Fernald and Lesley-Ellis Children on Form Discrimination Training: with Unicolor and Multicolor Slides

	Unicolor series					Multicolor series			
				Errors					Errors	
N	CA	MA	First	Repetitive	N	CA	MA	First	Repetitive
					Fernald					
Elementary (24 slides)	28	6 years 10 months to 16 years 11 months	4 years 4 months to 8 years 10 months	1.5	.4	10	10 years 7 months to 15 years 1 month	5 years 3 months to 8 years 4 months	2.4	1.9
Intermediate (40 slides)	25	6 years 10 months to 16 years 11 months	4 years 4 months to 8 years 10 months	2.4	1.2	9	same as above	same as above	3.3	1.1
					Lesley-Ellis					
Elementary (24 slides)	9	4 – 6 years		.5	.0	11	3 years 5 months to 5 years 10 months		3.0	3.2
Intermediate (40 slides)	9	4 – 6 years		.9	.1	10	4 years 5 months to 5 years 10 months		3.6	.4

TABLE VII

Mean Errors of Fernald and Lesley-Ellis Children
on Pre- and Posttests (60 Slides) Analyzed
on the Basis of Window Position

	N	CA	MA	Left-to-right window position				
				1	2	3	4	5
				Mean Errors				
			Pretests					
Fernald	8	11 years 10 months to 14 years 7 months	4 years 11 months to 7 years 2 months	2.3	5.1	14.6	5.4	2.8
Lesley-Ellis	5	4 years 9 months to 6 years 3 months		2.6	5.0	19.8	4.4	2.8
			Posttests					
Fernald	10	11 years 3 months to 16 years	6 years to 8 years 10 months	1.6	2.1	2.4	3.3	1.9
Lesley-Ellis	6	5 years 10 months to 7 years		2.0	2.0	2.0	1.7	0.8

Two relationships are obvious. For both groups, before training, the highest number of errors was on window 3, the next highest on windows 2 and 4, and the lowest number of errors on windows 1 and 5. After training, the errors of both groups tended to be distributed evenly across the five windows. It should also be noted that the mean number of errors for both groups is lower for the posttests than for the pretests. Subsequent research showed that the location of the sample with respect to the matches was a significant condition influencing the selection of a match when the problem was extremely difficult. Errors could be increased on the first, middle, or last window by placing the sample over each of these windows.

G. Implications of Results

An overview of the results indicates that the training program developed with normal preschool children was effective in teaching many of the retarded children left—right concepts. For the most part, the retarded children did well on the early part of the training sequence (the elementary and intermediate sets) that dealt with discrimination of simple forms in rotated positions. However, they encountered difficulties with the later part (the advanced set) on rotated mirror-image discriminations. Success was approximately proportional to mental age. For both theoretical and practical purposes a more effective training sequence was desirable; consequently, further revisions were made.

As research progressed, it became apparent that changes in procedure were necessary in order that the influence of discriminative stimuli (the forms) and the reinforcing stimuli (the contingencies) be clearly separated. It was essential that each S receiving training could demonstrate by his own performance that the contingencies being employed were *functional for him.* In other words, the light, the chime, and progress in the program following a correct response, had to have strengthening effects, and the representation of the previous slide, following an incorrect response, weakening effects. From nonsystematic observation, it seemed that the contingencies used were functional for the most part. The Lesley-Ellis children were delighted with their correct matches and somewhat distressed about their incorrect matches. The Fernald children also seemed pleased with their correct responses, but they were not overly concerned with their incorrect matches. Another observation deserves reporting: The Lesley-Ellis children were reluctant to come to the laboratory for repeated sessions; the Fernald children, on the other hand, were enthusiastic about coming and were eager to remain for long periods, although during the sessions they displayed considerable extraneous behaviors, e.g., nudging windows with the nose, fingering all the windows before responding, and making frequent unrelated comments. However, lacking systematic, objective data on the functional properties of the contingencies for individual Ss, one cannot tell whether serious variations in a child's performance were the result of poor programming, ineffective reinforcers, or both.

With respect to revision of the program, an analysis of errors by the retarded children suggested that training in the discrimination of nonmirror-image rotated forms (part of the elementary set and all of the intermediate set) contributed little to the terminal behavior of discriminating rotated mirror images. Hence, a revised program might start with mirror-image discriminations at the simplest level of vertical plane rotation, that is, with all forms in the upright position.

To reveal more clearly the conditions and processes of left−right conceptualization, the stimuli in the revised program were limited to one form. Such a program could also be expected to produce added information on generalization.

IV. MODIFICATION OF PROCEDURE AND
REVISION OF STIMULUS MATERIAL

A. Base Line and Contingencies

The experimental procedure described above was modified on additional samples of normal and retarded children to include base-line performance on 30 slides, each of which displayed simple upright forms—none of the forms in this series was rotated in the vertical plane, and none was a mirror image of any other form in the same slide. Subject was required to make the 30 matches during one session and to repeat this task in subsequent sessions until his performance reached stability, which was defined as having similar rates of matching in two successive sessions, and not more than two errors. The criterion of similarity: The terminal points of the curves on two successive sessions did not deviate by more than 5 mm from a point midway between them.

The contingencies were altered as follows: (a) A correct match produced a colored wooden bead in addition to the light, chime, complete blackout, and appearance of the next sample. The bead rolled down a tube into a clear plastic box, readily visible to the child but not attainable. (b) An incorrect match produced a mild, brief buzz and a blackout of the lower windows, making it necessary for S to press again on the same sample in the upper window. This sequence was repeated with each incorrect response until the correct match occurred. The back-up contingency described in Section II was eliminated.

The contingency for a correct match, after one or more errors, was light, chime, and forward movement in the program, but no bead. In other words, light, chime, blackout, forward movement in the program, *and* bead followed only *first* correct matches; light, chime, blackout, and advancement in the program came after correct matches that had been preceded by one or more incorrect matches to the same slide. The addition of the bead to the other contingencies for a correct response on the first try was designed to strengthen, differentially, behavior leading to a correct match on first exposure. In this way, S was encouraged not only to make the correct response but to do so for the "right reason"— for responding to the critical cue or cues.

At the end of each session, the beads were exchanged for toys, candies, or pennies on a ratio basis, and S was permitted to choose any combination of objects presented. Subject learned the token "value" of the beads during the first session by exchanging a few beads at a time for "goodies" at successively increasing intervals.

The following is an account of revised instructions: Pointing to sample on the first slide, E says, "See this? Push on it and see what happens." (Choices appear.) Pointing to the five choices, E says, "Find one like it here." (Subject points to correct form.) "Yes. Push on it and see what happens." (Light flickers, chime sounds, bead rolls into plastic box, slide blacks out, and next sample appears.) "That means you were right." Pointing to the new sample, E says, "Push on it again. Go ahead." (Subject makes correct response.) "That's right." The experimenter says,

"That's right" following the next two correct matches. If *S* makes an error at any point, the instructions are repeated from the beginning.

Pointing to the sample of the fifth slide, *E* says, "Let's find the one that is *not* like this one and see what happens." (Subject makes incorrect match which is followed by buzz and blackout of choices.) "That means you were *wrong*." Pointing to the sample again, *E* says, "Push on it again." (Choices appear.) "Find the *right one* this time. Go ahead." The experimenter returns to the control room to observe and monitor the apparatus.

Curve *A* in Fig. 6 shows a base line achieved by Ann, a 5-year-old normal girl attending a day-care center. She participated in the experiment on alternate days. In the fourth session, during which these data were gathered, Ann made no errors (no pips in the curve), and her rate of matching met the criterion of a stable base line. She was given the pretests in the next session.

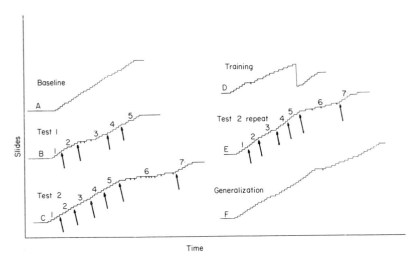

Fig. 6. Cumulative curves of the performances of a 5-year-old normal girl on the revised method involving baseline (*A*), test 1 on mirror-image discrimination (*B*), test 2 on rotated mirror-image discrimination (*C*), training on rotated mirror-image discrimination (*D*), test 2 repeated (*B*), and test of generalization (*F*).

The base-line technique was used in a study with 14 retarded boys in residence at the Rainier School, Buckley, Washington. Their average age was 11 years, with the youngest being 8 years 9 months and the oldest 13 years 7 months. Their Peabody mental age average was 4 years 10 months, with a low score of 3 years 10 months, and a high score of 6 years 3 months.

The range of base-line rates is shown in Fig. 7. The subject with the highest rate of matching is shown on the far left (curve 1), the S with the lowest, on the far right (curve 6). Not all 14 base lines are in Fig. 7 since many duplicated those shown: one resembled curve 1, two were like curve 3, two like curve 4, and three like curve 5. An average of 8.5 sessions was required for these S's to meet the criteria of stable performance. The fastest S met the requirements in four sessions; the slowest in 17.

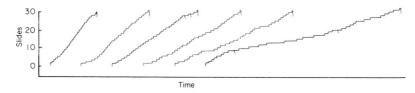

FIG. 7. Cumulative curves of six base-line performances of retarded boys ranked in order of match-to-sample response rate.

The group was too small to draw reliable conclusions about relationships between number of sessions to reach stability and slope of base-line performance on one hand, and chronological age, mental age, length of institutional residence, and educational achievement, on the other.

Obtaining stable base lines of this sort not only provides E with indispensable information regarding the functional properties of the contingencies used but also assures him that S has mastered the operation of the apparatus prior to the manipulation of the experimental condition and that the length of sessions during base-line training did not produce performance decrements attributable to satiation, boredom, or fatigue.

It should be pointed out in passing that the range of slopes obtained could have been constricted by manipulation of contingencies, i.e., by changing the reinforcement schedule from continuous (CRF) to differential reinforcement of high rates (DRH). Because there was no reason to have each S start with the same base-line rate in this study no such manipulation was attempted.

B. Pretests, Posttests, and Generalization Tests

The subjects who achieved stable baselines were given test 1 to determine whether they could discriminate mirror-image forms from nonmirror-image forms in the upright position. This test consisted of

25 slides: the first five were the same as base line; the second five were also like the slides in the base-line series except that the forms were rotated or tilted 30 degrees to the right or left; the third block of slides had only upright flag forms with four mirror images of the samples as distractors; the fourth group were like the second five; and the fifth, or last five, were the same as the first five. The rationale for the construction of test 1 was as follows: The first five slides from the base line were included to see whether the base-line performance was maintained on the test day; the second five with forms similar to the base-line slides but tilted in the vertical plane were to see whether minor variations in base-line stimuli produced disruption in performance; the third five were to test S's ability to make mirror-image discriminations on forms in an upright position; and the fourth and fifth blocks of slides each were to determine whether taking the mirror-image discrimination test had a disruptive effect on making simple discriminations.

A sample performance on test 1 by Ann is shown in Fig. 6, curve *B*. There the five sets of five slides each are designated numerically and are separated by arrows. Her rates of matching on the first, second, fourth, and fifth blocks are similar to her rate on the base-line series (curve *A*). Her rate decreased on the third block, which consisted of mirror-image discriminations among upright flags. As the pips in the curve show, she also made two errors on the first mirror-image discrimination, and one on the second.

If an S made mismatches on three or more of the slides in the mirror-image block, he was given training in mirror-image discrimination that consisted only of upright flag forms (more about this series, called the "flag-bar set," in Section IV, C). If an S made only one or two errors on the mirror-image block, he was given test 2 to see whether he could make mirror-image discriminations of forms rotated in the vertical plane. Test 2 consisted of 35 slides: 25 slides of test 1, five slides with flag forms having rotated mirror-image distractors and five slides from the base-line set. The rationale for the construction of test 2 was the same as for test 1.

If an S made correct matches on three or more of the slides in the rotated mirror-image block, he was eliminated from the study. However, if he made three or more errors in this critical sequence, he was given training on a rotated mirror-image set. Our sample subject, Ann, made nine errors on the rotated mirror-image part of test 2, and was therefore given this training (see curve *C*, Fig. 6). Her performance on the 16-item rotated mirror-image sequence—one error and a fairly constant rate of matching—is shown in curve *D*. Responses after the reset of the recording pen were to base-line slides.

After training on the rotated mirror-image discrimination, S was given test 2 again to evaluate the training on familiar material, and a generalization test to see whether training "carried over" to new forms. The generalization test consisted of 45 slides: five from baseline, five nonmirror-image, tilted forms; five upright mirror-image forms with flags; five rotated mirror-image forms with winged L's; five rotated mirror-image forms with square Z's, five upright mirror-image forms with flags; five nonmirror image, tilted forms; and five from base line, in that order.

On the repeat of test 2, Ann made three errors (curve E in Fig. 6), one on each of three slides in the rotated mirror-image segment of the test. As curve F shows, she made only one error on the generalization test, and her rate of matching was relatively constant throughout.

C. Training Programs

In Section II, the mirror-image training program was described as consisting of an elementary set with upright and 30-degree tilted forms, an intermediate set with nonmirror-image rotated forms, and an advanced set with rotated mirror-image forms. The revision of this program resulted in two sets: one with upright mirror-image forms and one with rotated mirror-image forms. Furthermore, the advanced set in the program described in Section II had mirror-image forms of the flag, square Z, and winged L faded-in by the gradual modification of the square C, inverted winged L, and cross, respectively. In contrast, the revision had only the flag form with mirror images faded-in by manipulating the *size* of the upper part of the form. Finally, the earlier program always displayed five choices with combinations of seven forms (see the left-hand column of Fig. 2) while the revision had two, three, four, or five choices, all with some variation of the flag form.

The first program in the revised series (A) consisted of 38 slides. Of these, all but the last two slides contained two choices; the last two had five choices. The first frame in this sequence showed the vertical bar or staff (the usual staff of the flag form), and a flag form with the upper part in the shape of a horizontal rectangle three times the size of the flags in Figs. 2, 3, and 4. In succeeding slides, the vertical bar gradually acquired a "flag" and the rectangular flag gradually contracted until both were identical (square) except for their left−right orientation. Throughout the series all forms were systematically presented as samples and as choices in all five choice locations. In the last two, which had five alternatives, the distractions were four mirror-image forms of the sample. Actually, the last two slides were the same as the mirror-image test slides in test 1.

Series A was explored on nine normal children from the Seattle Day Care Center. Ranging from 3 years 8 months to 5 years, the average age of the children was 4 years 5 months.

This group made an average of 7.3 errors on 5.6 slides with a range from 3 errors on three slides to 14 on eight slides. Their pre- and posttests were about the same with only one child passing the posttest. The inadequacy of the series was not apparent in the mean number of errors but showed up in their distribution over the slides. For example, the mean number of errors for the first three quarters of the series (29 slides) was only 2.4, whereas the mean number of errors for the last quarter (nine slides) was 5.1. Hence, the greatest part of the series was too easy for the group and did not contribute to training while the last small segment was too difficult to maintain the desired matching behavior. Consequently, a revision was undertaken in which many of the slides in the first part of the program were eliminated and new slides were added to the second part. Furthermore, the slides were arranged in four cycles with the number of choices increasing from two to five. Of the 36 slides constituting the revised set (Aa), 14 were in the first cycle, eight in the second, eight in the third, and six in the fourth cycle.

The Aa series was explored on a normal preschool group and a retarded institutionalized group. The normal group of nine children between the ages of 4 and 5 years attended the nursery school of the Developmental Psychology Laboratory at the University of Washington. These preschoolers averaged 15 errors on 6.6 slides, with individual performance ranging from two errors on two slides to 22 errors on 10 slides. One child refused to continue on slide 32 after 12 errors on five slides. Once again, the distribution of errors indicated that the first part of the series was too easy and the last part too difficult. There were no errors on the first half of the series, a mean of 5.1 errors on a mean of four slides on the fourth quarter.

The retarded group, composed of five boys from the base-line study described in Section IV, A, had a mean age of 11 years 4 months, and a mean Peabody mental age score of 4 years 10 months. They made a mean of 8 errors on 6.8 slides with a range from 4 errors on four slides to 12 errors on seven slides. The distribution of errors resembled that of the normal group: a mean of one error on the first half, a mean of 1.6 on 1.2 slides for the third quarter, and a mean of 5.2 errors on 4.1 slides for the fourth quarter of the series. Only one S passed the posttest with one error while making four on two mirror-image slides in the pretest. The performance of the other four boys was about the same on both tests.

A modification of this series (AA) made up of the same 36 slides in the Aa series, plus 10 slides similar to the criterion test slides (all with four mirror-image distractors) added to the end of the set, was explored on five other retarded boys who had participated in the base-line study. The mean age of these boys was 11 years 4 months, and the mean Peabody mental age score was 5 years 2 months. The mean number of errors was 94.4 on 15.4 slides with individual errors of 2, 34, 52, 149, and 235. The mean number of errors in the pretest was 93.6, and on the posttest 48.6. One S who "missed" all five mirror-image discriminations in the pretest passed the posttest without error. The pre- and posttest performances of the other four boys were about the same.

On the basis of these data, the flag-bar series was still inadequate as the basis for developing an effective history for left—right conceptualizing behavior. It seems that the early part of the program fails to bring the child's behavior under the kind of stimulus control required by the task. Adding 10 criterion slides to the end of the set did not help; it served only to emphasize that the necessary prior learning had not taken place.

On the basis of the above reasoning, having a S repeat the set will not improve his performance. To verify this inference, the 36-slide Aa sequence was given three times to one of the Ss attending the University of Washington nursery school. The subject made 22 errors the first time, 22 the second time, and 19 the third time. The errors were concentrated around the same slides beginning with slide number 22.

Any statement on the relative efficacy of programming mirror-image discriminations by manipulating the size of the flag form must wait until the flag-bar sequence has been modified, and then compared with the construction procedure described in Section II, D.

We turn now to the training series on the discrimination of rotated mirror-image forms. This sequence of 37 slides started with two-choice items tilted 30 degrees, to the right or left, and ended with five-choice tasks rotated through 360 degrees. Like the flag-bar series, the tasks were ordered in cycles with an increasing number of choices. The first cycle, with six slides, went from two choices to three, with increases in rotational positions; the second, with four slides, also went from two choices to three but had still further increases in vertical-plane rotations; and the third and last cycle, with 27 slides, from two choices to five, with still further increases in vertical-plane rotations culminating in 360 degree deflections as shown in slide 5-38, Fig. 4.

Data on this set are from performances of five retarded boys also from the base-line study. Four of these Ss passed test 1 without previous experience on a mirror-image training program, and one passed the test after training on the flag-bar Aa series. The mean chronological age of this group was 10 years 3 months; the mean Peabody age score was 4 years 5 months. The average number of errors made on the training series was at least 28.4. The average is said to be "at least" 28.4 because one S stopped responding after he had made 33 errors. On the pretest, three of the Ss refused to complete the series; only one refused on the posttest. Inspection of the data revealed that errors on the training series were distributed throughout. Hence, the next revision should incorporate slides which expand the training at all stages of vertical-plane rotation. Furthermore, the strategy of increasing the number of matches requires empirical solution. Consideration should be given to such questions as: Should the series start with a two-choice cycle and remain at that level until terminal behavior is attained? Should the procedure then be repeated with three choices, and again with four choices, and once more with five choices? Or, should the series start with five choices and move very gradually to final terminal behavior?

D. Summary of Revised Procedure

The following was the sequence of the revised procedure:
(1) Establishment of stable base-line performance on 30 slides with upright nonmirror-image forms.
(2) Administration of test 1 to determine whether Ss could discriminate upright mirror-image forms from nonmirror-image flag forms.
(3) Training on upright mirror-image sets for Ss who "failed" test 1. Retest on test 1 to determine the effectiveness of training.
(4) Administration of test 2 to Ss who "passed" test 1 before or after training on the upright mirror-image program.
(5) Training on rotated mirror-image program for Ss who "failed" test 2. Retest on test 2 to ascertain the effectiveness of the training program.
(6) Administration of generalization test to see whether the training on flag forms increased performance on similar tasks involving square Z and winged L forms.
(7) Revision of programs on the basis of error distributions and repetition of the training procedure to evaluate the effectiveness of the procedure.

V. DISCUSSION

This research explored the ingredients of an experimental history enabling a child, normal or retarded, to perform a left – right concept formation task. Specifically, the problem was: What stimulus material and what procedure instructs a child to discriminate geometrical forms differing in left—right orientation and in vertical-plane rotational position?

The study consisted of two phases, the first described in Sections II and III, the second described in Section IV. In the first investigation, which involved 90 normal and 89 retarded children, the experimental history consisted of training in form discrimination, mirror-image discrimination, and rotated mirror-image discrimination, presented as a five-choice, match-to-sample problems. Mirror-image discrimination training was based on fading-in, by construction, mirror images of three forms—flag, square Z, and winged L. Contingencies for a correct response were a light, a chime, and progress to the next slide; for an incorrect response, the contingencies were a blackout of the choices and a sound resulting from the operation of the apparatus. An incorrect match led to re-presentation of the same task until the correct match was made. A correct response *preceded* by one or more incorrect responses was followed by the re-presentation of the *previous* slide. Analyses of error frequencies and differences between the pre- and posttests indicated that the program developed on the normal children was reasonably serviceable for the retarded Ss. However, the retarded Ss were more prone to make repetitive errors.

Many of the Ss who started the program did not complete it. Among these were many Ss who mastered discrimination of upright forms with mirror-image distractors and did not make discrimination of rotated forms with two, three, and four rotated mirror-image distractors. In general, there was for the retarded Ss a positive relationship between progress in the program and mental age score.

The research in phase two generated from questions raised in phase one. For example: How might differences in the functional properties of contingencies for a correct match be better controlled? How might the contingencies for an incorrect response be altered to simplify analysis? Should training start with mirror image rather than form discrimination? Would it be better, for purposes of analysis, to use one rather than three forms in mirror-image discrimination training? Is there a more effective way to fade-in mirror image forms and to program rotated mirror-images stimuli?

In phase two of the study, contingencies for a correct match were a light, a chime, tokens (beads, negotiable for candy and toys), and movement to the next slide; for an incorrect match, a buzz, a blackout of choices, and a mild sound from the operation of the apparatus. A correct match *after* an incorrect match or matches resulted in the light, chime, and movement to the next slide, but no token. A base-line series was added and consisted of upright forms shown in the right-hand column of Fig. 2. The pre-, post-, and generalization tests were refined and extended, and the mirror-image training program was modified to consist only of the flag form, the mirror image of which was faded in by manipulating its size. In addition, the order of training was changed: first, discrimination training on upright forms (base line); second, mirror-image discrimination training on upright flag forms; and, third, rotated mirror-image training on rotated flag forms. Nonflag forms appeared only in the base-line set.

It was difficult, on the basis of data collected on two normal and two retarded groups of children, to evaluate the revised fading-in strategy and order of training sets. More obvious was the indication that the mirror image and the rotated mirror-image series needed another revision before gathering the data essential for these determinations.

A general comment is in order at this point. The fading-in technique proved, by far, most promising for the development of left–right concepts. Less obvious than this observation and more perplexing were questions like these: What specific aspects of the forms should be manipulated in the fading-in procedure? What should be the order of subsets in building complex conceptualizing behavior (in this case, rotated mirror-image discriminations)? How much training should be given for each stimulus change to effect a smooth performance through the series?

The first problem concerning the stimulus dimension to be manipulated is most difficult because of the many ways in which fading-in can be accomplished. In the absence of data, a working principle was used: vary that part of the form which includes the cue essential to the discrimination. The assumption here is that the key task in building a geometrical concept is to provide a situation which will bring the *S*s attending behavior under the control of that aspect of the stimulus which will be reinforced. In this study, the salient aspect was the relationship between the vertical and horizontal parts of the form. Hence the fading-in procedures involved the directional indicators of the forms. Nonmirror-image forms were transformed into mirror-image forms of the flag, square Z, and winged L in the first phase of the study, and the flag form was expanded and contracted in the second phase of the research.

The second question, pertaining to the order of subsets in building complex conceptualizing behavior, and the third question on the amount of training at each stage of stimulus change are not unrelated. In both, the problem is how to program stimuli so that each behavioral change is strengthened to the proper degree to effect the next discrimination. It is probable that zero or weak stimulus control results in repetitive errors within a frame and successive errors among frames, while strong stimulus control results in "perseverative" errors. In this primitive stage of research in delineating experimental histories, the only course open to an E is to be venturesome, to try different procedures, evaluate them on small groups, and revise them on the findings. Precisely that was done in this attempt to train Ss in discriminating rotated mirror images.

In this study, like that of Sidman and Stoddard (1966, 1967), the method was stressed. Clearly, the availability of a workable laboratory method would open the way for empirical-functional study of theoretical and practical problems in this area (Bijou & Baer, 1963). Relative to theoretical issues, the method could be a vehicle for an experimental analysis of Piaget-type concepts (e.g., Kessen & Kuhlman, 1962; Piaget, 1954; Sigel, 1964) and classical Gestalt problems, including perceptual constancy and figure-grouped relationships (e.g., Wohlwill, 1960).

With respect to practical problems, such a laboratory-type method could provide a functional framework for the diagnosis and treatment of learning disabilities such as reading retardation, aphasia, and articulatory difficulties (e.g., A. Holland & Mathews, 1963). For example, in the treatment of aphasia, a provisional program would be fabricated from all or parts of available programs and from materials and procedures in current use. The last section of the program would serve as a test to establish the behavioral competencies of the S at the beginning of training. There would also be a series of pre- and posttests for each subset in the program to evaluate behavior at each new phase of training. Performance would be monitored by data gathered on a day-to-day basis and revisions would evolve from analysis of findings. Finally, a series of generalization tests would be prepared and used to indicate what other modifications in the program were needed to produce the desired behavior in the appropriate situations. Procedures based on the kind outlined here would provide information on fabricating a history for developing new behavior or reestablishing old modes of responding. The prescription for accomplishing the task of building or rebuilding behavioral repertories would be described in empirical terms (accounts of procedures and materials), not in hypothetical terms, neurological or otherwise.

REFERENCES

Bijou, S. W. A functional analysis of retarded development. In N. R. Ellis (Ed.), *International Review of Research in Mental Retardation*, Vol. 1, New York: Academic Press, 1966. Pp. 1-19.

Bijou, S. W. & Baer, D. M. Some methodological contributions from a natural science approach to research in child development. In L. P. Lipsitt & C. C. Spiker (Eds.), *Recent advances in child development and behavior*. Vol. 1. New York: Academic Press, 1963. Pp. 197-231.

Hively, W. Programming stimuli in matching to sample. *Journal of Experimental Analysis of Behavior*, 1962, **5**, 279-298.

Holland, A. & Mathews, J. The use of a teaching machine in training speech sound discrimination for articulation therapy. *Asha*, 1963, **5**, 474-482.

Holland, J. G. Teaching machines: An application of principles from the laboratory. *Journal of Experimental Analysis of Behavior*, 1960, **3**, 275-287.

Holland, J. G. New directions in teaching-machine research. In J. Coulson (Ed.), *Proceedings of the conference on applications of digital computers to automated instruction*. New York: Wiley, 1963.

Kessen, W., & Kuhlman, C. (Eds.) Thought in the young child. *Monograph of the Social Research in Child Development*, 1962, **27**, No. 2.

Moore, R., & Goldiamond, I. Errorless establishment of visual discrimination using fading procedures. *Journal of Experimental Analysis of Behavior*, 1964, **7**, 269-272.

Piaget, J. *The construction of reality in the child*. New York: Basic Books, 1954.

Sidman, M. & Stoddard, L. T. Programming perception and learning for retarded children. In N. R. Ellis (Ed.), *International Review of Research in Mental Retardation*. Vol. 2. New York: Academic Press, 1966. Pp. 152-209.

Sidman, M., & Stoddard, L. T. The effectiveness of fading in programming a simultaneous form discrimination for retarded children. *Journal of Experimental Analysis of Behavior*, 1967, 10, 3-15.

Sigel, I. E. The attainment of concepts. In M. L. Hoffman & L. W. Hoffman (Eds.), *Review of child development research*. Vol. 1. New York: Russell Sage Foundation, 1964. Pp. 209-248.

Terrace, H. S. Stimulus control. In W. K. Honig (Ed.), *Operant behavior: Areas of research and application*. New York: Appleton, 1966. Pp. 271-344.

Wohlwill, J. F. Developmental studies of perception. *Psychological Bulletin*, 1960, **57**, 249-288.

ACKNOWLEDGMENTS

The assistance and support given by B. F. Skinner and J. G. Holland, Harvard Psychological Laboratories, made it possible to carry out the research conducted in the first part of this article. The assistance of Mrs. Janet R. Bijou in the preparation of the manuscript was indispensable to the completion of this task. The courtesies, which made it possible for the author to conduct the tests referred to in Section II, A, were extended by the principal of the Lesley-Ellis School, and Dr. Ferrell, the superintendent of the Fernald School. Their assistance in this matter is gratefully appreciated. The services of Mrs. Harriet Schultz and Mrs. Judith S. Thoft, who served as experimenters in the tests given in Section II, A at the Lesley-Ellis School and the Fernald School, respectively, were invaluable in exploring new procedures and in bringing the project to a conclusion. The work of Mr. L. Harper who served as research assistant made it possible to obtain the data from the tests conducted at Rainier School referred to in Section IV, A.

Verbal Learning and Memory Research with Retardates: An Attempt to Assess Developmental Trends

L. R. GOULET

WEST VIRGINIA UNIVERSITY, MORGANTOWN, WEST VIRGINIA[1]

I. INTRODUCTION

There is an increasing awareness of the analytical utility of verbal learning tasks in the study of the behavior of both normal and retarded children. The increased use of verbal learning tasks (e.g., paired associates, serial learning, transfer paradigms, and mediation paradigms,) has been followed by a number of systematic reviews of research and commentaries relating to method. For example, Keppel (1964) has indicated that the research literature reflects evidence which suggests

---

[1]This paper was written while the author was a Visiting Research Professor in Mental Retardation, Department of Psychology, St. Louis University and Cardinal Glennon Memorial Hospital for Children, St. Louis, Missouri.

that the processes involved in verbal learning of normal children are very similar to those of adults. Goulet (1968), in a later review, focused upon: (a) the applicability of theory developed in verbal learning to the study of developmental learning processes in children; (b) the isolation of the effects of a number of experiential variables that covary with chronological age and thus affect both verbal and nonverbal behavior; and, (c) the similarity of verbal learning and nonverbal learning tasks (e.g., discrimination learning and reversal shift tasks) and the resultant overlap of data and theory with each type of task.

Parallel types of reviews have appeared which have focused upon learning in retardates (Baumeister, 1967; Belmont, 1966; Denny, 1964; Jensen, 1965; Lipman, 1963; Prehm, 1966b; Stevenson, 1963). However, most of these reviews have concentrated mainly upon the determination of whether there was a learning deficit in retardates when compared to normal children of comparable mental or chronological age. Indeed, most of the research related to learning in retarded children has had, as a primary purpose, the identification of such a learning deficit.

Denny (1964) has suggested that there are two types of deficits related to learning ability which may be identified when retardates are compared to normal children. The first type, a low-MA—low-IQ deficit, refers to inferior learning performance by the retarded when they are compared to matched-CA normal children. The second type, a low-IQ deficit, results specifically from a low IQ and may be identified when retardates are compared to normal children who are matched with them on MA. Of course, the differentiation of learning deficit as to type was the result of a functional analysis and was based upon the types of conclusions that may be made from the usual experimental designs involving normal—retardate comparisons. That is, the typical design (Type I), where the learning rate of retardates is compared to normals matched on MA, suggests a low-IQ deficit, whereas the design involving retardates and CA controls (Type II) suggests the existence of a low-IQ deficit or a low-MA—low-IQ deficit since the normal children have both higher MA and IQ scores.

The third type of design, used infrequently, includes two matched samples of normal children, one equated on MA and the other on CA, for each group of retardates (Type III). The latter design is the least efficient in terms of numbers of subjects and experimental time but certainly yields more information to the investigator concerned with identifying the nature of the deficit in retardates.

While a large volume of research related to verbal learning may be found which involves normal—retardate comparisons, very little research is avilable which attempts to assess the changes in the learning of retardates that may be attributable to maturation or the effects of variables that covary with age. Similarly, little research has been oriented to assessing stages of development that covary with the presence of certain abilities (e.g., mediation). Research of the latter type is certainly available which traces the interaction of development and learning processes in normal children (e.g., Jensen & Rohwer, 1965; T. S. Kendler, 1964; H. H. Kendler & Kendler, 1962). The purpose of this article is to review the available research utilizing retarded subjects within the framework of identifying developmental trends together with reviewing the research which contrasts the learning of normal and retarded children. Secondary purposes relate to expanding upon the methodological commentaries of Berkson and Cantor (1962), Prehm (1966b), and Baumeister (1967). In addition, possible ways of circumventing methodological problems in learning research with retarded children are suggested.

II. VERBAL LEARNING AND MATURATION-EXPERIENCE EFFECTS

The utility of verbal learning tasks to study the behavior of retardates must be considered from a number of different points of view. The first of these relates to the implications for understanding retardate behavior that may be generated from theory in verbal learning. These implications are not obvious, especially since the theory has been derived almost exclusively from data collected using adult Ss. In addition, these implications must be considered as they apply to the behavior of retardates and retardate development as differentiated from that of normal children. On a more practical note, verbal learning tasks, in order to have functional utility, must be sufficiently analytical to permit more than the mere demonstration of a learning deficit. The focus must be toward the delineation of the process or processes in which the retardates are deficient, in addition to the identification of the course of retardate development.

The implications of theory in verbal learning for the understanding of retardate behavior primarily concern the effects of variables that covary with chronological age rather than with intellective variables (e.g., MA and IQ). In other words, extrapolations from theory in verbal learning are oriented to variables whose effects change systematically with increased experience, or according to the present definition, increased CA. This implication highlights a methodological problem in research concerned with comparing differences in the behavior of retarded and matched-MA normal children. For example, consider an experiment involving a paired-associate task of six paired highly familiar pictures. These materials are, most likely, more familiar to the retardates because they are older and this facilitating effect would be considered to offset, at least in part, the IQ deficit deemed to be present in retardates. Research of this nature must provide a proper control for the effects of CA, either by using materials which minimize the effects of past experience or by including both CA and MA control groups in the experiment. Further discussion relevant to this problem is presented at various places throughout the article. It is important to note here that, except for the differential effects of CA (experience), theory in verbal learning applies mutually to the development of normal and retarded children. However, the differential effects of CA as reflected in the transfer of prior or preexperimental learning to new tasks makes it difficult to differentiate the type of learning deficit in retardates as being attributable to either a low-IQ or a low-MA — low-IQ deficit as Denny (1964) has attempted to do.

The above assumption regarding the effects of CA on behavior deviates somewhat from that presented by Jensen (1965). He stated that IQ, as a quantitative estimate, represents *rate* of learning and that the product IQ × CA (which is equivalent to MA) represents the total amount learned. It follows from Jensen's analysis that the cumulative effects of past experience as reflected by CA are entirely dependent upon the individual's IQ and that these effects would be identical for a retardate and a normal child of comparable MA. As mentioned above, Jensen's analysis implies that the effects of CA are negligible except in interaction with IQ. It is the contention here that there are some preexperimental effects of CA that are independent of those represented by MA. In other words, there may be two different types of effects of past experience on new learning.

The above distinction regarding the effects of CA and IQ × CA (MA) is made most clear when the distinction is made in the context of discussing transfer of training. Concern with the behavioral effects of "old" learning on "new" learning may be identified with the basic transfer of training paradigm. Theorists in verbal learning have distinguished between two types of transfer, specific and nonspecific, each of which may be shown to have concomitant effects upon the acquisition of a learning task. Nonspecific transfer is positive in direction and results from practice on earlier tasks regardless of the similarity or stimulus response relationships between earlier and new (transfer) tasks. For example, nonspecific transfer would be reflected in learning a paired-associate (PA) task if other PA tasks had been learned earlier even though the PA lists learned earlier consisted of formally or conceptually different materials. This phenomenon has been called "learning how to learn" or "learning set" (Hamilton, 1950; Harlow, 1949). Specific transfer, on the other hand, may be positive or negative in direction and is dependent upon the similarity or relationship between the new learning tasks and earlier learning. For example, there would be a large amount of positive (specific) transfer in learning to spell the word "mountaineer" after having first learned the word "mountain."

The present distinction between the two types of transfer effects dependent on CA may be dichotomized according to whether they are attributable to specific or nonspecific transfer. It is suggested that the effects owing to CA, independently of IQ, are those related to specific transfer from preexperimental learning and that resulting from the function IQ × CA are a function of nonspecific transfer (learning to learn) from prior learning.

As an example, much of the verbal learning research with retardates utilizes highly familiar pictures as stimulus materials. These pictorial stimuli are, most likely, more familiar and more available for recall to retardates than to normal children simply because these materials have been seen more often. This result (specific transfer) may be considered to result primarily from CA if other relevant variables, e.g., school experience, are controlled. On the other hand, the transfer from learning to learn may be considered to be a function of "total amount of prior learning" and may thus be represented by the function IQ × CA. As will be seen later, the results of much of the research involving normal − retardate comparisons may be considered to be confounded by the differential specific transfer if the retarded and normal Ss are equated on MA (Type I) and by differential nonspecific transfer if Ss are equated on CA (Type II). However, in equal MA comparisons, it is possible to minimize the differential amounts of specific transfer if unfamiliar stimulus materials are used. This problem is discussed in further detail below.

It is interesting to explore some of the implications that may be derived from the above analysis regarding the transfer of preexperimental learning to new tasks. With the use of a Type I design, results indicating equal or superior rates of learning for retarded as compared to normal samples may indicate, not that there is an absence of a low-IQ deficit, but that the facilitating effect resulting from the greater familiarity of retardates with the learning materials offsets such a deficit. Similarly, studies utilizing Type I designs and demonstrating superior learning for normals do indicate the presence of a low-IQ deficit in retardates, but here, there is possibility of underestimating the absolute degree of the deficit.

The studies involving Type II designs are confounded by greater learning-to-learn transfer of normal children. The implication here can be tested experimentally, namely, that retarded children will profit more from learning-to-learn training than normal children who are equated on CA. This prediction follows because learning-to-learn functions are typically negatively accelerated for older, more experienced Ss but usually involve an initial period of positive acceleration for younger, less experienced Ss (see Harlow, 1959). According to the present analysis and that of Jensen (1965), retardates are less experienced and thus, should profit more from practice designed to familiarize Ss with the nature of the experimental task. This analysis is also applicable for comparisons of retardate samples equated in CA but varying in MA and IQ. It should be mentioned, however, that this implication holds only for learning-set experiments where Ss are taken to a criterion of mastery on each task before the initiation of succeeding problems. The above analysis also implies that studies utilizing Type II designs should provide retarded Ss with some learning-to-learn experience prior to practice on the experimental task. The prediction here would be that the learning-to-learn transfer would be greater (relatively) for retardates than for normal children after an equivalent amount of preliminary practice. Such learning-to-learn practice would more properly equate normal and retardates on the degree of preexperimental transfer with the resultant being that learning deficits could be assessed with a minimum of confounding.

It should also be noted that such factors as institutionalization and school training would interact with intellective variables to determine learning-to-learn transfer. Kaufman (1963) has provided support for this contention when he found that noninstitutionalized retardates acquired a learning set faster than a group of retardates matched on MA and CA but residing in an institution. He also found that CA was positively correlated with rate of learning over the first few object-quality discrimination problems even though the effects of past experience (CA) were not specific to the learning-to-learn task. The latter results imply that the effects of CA may have an influence on the degree of initial learning-to-learn transfer quite independent of those reflected by the interaction of IQ × CA (MA), again in line with the present assumptions regarding the effects of this variable. For a review of the learning-to-learn research with retardates see Kaufman and Prehm (1968).

Research comparing normals and retardates which is unconfounded by differential preexperimental transfer is very important in that both the nature and magnitude of the *learning* deficit in retardates can be assessed. In fact, research of this nature may yield evidence suggesting that only one type of deficit, the low-IQ deficit, is present for retardates, with the low-MA—low-IQ deficit being a composite of a low-IQ deficit and a smaller degree of learning-to-learn transfer. Also, with more adequate control of preexperimental transfer effects, there is the possibility of identifying the *type* of learning deficit. For example, the deficit may be attributable to deficiencies in associative learning or to inadequate storage and retrieval mechanisms. Jensen's (1965) analysis making IQ isomorphic with rate of learning and MA synonymous with total amount learned leads to the implication that one type of learning deficit is present in retardates. This deficit would be, in Denny's terminology, a low-IQ deficit. In fact, under conditions where preexperimental transfer effects were negligible, the analyses of Denny (1964) and Jensen (1965) may be considered to be quite similar. However, Denny did not identify the nature of the difference between a low-IQ and a low-MA—low-IQ deficit. Additionally, neither Denny nor Jensen functionally differentiated between specific and nonspecific sources of preexperimental transfer.

III. METHOD AND RESEARCH DESIGN

On a very gross level, the research involving retarded Ss can be grouped into two basic categories. The first type is that which is designed to identify the existence or nature of the learning deficit in retardates. Experimental designs of this type are, of necessity, comparative in nature and usually consist of normal—retardate comparisons where matching (statistical or experimental) is performed on some intellective or maturational variable. The second type of experiment utilizes only retarded Ss and has the primary purpose of understanding the behavior of retardates independently of a "normal" reference group. Designs of this nature may involve the comparison of comparable groups of retardates who each perform under a different experimental treatment or the design may compare groups of retardates differing in MA (or CA and IQ) under identical treatments.

The comparative studies, those involving normal—retardate comparisons or those where intellective variables are included, are subject to a number of fundamental problems. This is true especially for the single factor designs where the factor constitutes an organismic variable. The first problem, suggested as the most fundamental by Baumeister (1967), is that of insuring that the task measures the same psychological processes for each of the groups of Ss. This difficulty limits the conclusions that may be drawn from experimental results but does not constitute sufficient cause for eliminating comparative studies. Later research utilizing the same task, together with increased experimental precision, may be regarded as providing answers to this problem and, whatever the result, the comparative differences found in performance yield information of considerable theoretical and functional interest.

The second problem, also discussed in detail by Baumeister (1967) and by Prehm (1966b) relates to problems in measurement when ability is varied. The experimental task chosen may be too easy for one or all of the groups of Ss with the result being that learning takes place too quickly to demonstrate differences in performance between groups. A similar measurement problem obtains when the experimental task proves too difficult for one or more of the groups of Ss. These problems in measurement can, in most cases, be solved by systematic pilot or preliminary testing.

A third problem which limits generalization from results can be traced to inadequate design rather than methodological difficulties. Quite a number of the studies involve comparisons of normal and retarded children on a single treatment. The results of these experiments pose a difficult problem of interpretation. If the normal children are found to be superior to retardates, the conclusion of a general, all-inclusive, learning deficit in retardates may indeed be tenuous. Admittedly, the difference does provide some evidence regarding the variables or learning tasks under which the behavior of retardates is inferior to that of normals. However, studies of this nature provide no evidence regarding the relative or absolute changes in the degree of retardate inferiority at various points along the age span. Moreover, the conclusions from such experiments may not indicate a general learning deficit but rather an interaction between task (environmental) and organismic (subject) variables. Figure 1 presents the results of a hypothetical experiment involving a comparison of normal and retardate performance at each of two levels of a task variable. It is shown in Fig. 1 that if the retarded and normal samples had been compared only under treatment 2, a conclusion of a general retardate deficiency would have been suggested, whereas the opposite conclusion would have been suggested if the Ss had been compared only under treatment 1. The results, and the limited nature of the conclusion, become apparent only when the results of the complete experiment are presented in the form of the interaction between the task and subject variables.

The importance of research resulting from the use of designs permitting the assessment of the interaction between task and subject variables is obvious. However, there is a striking paucity of learning research with retardates which compares normal and retardate per-

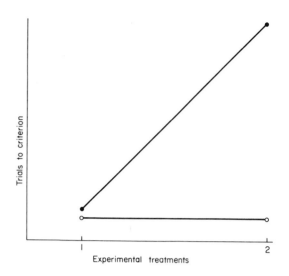

Fig. 1. Hypothetical experiment displaying interaction of task and subject variables for
(○) normal and (●) retarded children.

formance or retardates at different ages at various levels of a task variable. This is in direct contrast to the learning research identified with developmental psychology which, almost without exception, permits the assessment of age-task variable interactions. The reasons for this disparity are not apparent inasmuch as the developmental psychologist and the psychologist interested in the processes of the mentally retarded share many of the same interests and methodological concerns.

IV. PAIRED-ASSOCIATE LEARNING

A. Equal CA Comparisons

The paired-associate learning of normal children has been found to be superior to that of retarded children in five studies where CA has been controlled (Baumeister, Hawkins, & Davis, 1966; Lance, 1965; Madsen, 1963; Ring, 1965; Ring & Palermo, 1961) whereas four studies (Akutagwa & Benoit, 1959; Berkson & Cantor, 1960; Eisman, 1958; Vergason, 1964) have found no differences between retardates and normal children. These conflicting results represent a common state of affairs in the research comparing normals and retardates. To draw a general conclusion from results of this nature is difficult since the disparity may result from differences in Ss between studies, the different CA, MA, and IQ of the Ss tested, the materials or method used, the minimal or nonexistent learning deficit in retardates, or to a number of other factors. For this reason, it is of interest to compare the studies in terms of the overlap between them along the variables that are typically reported in the section on method. Table I presents this information for the studies utilizing Type II designs under standard PA conditions of low intralist similarity and the anticipation method of presentation.

The information in Table I includes the typical demographic data (mean CA, mean MA, and mean IQ of the retarded samples), the type of stimulus materials used, presentation rate, whether or not the retarded Ss were institutionalized, and the experimental results. Information is absent from some of the cells because the authors omitted these data in the report. However, the mean MA or IQ figures, where absent, can be derived with a small degree of error. Except where noted, the matched, normal samples had mean IQ scores approximating 100 and had comparable CA (Table I) or MA (Table II) scores to those of the

TABLE I
SUMMARY DATA FOR PAIRED-ASSOCIATE EXPERIMENTS: CA MATCHED

Experiment	CA[a]	MA	IQ	Materials	Presentation rate (seconds)	Institutionalized	Result
Akutagwa & Benoit, 1959	9, 12	—	79	8 paired pictures	4:4	Yes	N = R
Berkson & Cantor, 1960	12	8.2	70	6 paired pictures	Unpaced	No	N = R
Eisman, 1958	14	—	68	7 paired pictures	Unpaced	No	N = R
Lance, 1965	14	—	65	6 trigram-number pairs	5:5	No	N > R
Madsden, 1963	14	—	67	10 paired pictures	2:2	No	N > R
Ring, 1965	14	—	74	8 paired pictures	2:2, 4:2	No	N > R
Ring & Palermo, 1961	14	12.6	76	8 paired pictures	3:3	No	N > R
Vergason, 1964	14	—	67	13 paired pictures	3:3	No	N = R

[a] Rounded to nearest year.

retardates. Different IQ tests were used both within and between the studies and no reference to the tests used are included here.

Even a cursory glance at Table I reveals the striking similarity between Ss, method, etc., among studies. For reasons unknown, six of eight involved a retarded sample which had a mean CA of approximately 14 years. This means, of course, that few data are available which compare retardates and matched-CA controls at other points in the age span. Also, the IQ scores between studies covers the range only between 65 and 80 (approximately) and MA range between 11 and 13 years (approximately). In other words, there is little possibility of tracing developmental changes in retardate behavior or of establishing differential effects of selected variables on the PA learning of retardates of different ages. With one exception (Lance, 1965), highly familiar pictures or numbers were used as stimulus materials. The lists involved between six to eight pairs with the exception of Vergason (1964) who used 13 paired pictures.

A detailed examination of the data in Table I reveals that three of the studies which found equal learning rates for the normal and retarded samples (Akutagwa & Benoit, 1959; Berkson & Canton, 1960; Eisman, 1959) used presentation rates which were longer than the 2:2- or 3:3-second rates of the remaining experiments. These results suggest that longer periods for anticipation and/or presentation of the PA pairs facilitates the PA learning of retardates. Additionally, these data suggest that the retardates' low-MA—low-IQ deficit may be one of an inability to process information at relatively fast, paced rates. Ring (1965) has also suggested this possibility and this conclusion is partially supported in her data. She found a marked inferiority of retardates when the materials were presented at the conventional 2:2-second rate, with a greatly reduced difference in normal-retardate performance when the PA list was presented at a 4:2-second rate. The interaction of rate × sample, however, did not reach statistical significance. Baumeister et al. (1966), who manipulated the rate of presentation of PA pairs with a mixed list also found that their retardate samples profited more from longer presentation rates, whereas normal samples equated on MA or CA were not affected significantly by item exposure time.

Furthermore, Madsen (1963) and Dent and Johnson (1964) found that distributed practice greatly facilitated the PA learning of retarded samples (relative to a massed practice condition) but had minimal effects upon the performance of average or above-average children (Madsen, 1963). The data from the normal children approximated those found using adult Ss (e.g., Underwood, 1961); but as mentioned earlier, the performance of the retarded sample was greatly facilitated under conditions of distributed practice. The data also provide further support for the assumption that retardate learning (performance?) is hindered under conditions where the information must be processed in short periods of time.

One study (Lance, 1965) did find the more typical result of normal superiority in PA learning even under a slow rate of presentation. However, he used more complex PA stimuli (nonsense syllables). These stimuli were, most likely, unfamiliar to the children (both normal and retarded), thus minimizing the differential *specific* transfer between the two samples (see above). There is also the possibility that retardates find it difficult to learn complex or unfamiliar materials. This possibility is discussed in detail below.

B. Equal MA Comparisons

Table II presents summary data for the PA experiments involving normal and retarded children matched on MA. Again, as with the experiments cited in Table I, there are few data on PA learning in retardates at a number of different ages. As may be seen in Table II, four of the seven studies cited found no differences between the normal and retarded samples in rate of learning (Cantor & Ryan, 1962; Girardeau & Ellis, 1964; Heckman, 1966, Ring & Palermo, 1961), when the Ss were matched on MA, whereas three studies report normal superiority (Iscoe & Semler, 1964; Jensen, 1965; Rieber, 1964).

Interestingly, two of the studies reporting superiority of normals used institutionalized retardates as Ss. In contrast, all but one of the studies (Heckman, 1966) reporting equal rates of learning between the two groups of Ss used noninstitutionalized retardates. These data, then, suggest that institutionalized retardates are inferior to normal Ss even when the MA is equated between groups. However, the fact of being institutionalized rather than retardation, per se, seems to be the major factor responsible for this deficit. Of course, the possibility remains that this inferiority may result from subject variables responsible for institutional placement rather than the environmental deprivation attributable to the institution. Baumeister *et al.* (1966) have also reported that the institutional setting is detrimental to PA learning.

V. PAIRED-ASSOCIATE LEARNING AS A FUNCTION

A. Two-Stage Analysis

Paired-associate learning has been conceptualized as involving two stages, a response—recall stage in which the responses are integrated

TABLE II
SUMMARY DATA FOR PAIRED-ASSOCIATE EXPERIMENTS: MA MATCHED

Experiment	CA[a]	MA	IQ	Materials	Presentation rate (seconds)	Institutionalized	Result
Cantor & Ryan, 1962	9	6.6	72	6 picture pairs	6:5	No	N = R
Girardeau & Ellis, 1964	13	8.4	66	10 word pairs	3:3	No	N = R
Heckman, 1966	17	10.6	—	5 Japanese character- picture- pairs	2:2 2:4 2:8 2:10	Yes	N = R
Iscoe & Semler, 1964	12	6.8	—	6 picture pairs	5 second	Yes	N > R
Jensen, 1965	24	9.3	58	8 picture pairs	Subject- paced	Yes	N > R
Rieber, 1964	12	8.3	70	3 picture color- word pairs	2:2	No	N > R
Ring & Palermo, 1961	14	12.6	76	8 picture pairs	3:3	No	N = R

[a] Rounded to nearest year.

(learned) and available for recall as functional units, and an associative stage in which each response is associated with some aspect of its stimulus (Underwood, Runquist, & Schulz, 1959; Underwood & Schulz, 1960). The two-stage analysis has had major utility in the study and understanding of PA learning. For example, it is possible to determine the effects of selected experimental variables upon acquisition under each stage. Additionally, the stage analysis shows promise in terms of permitting greater understanding of the processes underlying the learning deficit in retardates in addition to permitting insight into how these processes are modified as a function of age and intellective status in both normal and retarded children.

No published research involving retarded Ss has measured acquisition separately for the response-learning and associative stages during PA learning. However, this has been done in research utilizing adult Ss (e.g.,

Postman, 1962) and with normal sixth-grade children (Carroll & Penney, 1966). This technique typically involves a determination of the trial where a response was first given and the trial where the response was first paired correctly. The first-given measure is used as the index of the response learning stage, while the difference between the first-given and first-pairing measures serve as an index of the associative stage. Response learning may also be estimated by testing for free response recall at different stages during PA learning (e.g., Jung, 1965; Underwood *et al.*, 1959) and the associative stage may be measured if an associative matching task (which eliminates response learning) is used in place of a PA task (Horowitz, 1962; Saltz, 1961). Ekstrand (1966b) discusses the relative merits of these techniques.

The major utility of the stage analysis is that it may permit the delineation of the factor or process responsible for the retardate learning deficit. As an example, this factor may be localized in the response-learning stage. With this assumption, a likely possibility for a causal variable would be the differential frequency of exposure to the printed and spoken language, making response terms less available for retardates at the onset of PA learning. As mentioned earlier, this factor may be controlled by using stimulus materials which are unfamiliar to all *S*s. A second possibility would be a deficit in the memory storage and retrieval mechanisms, this factor being attributable to organic or physical deficit rather than to environmental factors.

On the other hand, a very likely factor responsible, at least in part, for the retardate learning deficit is an associative-learning deficit. There is no research which permits the assessment of associative learning in retardates in the absence of response learning. Prehm (1966a,b) has suggested that PA learning research be presented in terms of a stage analysis, but no data of this type are currently available. In fact a series of experiments involving the study of learning in retardates using associative matching tasks would be of much interest. A number of individuals have suggested that retardates would be deficient in associative learning (e.g., Jensen, 1965; Lipman, 1963; Luria, 1960), but this assumption awaits experimental test.

The factor responsible for a deficit in associative learning could also result from maturational variables that vary with mental age and development independently of the degree of mental retardation. In this regard, H. H. Kendler and Kendler (1962) have suggested that pre-school children are deficient in mediational processes whereas older children are able to utilize mediators (at least those based on well-learned conceptual categories; i.e., color, size). It can be expected, then, that the utilization of such subject-generated mediators would increase with age, being entirely absent in very young children or retardates who have a low MA. On the other hand, retarded children may themselves have difficulty in spontaneously utilizing mediators to facilitate PA learning, either because language habits are weak, because mediation does not occur spontaneously, or possibly because subject-generated mediators elicit a number of erroneous responses which interfere with PA acquisition. Stedman (1963) and Evans (1964) have found that retardates do emit a high degree of extralist errors (relative to normal children) in free recall where the stimulus items comprise a small number of the instances in conceptual categories represented in the list (e.g., trees.) Prehm (1966a) has also found that retarded Ss have difficulty in screening out intruding associative responses, e.g., language associates, in PA learning when stimuli were meaningful, familiar pictures.

The hypothesis of a deficit in the associative process for retardates may be tested with a PA task by the manipulation of intralist similarity; that is, retarded Ss would be expected to be more subject to interference generated from high intralist stimulus (or response) similarity than normal Ss. It should be mentioned, however, that the above prediction is applicable only when formal similarity (e.g., letter duplication) is manipulated. When similarity in meaning or conceptual similarity is varied, the intralist interference would be expected to vary directly with the strength, number, and complexity of the preexperimental language habits. Thus, in the latter case, retardates (with weaker language habits) would be less subject to interference than normal Ss.

Some support for this contention has been found by Iscoe and Semler (1964) and Semler and Iscoe (1965). They found that PA lists consisting of conceptually similar pairs (e.g., glove-shoe) were learned more quickly than lists consisting of conceptually dissimilar pairs (e.g., glove-bowl). This was true for both normal and retarded Ss. However, the data from their experiments are difficult to interpret because the results cannot be attributed solely to facilitation resulting from pairing conceptually related pictures (similar condition) or interference resulting from interpair conceptual similarity in the dissimilar condition; that is, examples of two pairs in the dissimilar condition were "banana-shoe" and "toothbrush-orange." It is possible that interpair conceptual similarity led to competing responses, which in turn, hindered learning. Therefore, the hypothesis of greater interference for normal than for retarded children under conditions of high intralist stimulus or response similarity remains to be empirically tested.

Wallace and Underwood (1964) have provided evidence that retarded Ss ($\overline{X}$ CA = 20.4; $\overline{X}$ IQ = 63) are not subject to interference from high interpair conceptual similarity in learning a PA list. They noted that high intralist conceptual similarity should facilitate free learning (i.e., free recall) in normal Ss because recall can occur on the basis of the category name. On the other hand, PA learning is hindered because of the associative interference resulting from high interstimulus and inter-response conceptual similarity. Furthermore, Wallace & Underwood assumed that retarded Ss are not subject to associative interference based upon conceptual similarity, the result of which leads to the prediction that both free learning and PA learning should be independent of the effects of this variable. Their results were in accord with expectation. Their data, however, do not provide evidence as to whether the minimal effects of conceptual similarity on free learning and PA learning in retardates is a developmental process or one associated specifically with a retardate deficit. That is, the absence of an effect of conceptual similarity may have been because of weak language habits (which would also be true of young, normal children) or that high conceptual similarity does not *spontaneously* lead to competing associations in retarded Ss. The normal, matched-CA Ss in the Wallace and Underwood experiment were college students, thus, no comparable data are available for young children. No studies using retarded Ss have involved the manipulation of intralist formal similarity.

Also in regard to associative learning, there has been no research which has measured the simultaneous acquisition of both stimulus-response (S−R) (forward) and response-stimulus (R−S) (backward) associations in the PA learning of retardates. Both adults (Feldman & Underwood, 1957) and normal children (Palermo, 1961) do form R−S associations while practicing on a PA list in the S−R direction although S−R recall typically exceeds R−S recall. Empirical research in this area may provide evidence related to the suggestion of an incidental learning deficit in retardates (Denny, 1964), whether the principle of associative symmetry (i.e., equal strength of S−R and R−S associations) holds for retarded Ss, and whether the principle of stimulus selection (e.g., Underwood, 1963) applies to the PA acquisition of retardates as well as that of adults. For a complete discussion of the implications of research on R−S learning to developmental processes, the reader is referred to Goulet (1968).

B. Meaningfulness

Response meaningfulness (M) has been found to be a potent variable in determining the rate of PA learning for both adults (e.g., Hunt, 1959) and fifth-grade children (Palermo, Flamer, & Jenkins, 1964). Presumably, these potent effects are owing to the difficulty in response integration for low M materials, with high M materials already being partially or completely integrated prior to practice on the PA task. It is to be expected that the differences in learning PA lists with high or low response M would increase with age because of differential exposure to high and low M materials. This prediction applies mutually to studies involving normal and retarded Ss and is subject to experimental test since norms do exist (Underwood & Schulz, 1960) which make it possible to construct PA lists with responses (e.g., bigrams and trigrams) which differ in frequency of occurrence in the printed language. The existence of these norms also makes it possible to construct lists with responses which are scaled on a variable which is independent of possible confounding by subject variables. That is, M covaries, at least within the intermediate range, with frequency of occurrence in the printed language for adults, but no data exist relevant to the frequency-M function with either normal or retarded children. Therefore, the use of materials scaled in meaningfulness according to adult norms in research with children (either normal or retarded) is subject to potential confounding.

Prehm (1966a) has found evidence that normal and retarded children learn high and low M lists at differential rates, with normal children learning high M lists more quickly than low M lists. The retardates learned low M lists more quickly than high M lists. However, in Prehm's (1966a) study, response M was confounded with list length and no unequivocal interpretation of these results can be suggested. Lance (1965), manipulating stimulus M, has found that M varies inversely with PA learning when children (either normal or retarded) serve as Ss, a finding somewhat contrary to the available data collected from adults (cf. Underwood & Schulz, 1960).

C. Presentation Rate

There have been a number of studies using retarded Ss where rate of presentation (or exposure duration) of PA lists has been varied (Baumeister et al., 1966; Heckman, 1966; Ring, 1965). Ring varied the anticipation interval while Baumeister et al. and Heckman varied the stimulus—response exposure interval. In general, these studies were initiated because of Bugelski's (1962) finding that "total learning time," i.e., the time that adults actually spent in learning a list of paired associates, was independent of the rate of presentation of the lists. Ring found a tendency for the PA learning of retardates to be facilitated under the longer (4:2-second) anticipation interval, with no concomitant effect for matched CA normal children. Baumeister et al. using a 5-

second anticipation interval and varying (1 – 8 second) stimulus –
response exposure durations for each of the pairs within the list, found
results comparable to those of Ring. However, a measure of total
learning time was not presented in either of these studies.

Heckman (1966) manipulating stimulus – response exposure duration
as a between subject variable, found that total learning time was inversely
related to exposure duration for both normal and matched-MA normal
children. Her data suggested that the number of repetitions of the
list rather than total learning time was the major factor determining
learning rate. Price (1963), by using a different method and normal
children as Ss, has also arrived at the latter conclusion.

It should be noted that Heckman's data are in conflict with those of
Ring and Baumeister et al. However, the data clearly indicate that presentation rate affects PA learning of adults and children in different
ways; i.e., trials to criterion on a PA list varies inversely with presentation rate with adults, while for normal children (Baumeister et al., 1966;
Heckman, 1966; Ring, 1965) the effect is minimal whether the anticipation interval or the stimulus – response exposure interval is varied. For
retardates, lengthening the anticipation exposure interval or stimulus –
response exposure interval apparently facilitates PA learning although
the effect is slight.

VI. SERIAL LEARNING

There have been a surprising number of studies investigating the
learning of retarded subjects with serial tasks. These have included
experiments involving normal – retardate comparisons where IQ was
varied (Barnett, Ellis, & Pryer, 1960; Ellis, Pryer, Distefano, & Pryer,
1960; McManis, 1965b; Pryer, 1960), where MA was matched (Cassel,
1957; Girardeau & Ellis, 1964; Jensen, 1965; McManis, 1965b) and
studies involving only retarded samples (Blount & Heal, 1966; McManis,
1965a). No studies have been reported where normal and retarded
children were matched on CA. The frequent use of the serial learning
task would not be expected on the basis of the amount of published
research which has involved normal children as Ss. Spiker (1960) has
speculated that the reason for the paucity of data on normal children
may be owing to the fact that serial learning is too difficult for the young
child or that the serial task has not proved to be a sufficiently analytical
task. For example, there is difficulty in isolating stimulus and response
functions of the individual items in serial lists.

There are two possible reasons for the large number of studies using
serial tasks. The first reason stems from the results of an early study by

McCrary and Hunter (1953) who found that the serial position curve was higher and more peaked for slow than for fast learners when the absolute number of errors that occurred at each serial position were plotted. However, when the data were transformed into a relative measure, percentage of total errors at each serial position, the serial position curve was identical for the two groups of Ss. The studies involving retarded Ss have attempted to extend this result.

A second possible reason for the use of the serial learning task with retardates has been its singular fruitfulness in differentiating between normal and retarded children. That is, without exception, normals are superior to retardates in serial learning even when the groups of Ss are matched on MA. As seen above, PA tasks do not differentiate between normals and retardates with the same degree of uniformity. It should be noted that Lance (1965) did find a trend toward an interaction of list length and diagnosis, with normal children learning a serial list more quickly than matched-MA retardates with long (eight- and ten-item) lists, and retardates learning slightly more quickly with a short (four-item) list. However, statistical analyses of these data were not reported.

The data collected using serial learning tasks suggest that, with the exception of a difference in a learning-rate constant related to IQ or MA, retarded and normal children learn the lists in much the same manner. That is, the bowed serial-position curve is found in the serial learning of retardates (e.g., Ellis et al., 1959), serial position cues are of comparable importance in the serial learning of both normal and retarded Ss (Lance, 1965), and verbal mediation instructions do not affect serial learning either for normal or retarded Ss (e.g., Jensen, 1965). Also, the relative distribution of errors as a function of ordinal position of the item is much the same for normal and retarded Ss (e.g., McManis, 1965b). Barnett et al. (1960) did find a tendency of fast learners (normal high school students) to make relatively more errors for middle items and fewer errors for the beginning items than slow learners (retarded Ss). However, these differences were slight. The rate of serial learning has also been found to vary directly with MA and IQ across a wide range of MA or IQ levels (Blount & Heal, 1966; Ellis et al., 1959).

In addition, McManis (1966) has found that the isolation of an item (printing the item in red) in a serial list facilitates the learning of that item for both retarded and normal Ss. However, isolation on the basis of meaningfulness (inserting a low M item in a list of high M items) did not lead to facilitation for the retardates but did for the normal Ss. While the latter results may not be specific to serial learning, they do suggest that retarded Ss may not be able to differentiate between verbal materials on the basis of frequency while normal Ss can (e.g., McManis, 1966).

This problem has been discussed in some detail earlier in the article, but in the present context, the inability to differentiate between high and low M items is most likely because neither type of item is highly familiar to the retarded Ss.

The series of experiments utilizing serial tasks, while leading to un-equivocal findings of superior learning for normal Ss, have not provided insight into the specific process or factor responsible for the retardate deficit. However, it may be interesting to speculate as to the possible reasons for the relative inability of retarded Ss to learn serial lists. One possibility relates to the greater implicit difficulty of serial lists relative to PA lists. That is, in serial lists, confusion may arise between the two types of functional stimuli (i.e., ordinal position and the preceding item) especially when longer lists are used. Then again, the learning of a serial list may involve interference stemming from confusion between the stimulus and response functions of each item. Future research most certainly should focus upon the delineation of the factors responsible for the retardate deficit.

VII. MEDIATION

A number of studies have been conducted which have had, as their major focus, the determination of whether mentally retarded children can use verbal mediators to facilitate learning. These studies have been based on the implicit premise that retardates are, in some manner, deficient in mediational ability and this assumption has been tested with a number of different types of PA tasks and with retarded Ss of different levels of ability (Berkson & Cantor, 1960; Jensen, 1965; Jensen & Rohwer, 1963b; Rieber, 1964).

The assumption of a retardate deficit in mediational ability has its basis in the theory of Luria (1960) and from indirect evidence in empir-ical research such as that which demonstrates that retardates learn a discrimination reversal more slowly than normal children (e.g., Heal, Ross, & Sanders, 1966).

Stated in the above manner, any demonstration that retardates could utilize mediational cues as well as normal children (matched on MA or CA) would seem to refute this contention. However, the demonstration of a smaller effect resulting from mediation in retardates may be shown *not* to carry as much weight. That is, any comparisons of normals and retardates on a task involving verbal mediation must take account of developmental trends in mediational ability in addition to the type of learning task which involves verbal mediators. In other words, lack of mediational ability may result from developmental factors rather than a retardate deficit; or the mediational deficit may be apparent only in certain tasks, with certain materials, etc.

The question regarding the presence of a mediational deficit in retardates may take a number of forms. That is, one question is, can retardates generate verbal mediators as cues to facilitate learning? It is well known that adult Ss utilize idiosyncratic mediators to learn paired associates (e.g., Bugelski, 1962) even though they are not specifically instructed to do so. Also, in line with developmental trends in mediational ability that have been demonstrated in transposition tasks (e.g., Kuenne, 1946) and with reversal shift tasks (e.g., H. H. Kendler & Kendler, 1962) it can be expected that the utilization of such subject-generated mediators would increase with age, being entirely absent at some point on the age continuum. Unfortunately, there is no available research using normal or retarded children which is similar to the experiment by Bugelski. There are data which provide evidence that both retarded and normal children can use mediational cues to facilitate PA learning under mediation-prompting instructions, (e.g., Davidson, 1964; Jensen, 1965; Jensen & Rohwer, 1963a, 1963b, 1965). Jensen and Rohwer (1965), however, have found that normal, kindergarten children are apparently unable to utilize such instruction-prompted mediators. This is an important finding in view of the fact that kindergarten children are presumably at a transitional stage between those who can and cannot mediate.

Jensen (1965) has found that the PA learning of retarded adults ($\overline{X}$ MA = 9.3 years) was markedly facilitated when they were instructed to mediate (i.e., construct sentences). In fact, the facilitation attributable to verbal mediation was superior to that of a group of matched-MA normal children. Jensen and Rohwer (1963a, 1963b) have also reported that retarded adults can utilize verbal mediators to facilitate PA learning under conditions when such mediated verbalization is prompted by instructions.

There is some research Iscoe & Semler, 1964; Semler & Iscoe, 1965) indirectly related to mediational ability, which does suggest that the performance of retarded Ss is hindered relative to matched-MA normals when the stimulus materials are abstract (paired pictures) rather than concrete (paired objects). However, the conclusions from these data are not unequivocal since these results may result from a deficit in conceptual ability or from some other factor related to the dimensionality of the stimulus materials. In this regard, see Stevenson and McBee (1958).

A series of studies by Paivio and his associates (Paivio, 1963; Paivio & Yuille, 1966; Paivio, Yuille & Smythe, 1966; Yarmey & Paivio, 1965) also relate to the abstractness—concreteness dimension and the PA learning of normal adults. In each of these studies the PA learning of nouns was easier when the nouns were concrete rather than abstract. Furthermore, the effect was much greater on the stimulus than on the response side of the pairs. These findings were interpreted in terms of the greater capacity of concrete nouns to evoke sensory- images which mediate response recall. This effect was clearly smaller when children served as Ss and suggestive evidence was provided for an interaction of stimulus concreteness with age, the effect increasing from the fourth to the sixth grade (Paivio & Yuille, 1966). There are no available data from retarded Ss involving PA learning with materials parallel to that of Paivio.

Berkson and Cantor (1960) have compared normal and retarded children matched on CA in a three-stage mediation paradigm [for a complete explanation of three-stage mediation paradigms see Horton & Kjeldergaard (1961)] where the mediator was based on laboratory-acquired associations. They found comparable mediated facilitation for the two groups of Ss even though the normal children learned the third (test) stage faster than the retardates. Rieber (1964) has also demonstrated mediated facilitation and mediated interference on a task involving transfer from a verbal to a motor PA task. Mediation was not found, however, unless the retardates were instructed to verbalize the PA pairs during training. Additionally, the magnitude of mediated interference was greater for the retarded than for matched-MA normal children.

In summary, the evidence strongly suggests that retarded Ss can utilize verbal mediators to facilitate PA learning. However, most of the studies relating to this problem have used retarded adults rather than younger children. The results provided by Berkson and Cantor do imply that retarded Ss with a relatively low MA are capable of utilizing verbal mediators effectively and the magnitude of mediated facilitation is apparently equivalent to that found with normal children of comparable MA (e.g., Davis, 1966). There has been no published work with retardates parallel to that with normal children which has investigated mediational processes using paradigms where mediational links are based, at least in part, on preexperimental language habits (e.g., Palermo & Jenkins, 1964; Wismer & Lipsitt, 1964).

VIII. TRANSFER OF TRAINING

Transfer of training has been a focus of interest for investigators interested in adult verbal learning but strikingly few studies have been reported which use retarded or normal children as Ss. There has been an increasing number of studies identified with the study of nonspecific transfer (e.g., learning set, warm-up) but these typically have involved nonverbal tasks (see Harlow, 1959). Keppel (1964) and Goulet (1968) each provide detailed reviews of the verbal learning studies with normal children, while Harlow (1959) and Kaufman and Prehm (1968) provide suggestive evidence of developmental trends in learning-to-learn factors that may be investigated with verbal learning paradigms. The primary concern here is with specific transfer factors.

There are three basic PA transfer paradigms, A-B, A-C; A-B, C-B; and A-B, A-Br. The designation implies that Ss learn two consecutive PA lists, List 1 which is designated as A-B, and a List 2 which is defined in terms of the similarity to List 1. For example, the A-B, A-C paradigm involves identical stimuli and unrelated responses on the two lists and the A-B, A-Br paradigm involves repairing the identical stimuli and responses on the two lists. It is appropriate here only to mention the basic theory underlying transfer of training. For a more complete presentation of the empirical and theoretical relations, the reader is referred to Martin (1965), Ekstrand (1966a), Postman (1961), Twedt and Underwood (1959), and Kausler (1966).

Whenever an A-B, A-C relationship holds between successive tasks, negative transfer occurs. This negative transfer is attributed to interference where the first-list associations (A-B) compete with the acquisition of second-list (A-C) associations. This A-B, A-C relationship holds between List 1 and List 2 S−R associations in the A-B, A-C paradigm and between List 1 and List 2 R−S association in the A-B, C-B paradigm. Both S−R and R−S associations are sources of interference in the A-B, A-Br paradigm.

The basic question concerns the applicability of transfer of training paradigms in the study of the associative processes of retarded children. Transfer tasks have proved to be useful in studying normal children. For example, Gladis (1960), by using the A-B, C-B paradigm, found that positive transfer increased with age, being negative for third-grade Ss and increasingly positive for fifth- and seventh-grade Ss. Goulet (1968) has suggested that younger children may be more prone to associative interference, and this implication holds equally for retarded Ss of low MA. However, the similarity of the transfer function for normal and retarded children remains to be determined. In the present context, White (1964) has noted that younger children generalize more than do older children and this assumption has found support in the work of Mednick and Lehtinen (1957) and White and Spiker (1960) who each used nonverbal tasks. White (1964) has also suggested that children are poorer at response inhibition when they are younger, possibly because they are unable to inhibit responding to negative cues (Spiker & White, 1959) and/or because they are more susceptible to associative interference; e.g., restraining earlier learned responses. The basic transfer paradigms each provide means of testing this premise in a situation which is free of confounding from sources of non specific transfer (i.e., learning to learn and warm-up) if Ss are compared under one of the experimental paradigms (e.g., A-B, A-C) and the usual control (A-B, C-D) paradigm.

Unfortunately, there are no data which provide for comparisons between normal and retarded children under one of the verbal transfer paradigms. In fact, there are no data relevant to transfer of training in retardates using verbal tasks. Retardates do perform more poorly than normal Ss under a discrimination reversal paradigm (Heal, *et al.*, 1966) and Rieber (1964) has found that retardates are more subject to mediated interference than normal children. Associative interference may possibly be a major factor responsible for any retardate deficit related to learning and recall.

IX. RETENTION AND MEMORY

A. Simple Retention

The present discussion is not meant so much as a review of relevant research as it is a commentary on differences between retention studies using retarded Ss and those using normal young and adult Ss. Belmont (1966) has provided a recent summary of the research on long-term memory and Denny (1964) and Lipman (1963) have provided earlier reviews. Further extensive discussion of the results of these studies would be redundant. In short, the results of most studies comparing the retention of retarded to normal Ss imply that no deficit is involved (e.g., Belmont, 1966).

The studies which have compared normal and retarded children on the retention of a single PA list over varying intervals of time are subject to difficulty in interpretation, both on methodological and theoretical grounds. Belmont (1966) has discussed a number of the methodoligical problems involved in the study of simple retention, presenting many of Underwood's (1954, 1964) comments in the context of retention research with retardates. The reader is recommended to each of these papers and also that of Anderson (1963) for a discussion of these problems in addition to suggestions as to how to circumvent the difficulties posed by research of this nature.

The research concerned with tracing the course of retention (or forgetting) of retardates over time, in most instances, has been predicated on the assumption that retardates suffer some structural deficit which results in greater memory loss than normal Ss after comparable periods of time. While research of this variety may indeed provide some evidence relating to a structural memory deficit, it should be noted that an alternative conception views forgetting to be largely a result of interference from well-learned language habits (e.g., Postman, 1961; Underwood & Postman, 1960). In this regard, the interference may be proactive; i.e., interference from language habits acquired prior to the to-be-recalled material; or the interference may be retroactive; (i.e., interference from letter- or word-language habits acquired after the to-be-learned material). In any event, the course of forgetting over time in retardates must be considered to be a joint function of a memory deficit (if indeed such a deficit exists), retroactive and proactive interference. Alternatively, forgetting may be attributable only to retroactive and proactive interference with superior retention in normal Ss being accounted for in terms of greater susceptibility to associative interference in retarded Ss.

Unfortunately, the experiments comparing normals and retardates on retention of a single list permit no degree of experimental control over nor empirical estimate of the variance which is attributable to retroactive interference, proactive interference, and the memory deficit in retardates. Thus, the available data suggesting that normal and retarded children forget at equal rates may imply that retardates have no memory deficit *or* that the combined effect of the potential sources of forgetting confound the retention function. For example, it is logical to assume that the degree of retroactive and proactive interference is greater for normal children than for retardates because of their more diverse experience, verbal and communication skills, reading ability, etc. As may be seen, experiments involving normal — retardate comparisons may be confounded by differential degrees of associative interference for the two samples of Ss. Thus, the two sources of forgetting, associative interference and memory deficit, may counterbalance one another, the resultant leading to the conclusion that the retention function for the normals and retardates is identical *and* that the potential factors responsible for forgetting contribute equally to the decrement in recall over time for the two samples of Ss.

There has been extremely little research investigating retention of single lists in normal children or adult Ss. The reasons for this most likely are because of the lack of experimental control over the intervening activities during the period between original learning and subsequent recall. Relatively sophisticated designs are possible which allow for empirical tests of theories of forgetting (e.g., Underwood & Postman,

1960). However, when subject variables (e.g., age) are included into the research design, the problems in interpretation become extremely difficult. This is especially true in normal—retardate comparisons where two or more different processes (e.g., memory deficit and associative interference) may be assumed to vary concomitantly.

Some comment should be made about associative interference and the manner in which it would affect retention in normal and retarded children. It has been mentioned earlier that retarded Ss may be more susceptible to such interference than normal children. This assumption is predicated upon data such as that of Heal *et al.* (1966) which demonstrate that these Ss have greater difficulty in discrimination-reversal tasks than do normal Ss. Little is known about this problem in terms of developmental changes in the difficulty of discrimination-reversal experiments either with normal or retarded Ss. This assumption, however, does not imply that there is a greater *amount* of interfering material (e.g., language habits) for retarded Ss. Indeed, as stated above, there may be a greater *degree* of retroactive and proactive interference in normal Ss because of their greater and more complex verbal experience. The possibility of the dual effects of associative interference makes the interpretation of experiments on simple retention even more difficult. It also points out the need to include demographic data relative to reading level of the Ss, environmental experience, etc., in the body of the text of articles which focus upon retention.

B. Retroactive and Proactive Inhibition

The most influential theoretical explanation of forgetting is the interference-theory conception which explains retroactive inhibition (RI) in terms of two factors, unlearning of verbal associations as a function of conflicting (or interfering) first-list associations and competition between the two sets of responses at the time of recall. Proactive inhibition (PI) is accounted for in terms of a single factor, response competition. The purpose here is not to summarize data and theory in this area since excellent, current reviews of this conception can be found elsewhere (Keppel, 1968; Postman, 1961).

The increased interest in RI and PI has been accompanied by the advent of appropriate control conditions and by refinements in methodological sophistication. The results of recent research has demonstrated that both RI and PI can be experimentally manipulated, making each subject to increased experimenter control (for discussion of control paradigms by which to assess RI and PI, see Barnes & Underwood, 1959; Melton, 1961; Postman, 1961). For example, it is possible to accelerate the rate of forgetting by utilizing a PI or RI paradigm which maximizes the amount of associative interference. As indicated in the section on transfer of training, associative interference occurs whenever an A-B, A-C relationship obtains between successive tasks. This A-B, A-C relationship may be in the form of competition between $S-R$ (forward) associations as in the A-B, A-C paradigm; between $R-S$ (backward) associations as in the A-B, C-B paradigm; or may involve competition between both forward or backward associations as in the A-B, A-Br paradigm.

The use of these paradigms to study RI and PI is obvious; i.e., they permit the study of the processes of forgetting over short periods of time (e.g., in one experimental session) and they permit a high degree of control over the amount and characteristics of the interfering associations. Thus, with the paired-associate A-B, A-C paradigm, the learning of the second list (A-C) is followed by the concomitant unlearning of the first-list (A-B) associations. Additionally, this unlearning (RI) is a direct function of the number of practice trials on the second list (e.g., Barnes & Underwood, 1959).

These PA paradigms have obvious utility for the study of retention processes in retardates, especially in research which consists of comparisons between retention functions of normal and retarded children. The different groups of Ss can be taken to a common criterion of learning on the first list thus providing a reasonable estimate of or equating of original learning for the samples studied. Also, the amount of interference can be equated between groups. With this experimental control there is the possibility of functionally accounting for the amount of variance attributable to a structural memory deficit in retardates and, in addition, determining the susceptibility of these Ss to associative interference.

In a search of the literature only two studies could be found which were concerned with comparisons in RI between normal and retarded children (Cassel, 1957; Pryer, 1960). Both of these studies utilized serial tasks and compared retardates and normals on recall of the first list after practice on a second list. Equal degrees of RI were found for normal and retarded Ss in both experiments. However, a number of reasons make the two sets of data difficult to interpret. The use of serial learning tasks makes it difficult to identify the source of interlist interference. This is especially true in Cassel's experiment where the second list (five items) shared three items in common with the first list (six items), with the resultant being that the recall of the "shared" and "unshared" items on the first list was confounded by differential response availability. Cassel did not analyze his data separately for these sets of items, and since the data on the degree of RI were not included in the report further interpretation is unwarranted.

Pryer's Ss did learn two unrelated lists and therefore his data were not counfounded by the latter variable. However, he did not include control Ss against which to evaluate the relative degree of RI for his samples of normal and retarded children. He presented his RI data in terms of a "savings" score which were, most likely, confounded by differential learning-to-learn transfer for the two groups of Ss. Further confounding in the two studies may have resulted from the possibility of differential overlearning of the first list between the two samples of Ss (see Belmont, 1966; Underwood, 1954, 1964, for a discussion of this problem).

In short, the research related to RI may be shown to be subject to a number of uncontrolled factors, with the only conclusion possible being that RI does occur in retardates. In the only study concerned with PI in retardates, House, Smith, & Zeaman (1964) found that recall decreased as a function of the number of previously learned PA lists. In their study, Ss learned 10 PA lists on successive days with retention on each list being tested 24 hours after it had been learned. The amount of recall after this retention interval decreased from 86% for the first list to 43% of the tenth list (after nine previous lists had been learned). Again, however, no control conditions were included in the experiment.

The study of RI and PI in normal children has also been neglected. However, it is possible to derive predictions from the current version of interference theory which relate to the interaction of RI and/or PI and development. For example, Koppenaal, Krull, & Katz (1964) studied RI and PI in preschool, kindergarten, and third-grade children under a design where the Ss learned successive lists conforming to the A-B, A-C paradigm and either recalled the first list (RI test) or second list (PI test) after a 24-hour retention interval. On the assumption from interference theory that the degree of RI and PI varies directly with the strength of preexperimental language habits, and with the additional assumption that the number and strength of language habits increases with age during childhood, it was predicted that the degree of RI and PI would decrease from the third grade to preschool Ss. The experimental results confirmed this prediction.

Experimental designs such as that used by Koppenaal *et al.* can easily be adapted to study retention in retarded children. These designs can be modified to assess RI and PI as a function of the interaction of preexperimental language habits with laboratory learning by including a retention interval long enough to involve preexperimental associative interference (e.g., Koppenaal *et al.*). Or RI or PI may be assessed merely as a function of associative interference generated in the laboratory if a design parallel to that of Barnes and Underwood (1959) is used. In any event, the use of these designs will facilitate the determination of the factors responsible for forgetting in retardates, whether it be owing to a structural memory deficit, a susceptibility to associative interference, or to well-learned language habits.

X. FREE RECALL AND ASSOCIATIVE CLUSTERING

There has been increasing interest in the study of free recall in adults, in normal children, and in mental retardates. The experiments in free recall are of three basic types and all involve the same basic procedure. Stimulus words or pictures are presented, one at a time, after which Ss are asked to recall as many of the stimulus items as they can in any order they wish. One of the types of experiments involves presenting a list of stimulus materials where the items may be organized or grouped into a number of conceptual categories, e.g., trees and animals (Bousfield, 1953; Bousfield & Cohen, 1955; Bousfield, Esterson, & Whitmarsh, 1958). The second type involves lists with items grouped on the basis of natural language associates (e.g., Deese, 1959; Jenkins & Russell, 1952; Wicklund, Palermo, & Jenkins, 1965), whereas the third type of experiment consists of lists comprised of associatively or conceptually unrelated materials (e.g., Laurence, 1966; Tulving, 1962, 1964).

The recall of verbal material based on conceptual or associative categories is superior to that of control lists presumably because Ss code or cluster items on the basis of the category name. Subsequent recall, then, can be based on this category name thus reducing memory load and facilitating retrieval. Tulving (1962, 1964) has also demonstrated that adult Ss spontaneously or subjectively "organize" verbal material presented for subsequent recall. For theoretical papers dealing with free recall and clustering, the reader is referred to Cofer (1965), Deese (1961, 1962), and Tulving (1962, 1964). The primary purpose here is to ascertain developmental trends in the free recall and associative clustering of normal children and to compare these data to those involving normal – retardate comparisons.

Bousfield (1958) compared third-grade, fourth-grade, and college students on associative clustering in a list of 25 stimulus pictures which could be grouped on the basis of five colors or five conceptual categories (e.g., birds and flowers) and found that both perceptual and conceptual clustering increased with age. More recently, Wicklund et al. (1965) presented fourth-grade Ss lists of highly associated word pairs and found that associative clustering was apparent in both the S−R and R−S directions. Additionally, the degree of clustering was found to be a direct function of the average associative strength of three sets of pairs of high-, medium-, and low-associative strength. These data suggest that children categorize word lists in much the same manner as adults although there is a tendency for such clustering to increase with age (Bousfield et al., 1958; Hess and Simon, 1964; Simon & Hess, 1965) at least from the fourth grade through college.

Laurence (1967) included groups of preschool and kindergarten children along with children in grades three through seven and confirmed the above conclusion. In fact, even the preschool children recalled a greater number of items from a list of conceptually related pictures (high C) than from a list of unrelated (low C) pictures. The latter results were unexpected inasmuch as "cognitive" theories of development such as that of Piaget (Flavell, 1963) hold that the cognitive processes of the preschool child are still at a stage where objects are treated largely as discrete events. However, in line with the prediction from theory in verbal learning (Deese, 1959; Underwood & Postman, 1960), the disparity in recall between high C and low C lists increased with age.

Laurence (1966) has also compared free recall performance and the degree of subjective organization (Tulving, 1962) on lists of unrelated pictures for children in grades one through four with samples of college and elderly Ss. She did find that the mean words recalled increased over trials for all Ss. However, the asymptote of performance was markedly lower for the children with a mean of approximately eight pictures recalled for the youngest Ss as contrasted to 16 recalled for the college Ss. Laurence suggested the possibility of an "effective list length" which is related to age and which is not exceeded even though additional practice trials are given [in this regard, see Miller (1956)].

When Tulving's (1962) measure of subjective organization (SO) was applied to the data, striking differences were found between children and adults. That is, SO increased only minimally over trials for the four groups of children and there were no differences in SO attributable to age. On the other hand, the adult Ss manifested rapidly increasing SO scores as a function of practice. Apparently, children as old as those in the fourth grade are not prone to a high degree of spontaneous organization in free recall. This is in contrast to the relatively high degree of associative clustering when word lists may be grouped according to well-learned conceptual categories (Bousfield et al., 1958) or associatively related word pairs (Wicklund et al., 1965).

There have been six studies in which associative clustering has been studied in retardates (Evans, 1964; Gerjuoy & Spitz, 1966; Osborn, 1960; Rossi, 1963; Stedman, 1963; Weatherwax & Benoit, 1957). One of the studies (Rossi, 1963) compared groups of normal and retarded Ss matched on MA ($\overline{X}$=4.5, 7.25, and 10.0) with IQ ($\overline{X}$=48.3, 65.5, and 65.5), whereas a second study (Stedman, 1963) matched normal and retarded Ss on CA [$\overline{X}$=24.5 (approximately)] with IQ ($\overline{X}$=64). Gerjuoy and Spitz (1966) matched on both MA and CA [$\overline{X}$ MA=9.81; $\overline{X}$ CA=14.5 (approximately); $\overline{X}$ IQ=52.95, and 72.05]. Evans compared high and low IQ retardates [$\overline{X}$ IQ=46, 65 (approximately), $\overline{X}$ CA=30+(approximately)].

Rossi presented Ss with a list of 20 stimulus words consisting of five instances of each of four conceptual categories. The results indicated that normals and retardates clustered equally well and each MA group manifested increasing degrees of associative clustering over five training-test trials. The greatest difference in clustering between the normal—retardate groups occurred at the lowest MA level. Both Osborn (1960) and Weatherwax and Benoit (1957) compared organic and familial retardates with Osborn also including a matched-MA normal sample. The results of these studies were congruent; i.e., no differences between organic and familial retardates in the degree of associative clustering. In addition, Osborn found that retardates and matched-MA normals clustered equally well. Evans (1964) has also found that high IQ adult retardates slightly exceed low IQ retardates on free recall but these differences did not attain statistical significance. However, the IQ differences between the two groups of Ss were not large (see above), and a greater IQ difference may have provided a more adequate test of the hypothesis of increasing clustering deficits as a function of IQ.

Stedman (1963) compared normals and retardates in associative clustering on a list of items that could be grouped along semantic categories (e.g., synonyms and supraordinates). Recall and associative clustering were positively related to diagnosis when the Ss were matched on CA. Gerjuoy and Spitz (1966), also following Rossi's procedure, found that normal and retarded children, matched on MA, clustered equally well but that the retardates were much inferior to matched CA normals and college students. Again, clustering increased over trials. Gerjuoy and Spitz also found greatly increased amounts of clustering when the stimulus materials were categorized according to the associative clusters during training trials or when Ss were instructed to recall the stimulus items by categories during practice.

There has been no published research which has studied clustering in retardates using unrelated words as stimulus materials. As indicated above, Laurence (1966) found evidence suggesting that normal children show very little tendency to organize such materials. Whether retardates of comparable mental age do so with comparable materials remains indeterminate. However, Gerjuoy and Spitz (1966) noted that the individuals protocols of the retardates revealed many idiosyncratic, but consistent, associations. Such an observation is important for two reasons:

(1) it suggests a possible reason for the inferiority of retardates to matched-CA normals; that is, attempts to organize verbal materials in a subjective manner rather than on the basis of the well-learned categories implicit in the list itself may lead to interference in the retrieval or output phase of recall. Also, subjective organization may well be a less efficient manner of storing the materials.

(2) It points to the need for further research along the lines of that presented by Laurence (1966) using Tulving's SO measure.

The available data reveal that retardates and matched-MA normals cluster in much the same manner and in equal degrees. As with other types of learning research, however, most of the retarded Ss have been relatively old and only Rossi (1963) has varied MA for both retardates and normals. Further developmental research along these lines will certainly prove invaluable.

A final comment should be mentioned regarding the processes being studied when free recall performance is assessed. The studies using stimulus lists which are categorized on the basis of conceptual or asso-ciative categories basically reflect the Ss' ability to store and retrieve materials which are already clustered because of grammatical and linguistic experience. Differences between normals and retardates and within groups differing on MA (or CA and IQ) may reflect differences in the strength of such language habits *or* differential capacities to store and/or retrieve the *specific* stimulus materials. On the other hand, the studies using stimulus lists involving unrelated words may well tap differences in the Ss' ability to organize such materials rather than the capacity to utilize already well-learned organizational clusters. In any event, further research with both types of lists should provide much needed insight into the memory processes of retardates.

XI. SUMMARY

Perhaps the most clear problem for future research evolving from the preceding review is that of delineating the similarities and differences between retardate development and the development of the normal child. For example, to demonstrate that learning rate varies with MA in retardates is not, strictly speaking, a research problem oriented to understanding the behavior of retardates qua retardates as much as it is a problem related to the understanding of development or developmental processes. Similarly, to demonstrate that the learning rate of retardates is a constant proportion of that of MA-matched or CA-matched normal Ss at each point in the age continuum is not so much of theoretical interest as it is to demonstrate that the proportion *changes* as a function of age.

Empirical examples of this problem in the verbal learning literature are easy to find. As an example, the results indicating that high intralist conceptual similarity hinders the PA learning of normal adults but not that of matched-CA retardates (Wallace & Underwood, 1964) may indicate that retardates are not subject to associative interference resulting from this variable or that their language habits are not strong enough to result in associative interference. It is obvious that the latter explanation leads to an interpretation in terms of development qua development, whereas the former would indicate a retardate-specific deficit.

A general, inclusive statement summarizing the entire span of verbal learning research with retardates is impossible. However, it may be stated with some certainty that retardates and matched-MA normals learn verbal tasks at comparable rates. The lone exception to this conclusion may be normal—retardate contrasts involving serial learning. It should be mentioned, however, that data are not available relative to normal—retardate comparisons at various points along the age continuum, and the above conclusion does not preclude possible age-task interactions. Furthermore, the validity of this conclusion breaks down somewhat for institutionalized retardates. That is, the fact of being institutionalized seems to compound any learning deficit. There are suggestive data indicating that the associative processes of retardates are limited but, again, evidence is lacking as to whether the deficit is attributable to subject or environmental variables.

An attempt has been made to identify problems for future research, both those that identify themselves from a critical analysis of the verbal learning research with retardates and those that may be derived from data and theory heretofore concerned only with the verbal processes of normal children and adults. Close attention to the latter will prove to be of considerable interest both on methodological and theoretical grounds.

REFERENCES

Akutagawa, D., & Benoit, E. P. The effect of age and relative brightness on associative learning in children. *Child Development*, 1959, **30**, 229-238.

Anderson, N. H. Comparisons of different populations: Resistance to extinction and transfer. *Psychological Review*, 1963, **70**, 162-174.

Barnes, J. M. & Underwood, B. J. "Fate" of first-list associations in transfer theory. *Journal of Experimental Psychology*, 1959, **58**, 97-105.

Barnett, C. D., Ellis, N. R., & Pryer, M. W. Serial position effects in superior and retarded subjects. *Psychological Reports*, 1960, **7**, 111-113.

Baumeister, A. A. Problems in comparative studies of mental retardates and normals. *American Journal of Mental Deficiency*, 1967, **71**, 869-875.

Baumeister, A. A., & Guffin, J. Effects of conceptual similarity on serial learning and retention by retardates. *Journal of Educational Psychology*, 1967, **57**, 308-310.

Baumeister, A. A., Hawkins, W. F., & Davis, P. A. Stimulus-response durations in paired-associates learning of normals and retardates. *American Journal of Mental Deficiency*, 1966, **70**, 580-584.

Belmont, J. M. Long-term memory in mental retardation. In N. R. Ellis (Ed.), *International review of research in mental retardation*, Vol. 1. New York: Academic Press, 1966. Pp. 219-255.

Berkson, G., & Cantor, G. N. A study of mediation in mentally retarded and normal school children. *Journal of Educational Psychology*, 1960, **51**, 82-86.

Berkson, G., & Cantor, G. N. A note on method in comparisons of learning in normals and the mentally retarded. *American Journal of Mental Deficiency*, 1962, **67**, 475-477.

Blount, W. R., & Heal, L. W. Subject strategies and the effect of MA on learning rate and acquisition patterns of serial verbal material. *Psychonomic Science*, 1966, **6**, 185-186.

Bousfield, W. A. The occurrence of clustering in the recall of randomly arranged associates. *Journal of General Psychology*, 1953, **49**, 229-240.

Bousfield, W. A., & Cohen, B. H. The occurrence of clustering in the recall of randomly arranged words of different frequencies of usage. *Journal of General Psychology*, 1955, **52** 83-95.

Bousfield, W. A., Esterson, S., & Whitmarsh, G. A. A study of developmental changes in conceptual and perceptual associative clustering. *Journal of Genetic Psychology*, 1958, **92**, 95-102.

Bugelski, B. R. Presentation time, total time, and mediation in paired-associate learning. *Journal of Experimental Psychology*, 1962, **63**, 409-412.

Cantor, G. N., & Ryan, T. J. Retention of verbal paired-associates in normals and retardates. *American Journal of Mental Deficiency*, 1962, **66**, 861-865.

Carroll, W. R., & Penney, R. K. Percentage of occurrence of response members, associative strength, and competition in paired-associate learning in children. *Journal of Experimental Child Psychology*, 1966, **3**, 258-267.

Cassel, R. Serial verbal learning and retroactive inhibition in aments and children. *Journal of Clinical Psychology*, 1957, **13**, 369-372.

Cofer, C. N. On some factors in the organizational characteristics of free recall. *American Psychologist*, 1965, **20**, 261-272.

Davidson, R. E. Mediation and ability in paired-associate learning. *Journal of Educational Psychology*, 1964, **55**, 352-356.

Davis, J. K. Mediated generalization and interference across five grade levels. *Psychonomic Science*, 1966, **6**, 273-274.

Deese, J. Influence of inter-item associative strength upon immediate free recall. *Psychological Reports*, 1959, **5**, 305-312.

Deese, J. From the isolated verbal unit to connected discourse. In C. N. Cofer (Ed.), *Verbal learning and verbal behavior*. New York: McGraw-Hill, 1961. Pp. 11-30.

Deese, J. On the structure of associative meaning. *Psychological Review*, 1962, **69**, 161-175.

Denny, M. R. Research in learning performance. In H. Stevens and R. Heber (Eds.), *Mental retardation*. Chicago: University of Chicago Press, 1964.

Dent, H. E., & Johnson, R. C. The effects of massed vs. distributed practice on the learning of organic and familial defectives. *American Journal of Mental Deficiency*, 1964, **68**, 476-484.

Eisman, B. S. Paired-associate learning, generalization and retention as a function of intelligence. *American Journal of Mental Deficiency*, 1958, **63**, 481-489.

Ekstrand, B. R. Backward associations. *Psychological Bulletin*, 1966, **65**, 50-64. (a)

Ekstrand, B. R. A note on measuring response learning during paired-associate learning. *Journal of Verbal Learning and Verbal Behavior*, 1966, **5**, 344-347. (b)

Ellis, N. R., Pryer, M. W., Distefano, M. K., Jr., & Pryer, R. S. Learning in mentally defective normal and superior subjects. *American Journal of Mental Deficiency*, 1959, **64**, 725-734.

Evans, R. A. Word recall and associative clustering in mental retardates. *American Journal of Mental Deficiency*, 1964, **69**, 413-418.

Feldman, S. M., & Underwood, B. J. Stimulus recall following paired-associate learning. *Journal of Experimental Psychology*, 1957, **53**, 11-15.

Flavell, J. H. *The developmental psychology of Jean Piaget*. Princeton, N. J.: Van Nostrand,

Gerjuoy, I. R., & Spitz, H. H. Associative clustering in free recall: Intellectual and developmental variables. *American Journal of Mental Deficiency*, 1966, **70**, 918-927.

Girardeau, F. L., & Ellis, N. R. Rote verbal learning by normal and mentally retarded children. *American Journal of Mental Deficiency*, 1964, **68**, 525-532.

Gladis, M. Grade differences in transfer as a function of the time interval between learning tasks. *Journal of Educational Psychology*, 1960, **51**, 191-194.

Goulet, L. R. Verbal learning in children: Implications for developmental research. *Psychological Bulletin*, 1968, in press.

Hamilton, C. E. The relationship between length of interval separating two learning tasks and performance on the second task. *Journal of Experimental Psychology*, 1950, **40**, 613-621.

Harlow, H. F. The formation of learning sets. *Psychological Review*, 1949, **56**, 51-65.

Harlow, H. F. Learning set and error factor theory. In S. Koch (Ed.), *Psychology—a study of science*, Vol. 2. New York: McGraw-Hill, 1959. Pp. 492-537.

Heal, L. W., Ross, L. E., & Sanders, B. Reversal and partial reversal in mental defectives of a comparable mental age. *American Journal of Mental Deficiency*, 1966, **71**, 411-416.

Heckman, B. Varied exposure durations in paired-associate learning in normal and retarded children. *American Journal of Mental Deficiency*, 1966, **70**, 709-713.

Hess, J. L., & Simon, S. Extra-list intrusions in immediate recall as a function of associative strength in children. *Psychological Reports*, 1964, **14**, 92.

Horowitz, L. W. Associative matching and intralist similarities. *Psychological Reports*, 1962, **10**, 751-575.

Horton, D. L., & Kjeldergaard, P. M. An experimental analysis of associative factors in mediated generalization. *Psychological Monographs*, 1961, **75**, 11 (Whole No. 515).

House, B. J., Smith, M., & Zeaman, D. Verbal learning and retention as a function of number of lists in retardates. *American Journal of Mental Deficiency*, 1964, **69**, 239-243.

Hunt, R. G. Meaningfulness and articulation of stimulus and response in paired-associate learning and stimulus recall. *Journal of Experimental Psychology*, 1959, **57**, 262-267.

Iscoe, I., & Semler, I. J. Paired-associate learning in normal and mentally retarded children as a function of four experimental conditions. *Journal of Comparative and Physiological Psychology*, 1964, **57**, 387-392.

Jenkins, J. J., & Russell, W. A. Associative clustering during recall. *Journal of Abnormal and Social Psychology*, 1952, **47**, 818-821.

Jensen, A. R. Rote learning in retarded adults and normal children. *American Journal of Mental Deficiency*, 1965, **69**, 828-834.

Jensen, A. R., & Rohwer, W. D., Jr. The effect of verbal mediation on the learning and retention of paired-associates by retarded adults. *American Journal of Mental Deficiency,* 1963, **68,** 80-84. (a)

Jensen, A. R., & Rohwer, W. D., Jr. Verbal mediation in paired-associate and serial learning. *Journal of Verbal Learning and Verbal Behavior,* 1963, **1,** 346-352. (b)

Jensen, A. R., & Rohwer, W. J., Jr. Syntactical mediation of serial and paired-associate learning as a function of age. *Child Development,* 1965, **36,** 601-608.

Jung, J. Two stages of paired-associate learning as a function of intralist response similarity (IRS) and response meaningfulness (M). *Journal of Experimental Psychology,* 1965, **70,** 371-378.

Kaufman, M. E. The formation of a learning set in institutionalized and noninstitutionalized mental defectives. *American Journal of Mental Deficiency,* 1963, **67,** 601-605.

Kaufman, M. E., & Prehm, H. J. A review of research on learning sets and transfer of training in mental defectives. In N. R. Ellis (Ed.), *International review of research in mental retardation,* New York: Academic Press, Vol. 2, 1968, in press.

Kausler, D. H. *Readings in verbal learning: Contemporary theory and research.* New York: Wiley, 1966.

Kendler, H. H., & Kendler, T. S. Vertical and horizontal processes in human concept formation. *Psychological Review,* 1962, **69,** 1-18.

Kendler, T. S. Verbalization and optional reversal shifts among kindergarten children. *Journal of Verbal Learning and Verbal Behavior,* 1964, **3,** 428-435.

Keppel, G. Verbal learning in children. *Psychological Bulletin,* 1964, **61,** 63-80.

Keppel, G. Verbal learning and memory. *Annual Review of Psychology,* 1968, **19,** in press.

Koppenaal, R. J., Krull, A., & Katz, H. Age, interference, and forgetting. *Journal of Experimental Child Psychology,* 1964, **1,** 360-375.

Kuenne, N. R. Experimental investigation of the relation of language to transposition behavior in young children. *Journal of Experimental Psychology,* 1946, **36,** 471-490.

Lance, W. Effects of meaningfulness and overlearning on retention in normal and retarded adolescents. *American Journal of Mental Deficiency,* 1965, **70,** 270-275.

Laurence, M. W. Age differences in performance and subjective organization in the free-recall learning of pictorial material. *Canadian Journal of Psychology,* 1966, **20,** 388-399.

Laurence, M. W. A developmental look at the usefulness of list categories as an aid to free recall. *Canadian Journal of Psychology,* 1967, **21,** 153-165.

Lipman, R. S. Learning: Verbal, perceptual-motor, and classical conditioning. In N. R. Ellis (Ed.), *Handbook of mental deficiency.* New York: McGraw-Hill, 1963. Pp. 391-423.

Luria, A. R. *The role of speech in the regulation of normal and abnormal behavior.* Bethesda, Md.: U.S. Dept. of Health, Education, and Welfare, 1960.

McCrary, J. W., & Hunter, W. S. Serial position curves in verbal learning. *Science,* 1953, **117,** 131-134.

McManis, D. L. Position cues in serial learning by retardates. *American Journal of Mental Deficiency,* 1965, **70,** 471-473. (a)

McManis, D. L. Relative errors with serial lists of different lengths. *American Journal of Mental Deficiency,* 1965, **70,** 125-129. (b)

McManis, D. L. The von Restorff effect in serial learning by normal and retarded subjects. *American Journal of Mental Deficiency,* 1966, **70,** 569-575.

Madsen, M. C. Distribution of practice and level of intelligence. *Psychological Reports* 1963, **13,** 39-42.

Martin, E. Transfer of verbal paired-associates. *Psychological Review,* 1965, **72,** 327-343.

Mednick, S. A., & Lehtinen, L. E. Stimulus generalization as a function of age in children. *Journal of Experimental Psychology,* 1957, **53,** 180-183.

Melton, A. W. Comments on Professor Postman's paper. In C. N. Cofer (Ed.), *Verbal learning and verbal behavior*. New York: McGraw-Hill, 1961. Pp. 179-191.

Miller, G. A. The magical number seven plus or minus two: Some limits on our capacity for processing information. *Psychological Review*, 1956, **63**, 81-97.

Osborn, W. J. Associative clustering in organic and familiar retardates. *American Journal of Mental Deficiency*, 1960, **65**, 351-357.

Paivio, A. Learning of adjective-noun paired-associates as a function of adjective-noun word order and noun abstractness. *Canadian Journal of Psychology*, 1963, **17**, 370-379.

Paivio, A., & Yuille, J. C. Word abstractness and meaningfulness, and paired-associate learning in children. *Journal of Experimental Child Psychology*, 1966, **4**, 81-89.

Paivio, A., Yuille, J., & Smythe, P. Stimulus and response abstractness, imagery, and meaningfulness, and reported mediators in paired-associate learning. *Canadian Journal of Psychology*, 1966, **20**, 362-377.

Palermo, D. S. Backward associations in the paired-associate learning of fourth and sixth grade children. *Psychological Reports*, 1961, **9**, 227-233.

Palermo, D. S., Flamer, G. B., & Jenkins, J. J. Association value of responses in the paired-associate learning of children and adults. *Journal of Verbal Learning and Verbal Behavior*, 1964, **3**, 171-175.

Palermo, D. S., & Jenkins, J. J. Paired-associate learning as a function of the strength of links in the associative chain. *Journal of Verbal Learning and Verbal Behavior*, 1964, **3**, 406-412. (a)

Postman, L. The present status of interference theory. In C. N. Cofer (Ed.), *Verbal learning and verbal behavior*. New York: McGraw-Hill, 1961. Pp. 152-178.

Postman, L. Transfer of training as a function of experimental paradigm and degree of first list learning. *Journal of Verbal Learning and Verbal Behavior*, 1962, **1**, 109-118.

Prehm, H. J. Associative learning in retarded and normal children as a function of task difficulty and meaningfulness. *American Journal of Mental Deficiency*, 1966, **70**, 860-865. (a)

Prehm, H. J. Verbal learning research in mental retardation. *American Journal of Mental Deficiency*, 1966, **71**, 42-47. (b)

Price, L. E. Learning and performance in a verbal paired-associate task with preschool children. *Psychological Reports*, 1963, **12**, 847-850.

Pryer, R. S. Retroactive inhibition in normals and defectives as a function of temporal position of the interpolated task. *American Journal of Mental Deficiency*, 1960, **64**, 1004-1011.

Rieber, M. Verbal mediation in normal and retarded children. *American Journal of Mental Deficiency*, 1964, **68**, 634-641.

Ring, E. M. The effect of anticipation interval on paired-associate learning in normal and retarded children. *American Journal of Mental Deficiency*, 1965, **70**, 466-470.

Ring, E. M., & Palermo, D. S. Paired-associate learning of normal and retarded children. *American Journal of Mental Deficiency*, 1961, **66**, 100-107.

Rossi, E. L. Associative clustering in normal and retarded children. *American Journal of Mental Deficiency*, 1963, **67**, 691-699.

Saltz, E. Response pre-training: Differentiation or availability? *Journal of Experimental Psychology*, 1961, **62**, 583-587.

Semler, I. J., & Iscoe, I. Concept interference and paired associates in retarded children. *Journal of Comparative and Physiological Psychology*, 1965, **60**, 465-466.

Simon, S., & Hess, J. L. Supplementary report: Influence of inter-item associative strength upon immediate free recall in children. *Psychology Reports*, 1965, **16**, 451-455.

Spiker, C. C. Research methods in children's learning. In P. H. Mussen (Ed.) *Handbook of research methods in child development*. New York: Wiley, 1960. Pp. 374-420.

Spiker, C. C. & White, S. H. Differential conditioning by children as a function of effort required in the task. *Child Development*, 1959, **30**, 1-7.

Stedman, D. J. Associative clustering of semantic categories in normal and retarded subjects. *American Journal of Mental Deficiency*, 1963, **67**, 700-704.

Stevenson, H. W. Discrimination learning. In N. R. Ellis (Ed.), *Handbook of mental deficiency*. New York: McGraw-Hill, 1963. Pp. 424-438.

Stevenson, H. W., & McBee, G. The learning of object and pattern discriminations by children. *Journal of Comparative and Physiological Psychology*, 1958, **51**, 752-754.

Tulving, E. Subjective organization in free recall of unrelated words. *Psychological Review*, 1962, **69**, 344-354.

Tulving, E. Intratrial and intertrial retention: Notes toward a theory of free recall verbal learning. *Psychological Review*, 1964, **71**, 219-237.

Twedt, H. M., & Underwood, R. J. Mixed vs. unmixed lists in transfer studies. *Journal of Experimental Psychology*, 1959, **58**, 111-116.

Underwood, B. J. Speed of learning and amount retained: A consideration of methodology. *Psychological Bulletin*, 1954, **51**, 276-282.

Underwood, B. J. Ten years of massed practice on distributed practice. *Psychological Review*, 1961, **68**, 229-247.

Underwood, B. J. Stimulus selection in verbal learning. In C. N. Cofer & B. S. Musgrave (Eds.), *Verbal behavior and learning*. New York: McGraw-Hill, 1963. Pp. 33-47.

Underwood, B. J. Degree of learning and the measurement of forgetting. *Journal of Verbal Learning and Verbal Behavior*, 1964, **3**, 112-129.

Underwood, B. J. & Postman, L. Extra-experimental sources of interference and forgetting. *Psychological Review*, 1960, **67**, 73-95.

Underwood, B. J., Runquist, W. N., & Schulz, R. W. Response learning in paired-associate lists as a function of intralist similarity. *Journal of Experimental Psychology*, 1959, **58**, 70-78.

Underwood, B. J., & Schulz, R. W. *Meaningfulness and verbal learning*. Philadelphia: Lippincott, 1960.

Vergason, G. A. Retention in retarded and normal subjects as a function of amount of original training. *American Journal of Mental Deficiency*, 1964, **68**, 623-629.

Wallace, W. P., & Underwood, B. J. Implicit responses and the role of intralist similarity in verbal learning by normal and retarded subjects. *Journal of Educational Psychology*, 1964, **55**, 362-370.

Weatherwax, J., & Benoit, E. P. Concrete and abstract thinking in organic and non-organic mentally retarded children. *American Journal of Mental Deficiency*, 1957, **62**, 548-553.

White, S. H. Evidence for a hierarchical arrangement of learning processes. In C. C. Spiker and L. P. Lipsitt, (Eds.), *Advances in child development and behavior*. Vol 2. New York: Academic Press, 1964. Pp. 167-220.

White, S. H., & Spiker, C. C. The effect of a variable conditioned stimulus upon the generalization of an instrumental response. *Child Development*, 1960, **31**, 313-320.

Wicklund, D. A., Palermo, D. S. & Jenkins, J. J. Associative clustering in the recall of children as a function of verbal association strength. *Journal of Experimental Child Psychology*, 1965, **2**, 58-66.

Wismer, B., & Lipsitt, L. P. Verbal mediation in paired-associate learning. *Journal of Experimental Psychology*, 1964, **68**, 441-448.

Yarmey, A. D., & Paivio, A. Further evidence on the effects of word abstractness and meaningfulness in paired-associate learning. *Psychonomic Science*, 1965, **2**, 307-308.

Research and Theory in Short-Term Memory

KEITH G. SCOTT and MARCIA STRONG SCOTT[1]

University of Illinois, Champaign, Illinois

I. INTRODUCTION

A distinction between short-term memory (STM) and long-term memory (LTM) has frequently been assumed in research seeking to define a memory deficit in the retarded (Ellis, 1963). The very distinc-

[1] The preparation of this article was supported by Grant MH 07346 from the National Institute of Mental Health and Grand HD 02898-01 from the National Institute of Child Health and Human Development both of NIH, U.S. Public Health Service.

135

tion, defined arbitrarily as the difference between memory over a matter of seconds compared to that over a matter of hours, has been disputed in general theory of memory (Broadbent, 1958; Melton, 1963; Scott, Whimbey, & Dunning, 1967a, 1967b). Nevertheless, an interest in the difference between STM and LTM in the retarded dates back to Galton's interesting and amusing *Notes on "Prehension" in Idiots* (1887). Contained in that note is a discussion of the apparent strong LTM of retarded persons and evidence of their poor STM. Such observations form the basis for continuing interest in STM as an area that may provide an understanding, at least in part, of behavioral inadequacy in the retarded.

This article aims to provide an overview of recent work on STM in the retarded. The selection of material then is aimed at surveying the major trends, issues, and theories in an attempt to highlight what the authors see as important. Since the major impetus to research in the area seems to have grown out of data collected in the use of psychometric tests it is that area which is first discussed.

II. EVIDENCE FROM PSYCHOMETRICS

A. Digit Span as a Measure of Intelligence

Definitions of retardation typically center around the notion of a low IQ. If a poor STM is a major cause of behavioral inadequacy it might be expected that tests of digit span would correlate highly with total test score. This has been disputed by Wechsler (1949) who thought it among the poorest tests of general intelligence. There has been some tendency to devalue digit span as a test of intelligence as a result. Jensen (1964) made the important point that the test has a lower reliability than most Wechsler Adult Intelligence Scale (WAIS) subtests and when intercorrelations are inspected after correcting for attenuation it compares favorably with other subtests. Further, it shows substantial loadings on the general factor reported in Wechsler's (1958) factor analysis of the WAIS scales. The implication is that STM may be more closely related to intelligence than has been generally recognized. The ability to hold information in STM may be a critical skill in many, if not most, learning and problem-solving situations. In a simple discrimination, memory for what happened on the last trial plus what was reinforced seems clearly required for learning. In a more complex problem, to detect a dimension, strategy, or rule, memory for a sequence of trials is frequently required. The empirical fact that memory span is limited suggests that an individual with a brief span may lose much incoming information before he can process it into LTM; that is, a poor STM may provide a limited buffer storage system and thus reduce the probability that a given piece of information is permanently stored. Jensen (1964) has advanced a similar argument to account for the correlation between college students STM and their vocabulary ability. The general point is that STM is quite pervasive in intellectual functioning and clearly warrants careful study for those concerned with individual differences. Other evidence is provided by factor analytic techniques.

B. Factorial Studies—the Trace Factor

A series of studies of the Wechsler Intelligence Scale for Children (WISC) and the WAIS has attempted to show that a trace factor is present in the retarded but not in a normal population (Baumeister & Bartlett, 1962a, 1962b; Sprague & Quay, 1966). Other factor analyses, in a number of studies (e.g., Cohen, 1957; Gault, 1954; Hammer, 1950) would not lead to this conclusion. Depending on the method of factor extraction used, what loading is accepted as significant, and the age of the subjects, a memory factor accounting for up to 6% to 9% of the variance is found with both normal and retarded populations. It therefore appears that the same evidence exists for a trace factor in the general population as for the retarded. Dingman and Meyers (1966) pointed out that if a trace factor were unique to the retarded it would imply that the variability in this population was greater than in the normal population. Such a factor would *not* necessarily reveal a generally lower level of performance by retardates than normals. It follows that obtaining a trace factor in the normal population does not constitute negative evidence for a memory deficit in the retarded. Rather it suggests that the variability is continuous in the general population, a conclusion that is also consistent with Jensen's (1964) findings with a college population. The implication for retardation is that if this trace factor is general in the population, research should pay careful attention to general theories of memory. The laws considered are unlikely to be unique to the retarded subjects. Much useful information is likely to be gained with this general approach.

C. Patterning of Subtest Scores on Psychometric Measures

Since tests such as the WAIS and WISC were standardized on a normal population, a deficit in STM, as compared to general intellectual functioning, might be revealed by particularly low mean scores for retardates on digit span as compared to other subtests. Unfortunately, the WISC patterning reported has not always included digit span and reported patterns do not always cross validate (Baroff, 1959; Fisher, 1960).

Baroff found, with endogenous moderately retarded children, that digit span was a subtest of intermediate difficulty. Digit span was also found to be of intermediate difficulty by MacPhee, Wright and Cummings (1947) with adult, Negro retarded males in an analysis of the Wechsler-Bellevue verbal scale. Wechsler, Israel, and Balinsky (1941) reported for borderline retardates (IQ 66 – 79) that digit span was of intermediate difficulty although it appears relatively less difficult for a lower group (IQ 50 – 65). Similarly, Sandercock and Butler (1952) found digit span among the easier subtests on the WISC for retardates (IQ 45 – 86). Since in the literature difficulty is not always indexed in the same way, and in some reports tests are missing, a definite tabulation could not be arrived at by the present writers. However, it is clear from examination of those studies cited, and a considerable number of others with both normals and retardates, that digit span is not a particularly difficult subtest for the retarded on the Wechsler Scales.

On both the Illinois Test of Psycholinguistic Abilities (ITPA) (Kirk & McCarthy, 1961) and the Stanford-Binet, there is some evidence that tests involving STM are difficult compared to other items. Bateman and Wetherell (1965) presented averaged and typical profiles for the retarded that suggest a definite patterning on the ITPA showing a memory deficit. Their observations, however, are not supported by inferential statistics. On the Stanford-Binet a number of items requiring memory (e.g., digits forward, and memory for sentences) have been reported as among the more difficult for the retarded (Laycock & Clark, 1942; Margaret & Thompson, 1950; Sloan & Cutts, 1947; Thompson & Margaret, 1947).

In summary, the pattern of subtest difficulty depends on the particular test and probably results from the pool from which the items were drawn and the standardization. Unequivocal evidence for a memory deficit seems unlikely to be obtained with the instruments presently available.

D. Experimental Validation of the Trace Factor

The finding that STM items load on a trace factor has led to two attempts to use test scores to predict performance in the laboratory. Baumeister, Bartlett, and Hawkins (1963) derived trace scores for both normals and retarded subjects from the arithmetic, similarities, block design and coding subtests. The subtests were combined in proportion to their contribution to a trace factor in an earlier factor analysis (Baumeister & Bartlett, 1962a). These scores were intercorrelated with digit span scores and the number of trials to criterion on a double alternation task. Digit span was found to correlate significantly with the trace factor in both normal and retarded groups. Trials to criterion on the double alternation task however correlated with trace scores only for the retarded. Hawkins (1966) used the same method to calculate trace scores and examined their intercorrelations with digit span and performance on a visual recognition task for Chinese characters. When IQ was held constant the trace scores and performance scores correlated .41 for a brain-damaged group and .34 for a familial group. Only the former correlation was statistically reliable. The data add validity to the trace factor construct. Surprisingly, Hawkins did not obtain a significant correlation between trace score and digit span for either group.

E. Comment on Psychometric Evidence

The evidence clearly points to STM as an important parameter of variation in the performance of the retarded person. The fact that this is not uniquely true of this population certainly does not mitigate the need for further work. Psychometrics has provided a hypothesis and stimulation. From the laboratory we now need experimental evidence about process and theory involved in STM. From this information process defined rather than task-defined tests can be constructed and efficient techniques of training devised. This scientific process is likely to be facilitated by experimental studies of STM.

III. THEORETICAL INTERPRETATIONS

A. The Limited Channel Capacity Model of Broadbent

Based on research on listening, Broadbent proposed an influential model of memory and attention (1958). The tentative flow diagram he presented is shown in Fig. 1. The model supposes that the senses are bombarded with information of which only a limited amount can be processed. Some of this information may be held for a period of seconds in a short-term store called the S System. From this store a selective filter passes information, controlled by past experience, into the limited capacity channel or P System. It can pass through this channel into long-term storage, or it can be passed in a feedback loop into the short-term store much as in rehearsing an item to retain it. It can be seen that any deficiency in either the S or P System would have, as one manifestation, a general learning deficiency. For the present article the question arises of the relation among the capacity and efficiency of the S and P Systems, ability, and development.

The theory then might predict that retardates or young children have poor short-term memories and thus an impaired S System. Alter-

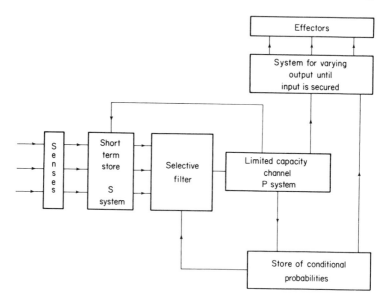

Fɪɢ. 1. The tentative information flow diagram for the organism presented by Broadbent to account for a variety of data including STM and multichannel listening (after Broadbent, 1958, p. 299).

natively, or in addition, the capacity of the P System might be restricted so that such subjects are able to attend to less information at once. It should be noted that the model has certain parallels of prediction both with Ellis's stimulus trace theory presented below and the attention theory of Zeaman and House (1963).

B. The Stimulus Trace Theory of Ellis

Within a long tradition of trace constructs from Müller and Pilzecher (1900) through Pavlov (1927), Kohler (1929), Hull (1952), and Mowrer (1960) among others (see Glickman, 1961), Ellis presented a theory which hypothesizes that the strength and duration of the stimulus trace is diminished in the subnormal individual. Further, it is speculated that the establishment of the adult form of the short-term memory function will show a developmental trend and that young children will show a stimulus trace deficit (Ellis, 1963, p. 140); that is, the stimulus trace will increase in both strength and duration as a function of age and intelligence.

Stated more formally the constructs of stimulus trace (s_t) and central nervous system integrity (n_i) are postulated. The former is defined by the observable stimulus (S) as the antecedent and by the subject's behavior (B) as the consequent. The stimulus trace model is presented in Fig. 2.

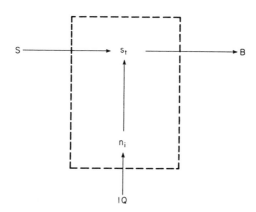

FIG. 2.   The stimulus trace model of N. R. Ellis. The symbols are explained in the text (after Ellis, 1963, p. 138).

The theory predicts a difference in retention both as a function of MA and IQ. In particular the prediction of interest has been that the slope of the forgetting curve will be greater for a group of low IQ subjects than for a group of high IQ subjects of equal CA. Equal MA subjects should perform similarly.[2] In terms of an analysis of variance design an interaction is predicted between intelligence and the retention interval. The most adequate design would be a MA by IQ by retention interval factorial. However, Ellis's prediction predated the first use of an MA by IQ factorial design (Harter, 1965) in retardation and such a design has yet to be employed in the study of memory.

By pointing to the probable role of memory in a number of tasks, Ellis predicted decrements in retardates' performances compared to that of normals on a wide range of tasks that include delayed response, reaction time, paired-associate learning as well as simple retention.

C.   Interference Theory

One of the most prominent theories of forgetting in general psychol-

---

[2] It should be noted that the stimulus trace theory was presented originally with data from adult and near adult Ss.

ogy is associated with interference theory (Postman, 1963; Underwood, 1957). The essence of this theory is that one or more stimuli may be associated with one or more responses and that in recall multiple associations with a given stimulus result in response competition, errors in recall, and forgetting. Thus, if a subject has an A-B association, and then learns an A-C association, at the time of recall B and C will compete. Which of these, B or C, will be dominant at the time of recall will depend on a number of factors. First, while the association A-C is being learned the association A-B is being extinguished at least in part; that is, the old habit gets weaker. Second, in the interval between learning A-C and the recall, the old association A-B will undergo some spontaneous recovery resulting in a gradual shift in favor of the old item as time passes or the length of the item list increases. Finally, at the time of recall, the strongest habit or association will be dominant.

Classically, two major paradigms should be identified. In the retroactive inhibition paradigm the sequence is learn List A, learn List B, recall List A. In this case the interference at the time of recall is from learning List B retroactive to learning List A. List B will interfere if the lists share common associations. The second major paradigm is that of proactive inhibition. In this paradigm the sequence is learn List A, learn List B, recall List B. Now the interference at the time of recall is from the previously learned, or proactive, List A. List A will interfere with List B if they share common associations.

For many years retroactive, rather than proactive, inhibition was thought to be the major cause of forgetting. In a key paper Underwood (1957), was able to show that in learning successive lists there was a systematic decline in performance and that proactive inhibition was of major importance. This finding has also been demonstrated by House, Smith, and Zeaman (1964) with the retarded.

Interference theory predicts that forgetting will vary as a function of the similarity of competing material and as a function of the number of successive lists or items. In a single session it predicts that items early in the series will be recalled better than items later in the series. Developmentally it might be expected that children would become more resistant to interference as a function of age. Also, children of higher intelligence might be expected to be less susceptible to interference than those of lower ability.

D. The Neural Theory of Spitz

In the tradition of Gestalt field theory, Spitz proposes that retardates, exogenous or endogenous, are characterized by a deficit in their neural functioning. Specifically, his position is that there is a slowed reaction of the electrochemical processes in the neural cells of the central nervous system (CNS), made manifest by weaker aftereffects and fewer reversals of the Necker cube (Spitz, 1963). These small aftereffects are seen as an indication that something is wrong with the underlying brain processes or structures. While the aftereffects are interpreted as implying inadequate "satiation," the theory does not include this as the only possible form of neural malfunction and is not critically tied to the Kohler-Wallach theory of satiation (Kohler & Wallach, 1944). It is therefore not a satiation theory of retardation (Zigler, 1967).

The theory has been presented in a series of four postulates:

"Postulate I.   In retardates, it takes longer to induce temporary, as well as permanent, electrical, chemical, and physical changes in stimulated cortical cells.

"Postulate II.   Once stimuli induce temporary chemical and electrical modification of cortical cells, it takes longer for these cells to return to their previous state.

"Postulate III.   In retardates, once stimuli induce permanent chemical and/or physical changes in cortical cells, it will be more difficult and take a longer period of time to switch consequent like—or relatively similar—stimuli away from these particular cell traces or current patterns so as to form new, or different, traces or patterns.

"Postulate IV.   In retardates, there is less spread of electrochemical activity from stimulated cells into the surrounding cortical field (Spitz, 1963, pp. 29—30)."

The upshot of this is that the subjective organization of material, as in "chunking" (Miller, 1956) or "clustering" (Bousfield, 1953) is interfered with in retardates who have a "noisy" transmission system resulting from CNS disturbance (Spitz, 1966). Stated in its most simple way the theory supposes that normals subject incoming information to an organizational process and that, in the retardate, the noisy system may produce a subjective disorganization.

In the area of memory some clear predictions follow from the theory. Since retardates are less likely than normals to organize efficiently many bits of information into fewer chunks, less total information can be permanently stored or learned. Therefore, a deficiency which appears to result from impaired STM may be due largely to the fact that information never reached storage, or reached storage in a disorganized state. However, since the system is, in effect, slow to change, any information which is permanently organized and stored is relatively more resistant to extinction or interference. It follows then that retardates should have better than normal LTM, relative to the amount originally learned.

IV. METHODOLOGICAL PROBLEMS

A. Comparative vs Process Approaches

In formulating theories about memory in retardation a central problem of strategy is how such theories should be related to general theory in psychology and to developmental theory in particular. Should such theories be concerned with differences between normals and retardates? Alternatively, should theory be concerned with writing the process laws of learning or memory that will define the conditions that control retardate behavior irrespective of how it differs from normal behavior? This latter approach as exemplified by the attention theory of Zeaman and House (1963) has been critized as not being of unique relevance to the behavior of the retarded (Zigler, 1966, p. 143) or not contributing anything special about mental retardation or how or why a retarded child suffers a defect in attention (Baumeister, 1967a). Zeaman has discussed this issue (1965) pointing out the problems of showing the uniqueness of retarded behavior, and the comparative approach has been shown to be fraught with problems (Baumeister, 1967b). The process theorist would hold that by systematically developing a theory, the place of development and intelligence can be defined by certain parameters of the theory and that the uniqueness of the laws is not essential. Such a theory is likely to benefit directly from relevant methodological developments in general psychology. On the other hand, the comparative theorist would argue that the specific causes of retardation are to be discovered more rapidly by the comparative approach even granted its difficulties. Some of the theories considered herein are more deeply rooted in retardation than others, but all are presented as of major relevance for at least some research strategies.

When a comparative approach is adopted the question of relevant comparison groups arises. Should the retarded child be compared with an equal MA or an equal CA peer? Retardation has been defined in terms of IQ rather than MA, and it has therefore been argued that a low IQ deficit is of major concern. On the other hand, from a developmental or a behavioral engineering point of view, MA is clearly important. Denny (1964) has argued for the use of two control groups, an equal MA and equal CA control. Such a design has been employed in a memory study by Neufeldt (1966). With the original retarded group, these two groups make up three cells of a 2 × 2 factorial design, MA × IQ, where these are orthogonal and CA is assumed to be irrelevant for purposes of interpretation. The design suggested by Denny is this exact factorial with, in the 2 × 2 case, one cell missing. Scott (1968) has discussed the problems of design and using appropriate control groups in more detail, and Zeaman and House (1967) have considered data on the irrelevancy of CA. Since both development and intelligence are of interest in studying memory, a full factorial design would seem to be optimal but it has yet to be employed in this area.

The many difficulties of comparative research suggest to the present authors that an understanding of process must precede comparative work for inconclusive outcomes may result from confounding of unknown variables with population variables. A strong background from general theories of memory could provide a theoretical framework in which variables are more likely to be explicated. Such a basis, often lacking in research with the retarded, could avoid problems that are well understood in research on memory with other subjects that tend to be neglected in research with the retarded. The next section considers such an issue.

B. Degree of Learning and Rate of Forgetting

Consider the retention, measured after an interval of time, for two groups of subjects. Let us say they manifest different levels of recall. It might simply be concluded that one group forgot more rapidly than the other. Such a conclusion is however only true in the case where both groups had reached the same level of original learning; that is, the habits or associations were of the same strength at the end of the practice trials and before forgetting had set in. When groups of subjects of different ability are being compared, or groups trained on material of different difficulty, the resulting research confounds degree of learning and rate of forgetting (Underwood, 1954, 1964). Belmont (1966) has shown that the greater part of research on long-term memory with the retarded has produced outcomes confounded in this fashion. Studies of STM face a similar problem.

In STM the general issue has been summarized by Underwood (1964). In the case of STM studies the typical problem has been to compare normal adult groups trained on differing items such as those of high and low association value. Underwood (1964) has raised a number of points relevant to STM. Two are particularly relevant. First, degree of learning may be appropriately assessed by a test of immediate recall, that is, with as nearly zero delay between learning and recall as is possible. Second, meaningful comparisons between recall of items learned to a criterion of 100% cannot be made since, depending on the rate of learning, one may be better learned than another. For example, items that are overlearned, or practiced beyond the degree of learning necessary for perfect performance on a test of immediate recall, will be remembered better than items that are not overlearned. As a solution, Underwood suggested that performance on items prior to the introduction of a retention interval should be below 100%. While this is a useful procedure in studying many process variables it could be unfortunate if research on normal—retardate comparisons were restricted to this.

The primary datum of a normal—retardate comparison lies in the difference between the performance of a normal person and a retarded person. Studies of discrimination learning indicate that the inclusion of overlearning is a powerful parameter in obtaining normal—retardate differences (e.g., Ohlrich & Ross, 1966). Indeed the effects of overlearning on intradimensional and extradimensional shift performance are related to both MA and IQ though parametric research manipulating amount of overlearning, and these population variables have yet to be done. If differences in STM were, or were not, established for some level of immediate recall below 100% it would not be a result that would necessarily hold for either higher or lower levels of recall. Degree of learning, and indeed the rate at which individuals differ in their ability to benefit from practice, must become one of the network of parameters relating STM to the individual differences that distinguish normals from retardates. The present authors would therefore suggest that comparative research, if it is to provide systematic answers, is properly preceded by an investigation of process. The problem becomes one of studying the role of individual differences in STM. The scientific question of the nature of forgetting in the retarded has not typically been thought of in this framework. Indeed, it has only recently begun in studies of adult STM (Jensen, 1964). Holding degree of learning to below 100% will provide at best a very partial answer.

C. Indexes of Recall

Traditionally, a number of different measures of memory have been employed. These include simple recall, relearning, recognition, reproduction, and anticipation. It has long been known that the memory thresholds for an item fall at different levels depending on the procedure used (Luh, 1922; Woodworth and Schlosberg, 1955). The upshot of this is that an interaction between degree of learning, procedure used in a memory test, and population differences may obtain. This argument has been presented elsewhere (Scott, 1968) and illustrated by some data from the literature. Again, parametric process information is needed in order to evaluate the products of comparative research.

V. EXPERIMENTAL DATA

A. Digit Span

Since digit span has figured in the literature on development and memory since the earliest reported observations (Galton, 1887; Humpstone, 1917; Jacobs, 1887) and it has been a standard item on intelligence test scales, one might expect that it would have been the subject of intensive experimental analysis with the retarded. Such is not the case. There is, however, important developmental data available. Jacobs found a steady increase in digit span with age, and Humpstone reported a correlation of .50 between age and digit span. Gates and Taylor (1925) compared a control group and an experimental group who had practice spread over 78 days. While the mean span of the experimental group did increase as a function of practice, $4\frac{1}{2}$ months later the groups were approximately equal. This and other material has been reviewed by McGeoch (1928), Blankenship (1938), and Munn (1954). These results suggest that STM goes through systematic developmental changes improving until adolescence (see Blankenship, 1938), much as is the case for general intelligence. There is also evidence for a decline in the aged (Inglis & Ankus, 1965; McGhie, Chapman, & Lawson, 1965). The ability also does not seem susceptible to practice in the sense of improving an underlying ability.

Hermelin and O'Connor (1964) compared the digit span of normal and retarded children approximately matched for MA. The recall intervals were 2, 6, and 12 seconds with three conditions of interpolation: silent, filled with the reading of unfamiliar words by E, and filled with the reading of familiar words by E. The immediate memory was found to be better for the normals than the retarded. The normals suffered greater interference from the unfamiliar words than did the retardates for whom the authors suggest they were probably meaningless. A highly significant interaction in the silent condition between groups and delay interval was the result of a steeper forgetting function for the retardates than for the normals. This result was replicated in a second experiment that included an immediate recall condition.

Recently, Fagan (1966) used memory for digits in a retroactive paradigm to test the prediction of Ellis's theory that the forgetting function for a group of retardates would have a greater slope than that for normals. However, Fagan matched subjects on MA and the experiment does not test Ellis' theory. He employed two conditions of interpolation: time alone and naming color cards. The forgetting rates for both groups were very similar though a main effect of IQ was obtained. Although these results are interesting and contribute to knowledge in the area, the experiment does not provide a critical test of Ellis's theory.

It appears in the above experiments that the groups compared may not have achieved similar learning since there are differences in performance on the immediate test. However, this is not easily interpretable and underlines the fact that simple digit span may not be simple at all. The immediate test is not like the retention of an individual item where immediate recall may be used as a measure of learning. The presentation of the digit series means that those digits later in the series are subject to more proactive inference (PI) than those that occur earlier. During recall interference comes from two further sources. First, there is retroactive inhibition (RI) from items that were presented subsequent to the digit recalled. Second, the act of recalling a digit can produce interference with the recall of a subsequent digit. It can be seen that as the subject makes successive recalls the number of digits producing RI decreases while the number of digits producing retrieval inhibition increases. This, coupled with possible primacy and recency effects, means that the psychological processes, in this superficially the most simple of intelligence test items, are quite complex. It may be important to note that Jensen (1964) has reported separate individual difference factors associated with RI and PI in college students' STM.

In an attempt to assess the relative contribution of encoding and decoding in digit span, O'Connor and Hermelin (1965) tested normal and retarded children, matched on MA and length of digit span. Digits were presented either in simultaneous or successive displays at different rates. Under the simultaneous condition, for fast rates only, the normals remembered better than the subnormals suggesting a limited input capacity in the latter. Under the successive condition both groups produced an optimal rate of one digit per .66 second. The authors interpreted their results as showing both an input restriction and a memory decay with only the former showing normal—retardate differences.

The finding that presentation rates substantially less than one digit per half-second produce poorer recall than slightly slow rates was also found by Headrick and Ellis (1964). They presented digits with a test using the method of partial report with a post stimulus cue. They found recall after zero delay was significantly poorer than for delays as great as 45 seconds. A significant difference between normals, high level retardates, and low level retardates, matched on CA was not obtained. Headrick and Ellis ascribe the poor performance in their zero delay condition to peripheral erasure of successive stimuli on the retina that is known as the "meta contrast effect" (Alpern, 1953; Raab, 1963). This could also explain the O'Connor and Hermelin result at high presentation rates and appears to be a perceptual, rather than a memory, effect. In STM studies rates of less than one-half to one second should be avoided unless these masking effects are the subject of interest.

Further analysis of digit-type tasks would both add to our knowledge about memory and add to the information available to test constructors in writing memory test items.

B. Dichotic Listening

Dichotic listening is the experimental procedure of presenting simultaneously a digit to each ear typically using stereophonic headphones. The procedure was first developed by Broadbent (1954) and figures prominently in his theorizing (1958). The task has been the subject of considerable research resulting in a good understanding of the controlling variables (e.g., Bryden, 1964; Dodwell, 1964; Yntema & Trask, 1963).

In dichotic recall, while various strategies are possible, the subject will typically recall the digits delivered to one ear and then those to the other. These are referred to as the first half-span and the second half-span. Inglis and Ankus (1965) report no changes with age for simple digit span for normal subjects (CA $11-70$) but a significant decline in the second half-span recalled. This result is interpreted by Inglis as owing to trace decay of the second half-span being held while the first is recalled. Recently, Neufeldt (1966) has contributed an important series of experiments with normal and retarded subjects. In a series of experiments, Neufeldt tested to find out if the STM capacity and/or the strategy of remembering dichotically presented digits was sensitive to capacity differences. He employed cultural and familial retarded children with two normal control groups one matched on CA and the other matched on MA. This is the design suggested by Denny (1964) and previously discussed. Influenced by Inglis's work, he considered CA an important variable. However, since Inglis had not been concerned with ability measures this could as easily reflect the correlation of CA and MA in a normal population. A partial replication extended to complete an MA x IQ factorial would be of interest.

In his first experiment, Neufeldt established the feasibility of using the dichotic technique with the retarded. He obtained the typical result that the first half-span was better recalled than the second. In the second experiment all the above groups were employed; in addition, the subjects were matched on simple digit span. First, considering Broadbent's perceptual store or P System, as indexed by the first half-set of digits, Neufeldt found the normal CA group to have a larger capacity than both organic and familial retardates as well as the normal MA control. The latter groups performed similarly, which suggests that most of the differences between groups were accounted for by MA. Second, considering the recycling short-term store or Broadbent's S System, as indexed by the second half-span of digits, the normal CA group was indistinguishable from the retarded in a short series but as the series lengthened a marked difference appeared. The retardates showed a much more rapid decline of recall output as a function of series length suggesting that their S Ssytems were characterized by more rapid decay of the memory trace. The normal MA group also performed significantly better than the organic retardates at a series length of two suggesting some difference in their favor in decay rates as compared to the retarded. In three subsequent experiments, Neufeldt manipulated the recall strategies that his subjects employed by manipulating rate of presentation and instructions. Both normal groups were found to be more flexible than the retarded.

It would be interesting to investigate further the relative contribution of MA, CA, and IQ in dichotic listening. With the normal CA control both MA and IQ are confounded. The relatively small differences between the normal MA group and the retarded groups suggest that MA rather than IQ is of importance although a full factorial would provide a more sensitive test. Perhaps the major contribution of Neufeldt's monograph is the demonstration of the usefulness of the technique and the fruitfulness of Broadbent's theory in the area of retardation.

C. Inhibition

Recent developments in memory theory have emphasized the importance of parallel findings of PI and RI effects in LTM and STM(Melton, 1963). Also, it is now believed that PI is a major cause of forgetting in adult subjects (Underwood, 1957). What then is the evidence for PI and RI in retarded subjects?

Hawkins and Baumeister (1965a) investigated the retroactive effects of interpolating 0, 1, 2, or 3 digit messages between presentation and recall of a digit message. The retarded adult women profited from repetition provided there was no intervening material between learning and recall. With even one intervening digit series repetition provided no facilitation. The normal women, however, while showing RI effects, did benefit from repetition even with three intervening series. The retarded thus appeared particularly susceptible to RI. In a subsequent and similar study (Baumeister, Hawkins, & Holland, 1967) it was found that interpolated digits were more interfering than letters, as interference theory would predict.

Borkowski (1965) investigated PI effects in STM as a function of intelligence using trigrams and bigrams with an individual item technique (see below). He obtained, in both studies, an interaction between IQ and amount of with-in session PI as indexed by the number of previous items in a session. It therefore seems that retardates may be very susceptible to interference, and this may account for much of their forgetting.

In the study of STM following the work of Peterson and Peterson

(1959), a technique of studying individual items has been developed. In this procedure a subject is typically presented with a trigram such as WRX, then, to prevent rehearsal, he counts backward by threes until a signal is presented for him to recall the item. Marked forgetting is obtained with normal subjects and both PI and RI effects have been demonstrated. This procedure has a number of advantages. First, the degree of learning may be properly assessed by an immediate test. Thus the learning and memory effects can be separated in comparing the acquisition of items of different degree of meaningfulness or in comparison of subjects of different age or ability. Second, the course of proaction can be studied item by item rather than list by list and comparisons made between LTM and STM. Third, the procedure can be adapted to use in a miniature experiment design (Estes, 1960; House & Zeaman, 1963). It then becomes possible to use each subject as his own control having eliminated practice effects. Fourth, parameters for theoretical analysis can be estimated from one part of the data and used to predict subsequent performance. This is particularly valuable for formal theorizing.

House and Zeaman (1963) reported significant RI in a miniature experiment using a Wisconsin General Test Apparatus (WGTA). The essence of their procedure, and those to be discussed below, was to present the child with a simple two-choice problem for one training trial using a candy reward. On this trial the subject must guess since he has not seen the stimuli before. This trial is analogous to the presentation of the trigram in Peterson's technique. It is followed either immediately, or after a period of time, by one or more test trials where the stimuli are presented and the child again makes his choice. Mean performance is calculated from a number of similar problems and can be compared with chance. House and Zeaman found significant interference on a third trial from a second test trial. Their series of experiments, aimed mainly at attentional mechanisms in learning, thus turned up a memory effect that has been the start of an emphasis in the work at their laboratory and in the unpublished thesis research of their students discussed below.

Klinman (1964) conducted a series of experiments following the miniature experiment model. Each memory task consisted of three trials: a training trial, an interpolated trial, and a test trial. Among her more important results is the examination of effects of similarity on RI. In this experiment the training trials consisted of á pair of planometric stimuli differing either in color or in form. One of the stimuli was randomly designated as correct and was reinforced with a candy using a noncorrection procedure. The intervening trials consisted of seven

kinds: Identity where the training trial stimuli were repeated; color—
form pattern (CFP), where a different color—form pattern from the one
used in training was employed; similar dot patterns (SDP) and dissimilar

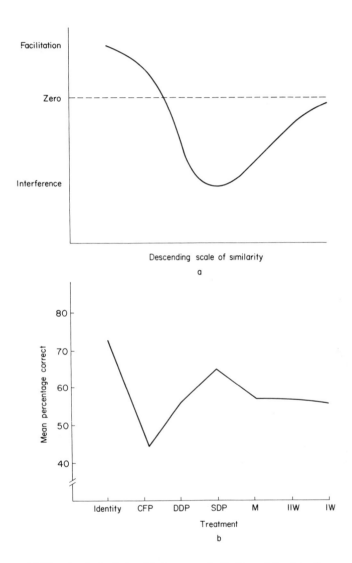

Fig. 3.   (a) The classical relationship between similarity and the interference with and
facilitation of retention following the Skaggs-Robinson hypothesis (after Robinson, 1927).
(b) A similar empirical function with the treatments in descending order of similarity,
from the data of Klinman. The symbols are explained in the text (after Klinman, 1964).

dot patterns (DDP), where the interpair similarity differed made two other conditions; and, finally, the remaining conditions consisted of presenting gray wedges to make the two-wedge (2W) and one-wedge (1W) conditions. These stimuli were judged to lie on a continuum of decreasing identity. Similarity effects are predicted by the well-known Skaggs-Robinson hypothesis (Robinson, 1927; Skaggs, 1925) shown in Fig. 3a. Klinman's result, presented in Fig. 3b, is in close agreement. It thus seems that similarity produces interference in the RI paradigm following the function originally proposed to account for normal adult performance. Wide generality of the obtained laws is implied.

In another study, Scott (1966) used an automated WGTA to provide better control of timing. Keppel and Underwood (1962) and Loess (1964) have clearly shown a marked with-in session PI effect using adult subjects, trigrams, and counting backward by threes to prevent rehearsal. Scott first overtrained his subjects on a color or a form problem and then used this as a task to intervene between a training and a test trial analogous to the use of the counting task. The training and test stimuli were other color and other form pairs. A rapid buildup of PI was obtained as can be seen in Fig. 4. The result is similar in form to that typically obtained with adult subjects and verbal stimuli. Scott's retarded children however performed poorly when asked to name the stimuli, and a negligible correlation was found between naming performance and per-

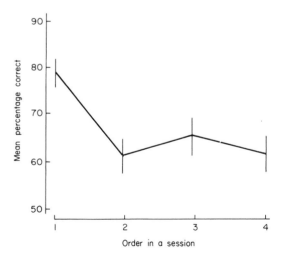

FIG. 4.   Performance as a function of serial position in a session for individual STM items. The data are from retarded subjects, but the function is similar to that obtained by Loess (1964) and others with college students (from Scott, 1966).

formance on the test trials. This suggests that the phenomenon is certainly not a purely verbal one. Similar functions were also obtained by Klinman.

D. Reaction Time

The reaction time (RT) of normal and retarded individuals has been compared in a number of studies. Berkson (1961) reviews these and shows that typically the RT of the retarded subject is characterized by a slower than normal voluntary response. The relation of this phenomenon to STM has been of some interest.

Terrell and Ellis (1964) investigated the RT of normals and defectives following a warning signal in a test of stimulus trace theory. The data were discussed by Ellis (1963) in some detail. Terrell and Ellis found that the RT for the normal subjects did not differ if the warning signal was continuous or if it consisted of a 1.5-second burst followed by an interval of time. Their retarded group however showed longer RTs under the latter condition compared to the condition where there was a continuous warning signal and the data were interpreted as showing a STM weakness in the retarded and supporting stimulus trace theory. A series of studies have attempted to explicate the variables in this task (Baumeister, Hawkins, & Koeningsknecht, 1965a; Hawkins, Baumeister, & Holland, 1965; Baumeister and Hawkins, 1966).

In one study a variation of the Terrell and Ellis result was obtained. Hawkins and Baumeister (1965b) used the same interval between warning signal and reaction signal for a whole block of trials, whereas Terrell and Ellis had varied this within blocks. Hawkins and Baumeister found that the unfilled condition resulted in faster RTs than the filled one with retarded subjects, a finding contrary to that of Terrell and Ellis. Under the regular condition a set may be formed rendering the warning signal less important. The outcome suggests that ability to vary a set, rather than STM, may be involved.

E. Recognition Experiments

Recognition tests have been used in a number of studies of retardate memory. Griffith (1960) examined the effects of retention interval and exposure time on the recognition of geometric forms with two groups of retarded young adults matched on CA. The subjects were assigned to a high IQ or low IQ group but MA differences were also present. She found significant effects of exposure time and group, but no significant interactions. Holden (1965, 1966, 1968) has investigated pattern recognition in a series of experiments using sequentially presented flashing lights that outline a letter. In each case he has used the design suggested by Denny (previously referred to): a retarded group which was matched with an MA normal group and a CA normal group. In the first study Holden manipulated the interstimulus interval between successive lights that made the letter pattern. The equal CA normal group performed significantly better than both the equal MA normal group and the retarded group. The MA normals also showed a more rapid decline than either of the other groups. Holden's second experiment was similar to the first except that he manipulated the duration of each light. The result showed a significant difference between all the groups with the MA normal and retarded groups showing a more marked decrement in performance as a function of decreasing stimulus duration than the CA normals. Holden interpreted his results as generally supporting Ellis except that he proposed that there was a CA effect as shown by his CA normal groups. It should be noted that in this design the equal CA normals were of higher MA than the other groups and MA and CA were confounded. An MA effect might provide a more suitable interpretation. In his most recent study, Holden required judgments of straightness or crookedness using rows or lines of lights instead of letters. In this study he failed to find group differences and suggested that this simple test of stimulus trace theory failed to support it. His previous results were attributed to stimulus organization factors and thus supported Spitz rather than Ellis. The data seem open to interpretation as supporting either theory. The retention interval required to form an organization for the letters would seem to be greater than for the lines.

In a study of perceptual memory with normal adults, retardates (mean MA 10-2, mean IQ 63.7) and groups of normal children of ages 8, 10, and 12 years, Belmont (1967) required judgments of whether a comparison light was brighter or dimmer than a standard light. The presentation of the standard and comparison was separated by 2, 5, 9.5, or 14 seconds in different blocks administered to each subject. Belmont found a significant shift in performance for all groups as a function of delay but no differences between groups. It was concluded that the outcome failed to support Ellis's position. Coupled with Holden's results, it does appear that the retention of very simple perceptual memory is not capacity sensitive with the subjects that have been tested.

Baumeister, Smith, and Rose (1965b) employed a perceptual recognition task for Chinese characters in a test of stimulus trace theory. They tested adult males of normal and subnormal intelligence and manipulated the complexity (number of items) and the retention interval using a display time of 6 seconds. They found main effects of complexity, delay interval, and intelligence as well as an interaction between intelligence and delay interval; that is, the retardates showed a greater rate of forgetting than the normals as Ellis would predict. In general, the recognition data have tended to support Ellis.

VI. The Relation of Theories and Data

With the present state of knowledge it does not seem useful to summarize with the aim of confirming or disconfirming any theory. Ellis's theory, coming earliest in the area, has been the most tested and has therefore been the most open to confirmation or disconfirmation. At times its predictions have been confirmed and other times they have not. Never conceived of as a complete theory of memory, it has nevertheless provided a major impetus and a point of focus. It is probably almost completely compatible with a more developed theory such as that of Broadbent where trace constructs again figure in a multifaceted system. Again, it has parallels in interference theory or the work of Spitz.

In view of its long dominating role in general psychology, interference theory has been strangely neglected, but when tested with retarded subjects the findings show remarkable parallels with classical results. Further studies are needed including work with picture and word stimuli that are of known association value with retarded and normal populations. This information is essential for comparative studies (Wallace & Underwood, 1964). Also, interference theory provides an important framework for examining the differences, if any, between STM and LTM. This distinction has been most generally assumed in the literature on retardation with little or no empirical evidence as a basis. A theory of memory in the retarded can scarcely neglect such an issue for long.

Two new techniques of experimentation show promise of major theoretical importance. These are the dichotic listening technique and the miniature experiment technique. Both provide bridges between research on attention (Broadbent, 1958; Zeaman & House, 1963) and memory. We have impressive evidence on the importance of attention in learning and STM in intellectual functioning. How do they relate? Zeaman and House (1963), for example, have been mainly concerned with the direction of attention but have seen the importance of span of attention in their multiple look models. These, however, have been rarely tested. What is the relation of attention span and memory span? How important is the subject's ability to organize or "chunk" or "cluster" material so that it may be attended to in a glance and brought into the range of memory span? These questions have not been the subject of intensive investigation. They are all related, and a complete theory will perhaps be formed eventually by combining much of several smaller theories developed around such topics.

In STM there are many processes to be delineated and parameters to be explored. Up to the present, probably 90% of the research has compared normal and retarded subjects. Such comparisons are unlikely to be meaningful unless a good deal of process information is available; otherwise, a small change of procedure can upset the outcome. It would seem that the time has come for a predominance of theory'guided process-oriented research as the proper precursor of comparative studies. When these are made, a factorial design, MA × IQ, would seem appropriate (Harter, 1965; Scott, 1968); that is, ability and development should be two parameters. If specific deficits exist for some etiological group they might then appear as aberrations of a developmental pattern.

Some data support the interpretation that intelligence may be defined by two parameters, not one. Harter (1965) reported separate and orthogonal relations among MA, IQ, and learning. Relevant evidence has been reviewed by Zeaman and House (1967) who also consider theories of intelligence. If MA is seen as an index of developmental level and IQ as a rate of development, various processes in memory may show different relations to IQ and MA. Jensen (1965) has suggested that serial learning ability predominantly reflects IQ and is relatively independent of MA, whereas the learning of material where spontaneous mediational processes are aroused in the learner also produces a correlation with MA. For example, IQ and MA should both correlate with performance on a meaningful paired-associate task. However, this interpretation is not clearly supported by the data. House (1963), for example, found a substantial correlation between probability of first recall on a serial learning task and MA. The general issue of the relation among ability, development, and STM remains an open and important question.

ACKNOWLEDGMENTS

The authors wish to thank Miss J. Pratt and Mr. R. Urbano for help with bibliographic material and reading the manuscript. They also wish to acknowledge discussion of the issue referred to in Section II,B with Drs. H. Quay and R. L. Sprague. They are indebted to Dr. N. R. Ellis for his comments regarding Section III,B, and to Dr. H. Spitz for comments on his theory referred to in Section III,D.

REFERENCES

Alpern, M. Meta contrast. *Journal of the Optical Society of America*, 1953, **43**, 648-657.
Baroff, G. S. WISC patterning in endogenous mental deficiency. *American Journal of Mental Deficiency*, 1959, **64**, 482-485.

Bateman, B., & Wetherell, J. Psycholinguistic aspects of mental retardation. *Mental Retardation,* 1965, **3**, 8-19.

Baumeister, A. A. Learning abilities of the mentally retarded. In A. A. Baumeister (Ed.), *Mental retardation. Appraisal, education, and rehabilitation.* Chicago: Aldine Press, 1967. (a)

Baumeister, A. A. Problems in comparative studies of mental retardates and normals. *American Journal of Mental Deficiency,* 1967, **71**, 869-875. (b)

Baumeister, A. A., & Bartlett, C. J. Further factorial investigations of WISC performance of mental defectives. *American Journal of Mental Deficiency,* 1962, **67**, 257-261. (a)

Baumeister, A. A., & Bartlett, C. J. A comparison of the factor structure of normals and retardates on the WISC. *American Journal of Mental Deficiency,* 1962, **66**, 641-66. (b)

Baumeister, A. A., Bartlett, C. J., & Hawkins, W. F. Stimulus trace as a predictor of performance. *American Journal of Mental Deficiency,* 1963, **67**, 726-729.

Baumeister, A. A., & Hawkins, W. F. Variations of the preparatory interval in relation to the reaction times of mental defectives. *American Journal of Mental Deficiency,* 1966, **70**, 689-694.

Baumeister, A. A., Hawkins, W. F., & Holland, J. M. Retroactive inhibition in short-term recall in normals and retardates. *American Journal of Mental Deficiency,* 1967, **72**, 227-231.

Baumeister, A. A., Hawkins, W. F., & Koeningsknecht, R. Effects of variations in complexity of the warning signal upon reaction time. *American Journal of Mental Deficiency,* 1965, **69**, 860-864. (a)

Baumeister, A. A., Smith, T. E., & Rose, J. D. The effects of stimulus complexity and retention interval upon short-term memory. *American Journal of Mental Deficiency,* 1965, **70**, 129-134. (b)

Belmont, J. M. Long-term memory in mental retardation. In N. R. Ellis (Ed.), *International review of research in mental retardation.* Vol. 1, New York: Academic Press, 1966. Pp. 219-255.

Belmont, J. M. Perceptual short-term memory in children retardates and adults. *Journal of Experimental Child Psychology,* 1967, **5**, 114-122.

Berkson, G. Responsiveness of the mentally deficient. *American Journal of Mental Deficiency,* 1961, **66**, 277-286.

Blankenship, A. B. Memory span: A review of the literature. *Psychological Bulletin,* 1938, **35**, 1-25.

Borkowski, J. G. Interference effects in short-term memory as a function of level of intelligence. *American Journal of Mental Deficiency,* 1965, **70**, 458-465.

Bousfield, W. A. The occurrence of clustering in the recall of randomly arranged associates. *Journal of General Psychology,* 1953, **49**, 229-240.

Broadbent, D. E. The role of auditory localization in attention and memory span. *Journal of Experimental Psychology,* 1954, **47**, 191-196.

Broadbent, D. E. *Perception and communication.* Oxford: Pergamon Press, 1958.

Bryden, M. P. The manipulation of strategies of report in dichotic listening. *Canadian Journal of Psychology,* 1964, **18**, 126-138.

Cohen, J. The factorial structure of the WAIS between early adulthood and old age. *Journal of Consulting Psychology,* 1957, **21**, 283-290.

Denny, M. R. Learning and performance. In J. A. Stevens and R. Heber (Eds.), *Mental retardation.* Chicago: University of Chicago Press, 1964.

Dingman, H. F., & Meyers, C. E. The structure of intellect in the mental retardate. In N. R. Ellis (Ed.), *International review of research in mental retardation.* Vol. 1, New York: Academic Press, 1966. Pp. 55-76.

Dodwell, P. C. Some factors affecting the hearing of words presented dichotically. *Canadian Journal of Psychology,* 1964, **18**, 72-91.

Ellis, N. R. The stimulus trace and behavioral inadequacy. In N. R. Ellis (Ed.), *Handbook of mental deficiency*. New York: McGraw-Hill, 1963. Pp. 134-158.

Estes, W. K. Learning theory and the new "mental chemistry." *Psychological Review*, 1960, **67**, 207-223.

Fagan, J. F., III. Short-term retention in normal and retarded children. *Psychonomic Science*, 1966, **6**, 303-304.

Fisher, G. M. A cross-validation of Baroff's WISC patterning in endogenous mental deficiency. *American Journal of Mental Deficiency*, 1960, **65**, 349-350.

Galton, F. Supplementary notes on "prehension" in idiots. *Mind*, 1887, **12**, 79-82.

Gates, A. I., & Taylor, G. A. An experimental study of the nature of improvement resulting from practice in a mental function. *Journal of Educational Psychology*, 1925, **16**, 583-592.

Gault, U. Factorial pattern of the Wechsler intelligence scales. *Australian Journal of Psychology*, 1954, **6**, 85-90.

Glickman, S. E. Perseverative neural processes and consolidation of the memory trace. *Psychological Bulletin*, 1961, **58**, 218-233.

Griffith, A. H. The effects of retention, interval, exposure time and IQ on recognition in a mentally retarded group. *American Journal of Mental Deficiency*, 1960, **64**, 1000-1003.

Hammer, A. G. A factorial analysis of the Bellevue tests. *Australian Journal of Psychology*, 1950, **1**, 108-114.

Harter, S. Discrimination learning set in children as a function of IQ and MA. *Journal of Experimental Child Psychology*, 1965, **2**, 31-43.

Hawkins, W. F. Trace as a predictor of STM of organic & familial retardates. *American Journal of Mental Deficiency*, 1966, **70**, 576-580.

Hawkins, W. F., & Baumeister, A. A. The effect of retroactive inhibition upon the digit-span performance of normals and retardates. *American Journal of Mental Deficiency*, 1965, **69**, 871-876. (a)

Hawkins, W. F., & Baumeister, A. A. Effect of duration of warning signal on reaction times of mental defectives. *Perceptual and Motor Skills*, 1965, **21**, 172-182. (b)

Hawkins, W. F., Baumeister, A. A., & Holland, J. M. Reaction time in retardates following variations in warning signal intensity and preparatory interval. *American Journal of Mental Deficiency*, 1965, **70**, 135-138.

Headrick, M., & Ellis, N. R. Short-term visual memory in normals and retardates. *Journal of Experimental Child Psychology*, 1964, **1**, 339-347.

Hermelin, B., & O'Connor, N. Short-term memory in normal and subnormal children. *American Journal of Mental Deficiency*, 1964, **69**, 121-125.

Holden, E. A., Jr. Temporal factors and subnormality in visual pattern recognition: A test of stimulus trace theory. *Journal of Comparative and Physiological Psychology*, 1965, **59**, 340-344.

Holden, E. A., Jr. Stimulus duration and subnormality in visual pattern recognition: A further test of stimulus trace theory. *Journal of Comparative and Physiological Psychology*, 1966, **62**, 167-170.

Holden, E. A., Jr. Interstimulus interval, locus redundancy, and mental subnormality in the perception of rectilinear dot progressions. *Journal of Comparative and Physiological Psychology*, 1968, in press.

House, B. J. Recalls versus trials as factors in serial verbal learning of retardates. *Psychological Report*, 1963, **12**, 931-941.

House, B. J., Smith, M., & Zeaman, D. Verbal learning and retention as a function of number of lists in retardates. *American Journal of Mental Deficiency*, 1964, **69**, 239-243.

House, B. J., & Zeaman D. Miniature experiments in the discrimination learning of retardates. In L. P. Lipsitt and C. C. Spiker (Eds.), *Advances in child development and behavior.* New York: Academic Press, 1963. Pp. 313-374.

Hull, C. L. *A behavior system.* New Haven: Yale University Press, 1952.

Humpstone, J. J. *Some aspects of the memory span test: A study of associability.* Philadelphia: Psychological Clinic Press, 1917.

Inglis, J., & Ankus, M. N. Effects of age on short-term storage and serial rote learning. *British Journal of Psychology,* 1965, **56,** 183-195.

Jacobs, J. Experiments in "prehension." *Mind,* 1887, **12,** 75-79.

Jensen, A. R. Individual differences in learning: Interference factor. *Cooperative Research Report No. 1867,* 1964, Department of Health, Education & Welfare.

Jensen, A. R. Rote learning in retarded adults and normal children. *American Journal of Mental Deficiency,* 1965, **69,** 828-834.

Keppel, G., & Underwood, B. J. Proactive inhibition in short-term retention of single items. *Journal of Verbal Learning and Verbal Behavior,* 1962, **1,** 153-162.

Kirk, S. A., & McCarthy, J. The Illinois Test of Psycholinguistic Abilities—an approach to differential diagnosis, *American Journal of Mental Deficiency,* 1961, **66,** 399-412.

Klinman, C. S. *Short-term memory in the discrimination learning of retardates.* Unpublished Ph.D. dissertation, University of Connecticut, Storrs, Conn., 1964.

Kohler, W. *Gestalt psychology.* New York: Liveright, 1929.

Kohler, W., & Wallach, H. Figural after-effects. *Proceedings of the American Philosophical Society,* 1944, **88,** 269-257.

Laycock, S. R., & Clark, S. The comparative performance of a group of old-dull and young bright children on some items of the Revised Stanford-Binet Scale of Intelligence, Form L. *Journal of Educational Psychology,* 1942, **33,** 1-12.

Loess, H. Proactive Inhibition in short-term memory. *Journal of Verbal Learning and Verbal Behavior,* 1964, **3,** 362-368.

Luh, C. W. The conditions of retention. *Psychological Monographs,* 1922, No. 142.

MacPhee, H. M., Wright, H. F., & Cummings, S. B., Jr. The performance of mentally subnormal rural southern Negroes on the verbal scale of the Bellevue Intelligence Examination. *Journal of Social Psychology,* 1947, **25,** 217-229.

Margaret, A., & Thompson, C. W. Differential test responses of normal, superior and mentally defective subjects. *Journal of Abnormal and Social Psychology, 1950,* **45,** 163-167.

McGeoch, J. A. Memory. *Psychological Bulletin,* 1928, **25,** 513-549.

McGhie, A., Chapman, H., & Lawson, J. S. Changes in immediate memory with age. *British Journal of Psychology,* 1965, **56,** 69-75.

Melton, A. W. Implications of short-term memory for a general theory of memory. *Journal of Verbal Learning and Verbal Behavior,* 1963, **2,** 1-21.

Miller, G. A. The magical number seven, plus or minus two: Some limits on our capacity for processing information. *Psychological Review,* 1956, **63,** 81-97.

Mowrer, O. H. *Learning theory and behavior.* New York: Wiley, 1960.

Müller, G. E., & Pilzecker, A. Experimentelle Beitrage zur Lehre vom Gedachtnis. *Zeitschrift fuer Psychol. Erganzbd,* 1900, No. 1.

Munn, N. L. Learning in children—memory. In L. Carmichael (Ed.), *Manual of child psychology.* New York: Wiley, 1954. Pp. 374-458.

Neufeldt, A. H. Short-term memory in the mentally retarded: An application of the dichotic listening technique. *Psychological Monographs,* 1966, No. 620.

O'Connor, N., & Hermelin, B. Input restriction and immediate memory decay in normal and subnormal children. *Quarterly Journal of Experimental Psychology,* 1965, **17,** 323-328.

Ohlrich, E. S., & Ross, L. E. Reversal and nonreversal shift learning in retardates as a function of overtraining. *Journal of Experimental Psychology*, 1966, **72**, 622-624.

Pavlov, I. P. *Conditioned reflexes*. London and New York: Oxford University Press, 1927.

Peterson, L. R., & Peterson, M. J. Short-term retention of individual verbal items. *Journal of Experimental Psychology*, 1959, **58**, 193-198.

Postman, L. Does interference theory predict too much forgetting. *Journal of Verbal Learning and Verbal Behavior*, 1963, **2**, 40-48.

Raab, D. H. Backward masking. *Psychological Bulletin*, 1963, **60**, 118-129.

Robinson, E. S. The similarity factor in retroaction. *American Journal of Psychology*, 1927, **39**, 297-312.

Sandercock, M. G., & Butler, A. J. An analysis of the performance of mental defectives on the WISC. *American Journal of Mental Deficiency*, 1952, **57**, 100-105.

Scott, K. G. *Some parameters of short-term recall*. Unpublished Ph.D. dissertation, University of Connecticut, Storrs, Conn., 1966.

Scott, K. G. Learning and intelligence. In C. Haywood (Ed.), *Psychometric intelligence*. New York: Appleton, 1968. In press.

Scott, K. G., Whimbey, A. E., & Dunning, C. Separate LTM and STM systems? *Psychonomic Science*, 1967, **7**, 55. (a)

Scott, K. G., Whimbey, A. E., & Dunning, C. A functional differentiation of STM and LTM. *Psychonomic Science*, 1967, **7**, 143. (b)

Skaggs, E. B. Further studies in retroactive inhibition. *Psychological Monographs*, 1925, No. 161.

Sloan, W., & Cutts, R. Test patterns of mental defectives on the revised Stanford-Binet Scale. *American Journal of Mental Deficiency*, 1947, **51**, 394-396.

Spitz, H. H. Field theory in mental deficiency. In N. R. Ellis (Ed.), *Handbook of mental deficiency*. New York: McGraw-Hill, 1963. Pp. 11-40.

Spitz, H. H. The role of input organization in the learning and memory of mental retardates. In N. R. Ellis (Ed.), *International review of research in mental retardation*. New York: Academic Press, 1966. Pp. 29-56.

Sprague, R. L., & Quay, H. C. A factor analytic study of the responses of mental retardates on the WAIS. *American Journal of Mental Deficiency*, 1966, **70**, 595-600.

Terrell, C. G., & Ellis, N. R. Reaction time in normal and defective subjects following varied warning conditions. *Journal of Abnormal and Social Psychology*, 1964, **69**, 449-452.

Thompson, C. W., & Margaret, A. Differential test responses of normals and mental defectives. *Journal of Abnormal and Social Psychology*, 1947, **42**, 285-293.

Underwood, B. J. Speed of learning and amount retained: A consideration of methodology. *Psychological Bulletin*, 1954, **51**, 276-282.

Underwood, B. J. Interference and forgetting. *Psychological Review*, 1957, **64**, 49-60.

Underwood, B. J. Degree of learning and the measurement of forgetting. *Journal of Verbal Learning and Verbal Behavior*, 1964, **3**, 112-129.

Wallace, W. P., & Underwood, B. J. Implicit response and the role of intralist similarity in verbal learning by normal and retarded subjects. *Journal of Educational Psychology*, 1964, **55**, 362-370.

Wechsler, D. *Manual of the Wechsler Intelligence Scale for Children*. New York: Psychological Corp., 1949.

Wechsler, D. *The measurement and appraisal of adult intelligence*. (4th ed.) Baltimore: Williams & Wilkins, 1958.

Wechsler, D., Israel, H., & Balinsky, B. A study of the sub-tests of the Wechsler-Bellevue intelligence scale in borderline and mentally defective cases. *American Journal of Mental Deficiency*, 1941, **45**, 555-558.

Woodworth, R. S., & Schlosberg, H. *Experimental psychology.* London: Methuen, 1955.

Yntema, D. B., & Trask, F. P. Recall as a search process. *Journal of Verbal Learning and Verbal Behavior,* 1963, **2,** 65-74.

Zeaman, D. Learning processes of the mentally retarded. In S. F. Osler and R. E. Cooke (Eds.), *The biosocial basis of mental retardation.* Baltimore, Maryland: The Johns Hopkins Press, 1965. Pp. 107-127.

Zeaman, D., & House, B. J. The role of attention in retardate discrimination learning. In N. R. Ellis (Ed.), *Handbook of mental deficiency.* New York: McGraw-Hill, 1963. Pp. 159-223.

Zeaman, D., & House, B. J. The relation of IQ and learning. In R. M. Gagne (Ed.), *Learning and individual differences.* Columbus, Ohio: Charles E. Merrill, 1967. Pp. 192-212.

Zigler, E. Mental retardation. In L. W. Hoffman and M. L. Hoffman (Eds.), *Review of child development research.* Vol. 2, New York, Russell Sage Foundation, 1966. Pp. 107-168.

Zigler, E. Familial mental retardation: A continuing dilemma. *Science,* 1967, **155,** 292-298.

Reaction Time and Mental Retardation

ALFRED A. BAUMEISTER AND GEORGE KELLAS

UNIVERSITY OF ALABAMA, UNIVERSITY, ALABAMA

I. INTRODUCTION

The swiftness with which an organism perceives and responds to its environment frequently is taken as an index of adaptability. Individuals who can process information rapidly and respond appropriately obviously have a distinct adaptive advantage over slower individuals. It is no accident that the concept of speed is inherent in most definitions and formal tests of intelligence. Moreover, many of the structured laboratory tasks employed in comparative studies of mental retardates incorporate speed as a measure of accomplishment. For instance, learning is often defined as the ability to make a specified response within a given interval. Speed is also an index of the complexity of a task, for the more complicated the central processes involved, the more time required to react. It is not unreasonable, therefore, to expect that an analysis of the factors that affect response latency may have some important implications for an experimental analysis and conceptualization of retarded behavior.

163

A. Reaction Time as a Unit of Measurement

Although a multitude of overt response measures involve timing, perhaps the purest and simplest is reaction time (RT). The venerable RT task has had a long and respected role in experimental psychology. In fact, studies using this procedure are so commonplace in the psychological literature that reaction time is often regarded as a specific inherent reflex pattern rather than as a dependent measure reflecting the operation of a number of internal processes. Actually, RT is a highly sensitive psychophysical measure that can be applied to a variety of contexts, not just simple stimulus—response (S—R) sequences.

There are several advantages that can be cited for the use of RT as a response measure in the study of individual differences in relation to adaptability. For one, RTs are highly reliable—the coefficients usually range from .80 to .95. Under relatively constant environmental conditions, RTs will remain stable over a considerable period of time. Related to this consideration is the fact that many measurements can be obtained upon the same individual. It is one of the few tasks that can be used for extensive within-subject comparisons of treatment conditions without introducing critical interpretation problems. Sequence effects, while sometimes present, usually do not represent a serious source of confounding. Variability owing to short-term practice is relatively minor, particularly if a brief warm-up period is allowed. The task usually does not involve a complicated set of verbal instructions and is easily communicated to even moderately retarded individuals. Moreover, it seems intrinsically motivating to most people, whether normal or retarded. In short, RT provides the basis for systematic comparisons of widely separated ability and age groups.

Many of the factors which affect reaction time have been studied thoroughly and are relatively well understood. Consequently, there is a considerable body of experimental literature that can serve as a point of departure for studying individual differences in gross adaptability. In addition, a number of theoretical models have been developed that can incorporate concepts relevant to both mental retardation and timing behavior. For example, one promising candidate that remains to be exploited in this connection is information theory (Bricker, 1955). Finally, it is important to note that the RT task provides a relatively "clean" context in which to study the interactive effects of intelligence and environmental variables. A high degree of experimental control over extraneous variables can be achieved in the measurement of reaction time.

Sometimes it has been convenient to analyze RTs in terms of input, central, and motor processes. Although such a conception of reaction time probably represents an oversimplification, it nevertheless has proved to be useful. An independent variable may be viewed as primarily exerting its influence at different points of the RT sequence, including receptor, central, and motor phases. Thus, a means is provided by which to experimentally analyze complex behavioral sequences into more elemental stimulus and response components. Higher "mental" processes such as discrimination, cognition, problem solving, attention, and conflict can be measured and quantified in terms of reaction time.

In summary, studies of reaction time may have implications for an understanding and analysis of impairments in cognition and other "higher processes." It should be noted that the focus here is less upon RT per se, than upon the environmental, task and organismic conditions which produce variability in this behavior. Central factors that involve integration and interpretation of the environment can be studied objectively beyond the efferent systems involved in the overt response. If the task is properly structured, RTs can be used to probe a variety of complex interactions between the subject and his environment.

B. The Reaction Time Paradigm

As with any widely applied experimental procedure, there have been numerous adaptations of the reaction time task. Nevertheless, certain features are common to most of these variations. Basically, there are three phases involved in the sequence of simple RT measurement: (a) presentation of a warning signal (WS) for some duration; (b) a blank interval, sometimes referred to as the warning interval (WI), following the termination of the WS; and (c) a reaction signal (RS). The warning and reaction stimuli are typically visual and/or auditory. The subject makes his response at the onset of the RS. The motor response is usually a finger lift or press, although verbal RTs are used occasionally. In fact, the choice of response in most experiments is arbitrary and a matter of convenience. The usual measure obtained is the time between presentation of the RS and the initiation or beginning of the response, i.e., latency of the response. Sometimes serial reactions are obtained by placing two or more RSs in a sequence. Another theoretically important implicit response is assumed to occur in relation to the WS. This covert response, frequently called "preparatory set," is regarded as preparatory to the reaction stimulus and can be objectively recorded in terms of muscular tension. It can also be inferred from the effects of certain temporal manipulations. It is this aspect of experimental concern that most clearly distinguishes current research from the classical literature on RT. We are at least as greatly concerned with response events that occur *before* as opposed to after the cue to react. Figure 1 depicts the essential features of the RT task. Most of the studies with mental retardates have focused upon certain aspects of the warning and reaction signals, such as intensity and complexity. It is also obvious that considerable attention might be directed to the temporal aspects of the task, particularly the interval separating WS and RS.

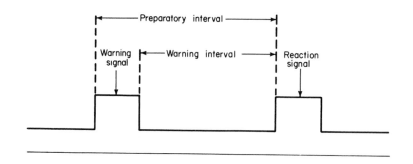

Time

Fig. 1. Reaction time paradigm. This figure illustrates the fundamental procedures typically utilized in the measurement of reaction time. A warning signal is presented for a brief period followed by a blank interval, referred to here as the warning interval. One of two procedures is employed in presenting the WIs: (a) a "regular" under which the same interval is presented over a number of trials and (b) an "irregular" in which different intervals are given from trial to trial. The WS and the WI taken together are designated the preparatory interval (PI). The reaction signal is the cue for the subject to make his overt response. Time to initiate the response usually constitutes the dependent measure.

II. Research Findings

An attempt was made to review all of the research in which the RT task, simple or complex, has been employed with retardates. Other investigations which incorporated speed as a dependent measure, but which did not conform to the general RT paradigm, were omitted from this survey. Studies deriving from or leading to some theoretical conceptualization of retarded behavior are covered a little more thoroughly than others. In an effort to put some findings in perspective, occasional references are made to the broader RT literature involving normal persons.

It should be noted, parenthetically, that these studies involving retarded subjects have general implications for understanding the processes underlying timing behaviors. For instance, some of the most systematic investigations of warning signal effects have been done with mental defectives. The fact that the research is conducted with retarded individuals in no way negates the contribution of the research to general behavioral theory and knowledge. However, the writers have the impression that, even with everything else equal, experimental studies involving deviant groups often are accorded second class status. There seems to be some subtle bias operating that lawful relationships established with certain subgroups of humans have relatively limited generalization. Without wishing to unduly press the issue, it should be stated that the problem of generalization is equally acute whether rats, sophomores, or retardates are the subjects of scientific inquiry. A lawful relationship is no less important for having been established with intellectually dull individuals.

A. Reaction Time as a Function of Intelligence

Although there have been some differences in conclusions regarding the relationship between intelligence and RT, the majority of studies indicate that speed and intelligence are positively related, at least within a certain range of ability. Ordahl and Ordahl (1915) were the first to formally note this relationship. Virtually every recent study in which normal and retarded subjects have been compared shows the latter to be markedly slower.

In conducting one of the first systematic studies of the relationship between intelligence and response speed, Scott (1940) found that normal children had faster RTs than retarded children of comparable chronological ages. Furthermore, the retardates were more variable as a group. The latter finding has been largely ignored, although as will be subsequently pointed out, it may have more theoretical significance than the factor of speed per se. Scott concluded that, beyond some level of ability (e.g., an MA of 6 or 7), further increases in intelligence are not associated with improvement in RT.

Even within the retarded group, mental ability and speed seem to be substantially related. Pascal (1953) reported a correlation of $-.61$ between MA and RT. He also suggested that the relationship is curvilinear. Ellis and Sloan (1957) found that MA, within a group of retardates, was a better predictor ($r = -.54$) of RT than chronological age ($r = -.27$). Obviously, the particular CA range sampled is a relevant consideration in interpreting these findings. Unlike previous workers, Ellis and Sloan did not observe a curvilinear function of RT on MA. Finally, Berkson (1960b) controlling for CA, length of institutionalization, and diagnostic category, found a reliable difference in response latencies between two groups of retardates differing in IQ. Those few studies which have failed to obtain a significant correlation between RT and intelligence (e.g., Holden, 1965; Wolfensberger, 1960) have either tested subjects within an extremely narrow range of ability or have employed older defectives.

It may be that a strong relationship between mental ability and RT is characteristic of only certain subgroups within the retarded population. Bensberg and Cantor (1957) obtained a substantial correlation between MA and RT for a group of defectives diagnosed as "familial." On the other hand, the correlation was not significant for a group of retarded brain-injured subjects. This is not an entirely unexpected finding in view of the fact that many brain-injured individuals have motor and/or sensory disabilities to some degree or another. Variability in RTs resulting from differences in IQs may be suppressed completely by the effects of sensory or motor involvements.

In most of the studies which bear upon the issue of the relationship between mental ability and speed, it is difficult to separate the effects of performance disability and intelligence. Clearly, low intelligence is associated with long response latencies; however, this relationship frequently appears to be confounded with motor or sensory defects. Less intelligent subjects are more likely to have impaired motor and sensory systems. Consequently, the correlation observed between intelligence and speed may be the fortuitous result of such defects. Additional evidence concerning the effects of motor disability comes from a study by Dingman and Silverstein (1964). Testing a large group of retarded subjects, these workers found that the association between intelligence and RT can be accounted for almost entirely by subject differences in motor integrity. Dingman and Silverstein emphasize the need to control for sensory and motor differences in research with the retarded. Certainly one would not wish to attribute behavioral differences between intelligence groups exclusively or directly to intellectual characteristics when other factors may be implicated.

In any event, it should be emphasized that studies showing a correlation between intelligence and RT or studies revealing a significant difference between intelligence groups represent a low order of functional analysis. In these cases little is learned about the source of the slowness that characterizes retarded individuals. The finding of differences between widely separated intelligence groups is not particularly surprising and may attest to nothing more than the reliability of the original diagnosis.

In general, it is far more meaningful to ask whether there is an *inter-*

action between the organismic variable of intelligence and some experimental variable; that is, do different intelligence groups display the same adjustment in speed to varying task and environmental conditions? What are the functions involved in RT that differentiate bright subjects from less bright individuals? In this context, one is concerned with relative rather than absolute differences. As Baumeister (1967) has previously pointed out, this kind of analysis is more in the tradition of comparative psychology and may lead to an experimental conceptualization of mental retardation. Much of the recent research on RT and intelligence is primarily concerned with interactions.

B. Reaction Time and Stimulus Intensity

Perhaps the most consistent finding in the experimental literature on reaction time is that RTs become shorter as the intensity of the signal to react is increased. This relationship is nonlinear, although its exact nature is open to question. Increments in intensity near threshold produce the greatest improvement in RT. Beyond some optimal level of intensity, the curve reaches an asymptote and further increases in intensity have little effect. Possibly different subject "sets" are operative when stimuli are weak as opposed to moderate and intense. Within a given context, there appears to be a physiological limit of speed.

Some evidence indicates that the intensity of the reaction signal is related to normal − retardate differences in RT. An interaction of these variables was recently reported by Baumeister, Urquhart, Beedle, and Smith (1964). The reaction signal in this case was a *change* from a variable ongoing level of stimulation to a higher level. The subject was shown a light with an initial intensity of .5, 4.0, or 7.0 ft-c. After a brief warning period, the intensity of the light was increased to 8.0 ft-c. The retardates were relatively impaired under the smallest intensity change as compared with the largest. Normals, on the other hand, were not affected. This may suggest that the normals tend to work closer to their irreducible minimum than retardates. One may speculate further that the retardates are characterized by some sort of attentional or arousal lag that is partly overcome by increased intensity of the relevant cues. The results are shown in Fig. 2.

The procedures employed by Baumeister *et al.* (1964) were rather unconventional in that the effective RS was a *change* in the ongoing level of stimulation. It has been suggested that this method of varying intensity produced results that are not directly comparable with those obtained from procedures in which the receptor is in a "normal" condition (see Teichner, 1954). The atypical finding that the more intelligent

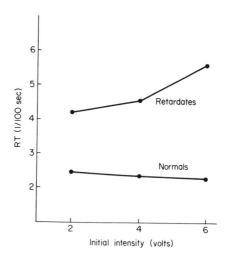

Fɪɢ. 2.   Reaction time as a function of stimulus intensity change. The curves represent the mean RTs of normals and retardates at three different levels of intensity change. The RS was a change from an initial intensity level of 2, 4, or 6 V (corresponding to .5, 4.0, and 7.0 ft-c, respectively) to 8 V (8 ft-c) (from Baumeister *et al.*, 1964).

subjects were not differentially affected by the different stimulus intensity changes probably results from the particular method employed. In addition to these considerations, the study by Baumeister *et al.* (1964) failed to equate threshold differences between the two intelligence groups. Such a control would seem desirable in view of the fact that the effects of intensity are dependent upon proximity of the stimulus energy to threshold.

In an effort to replicate the intensity by intelligence interaction effect using conventional procedures, Baumeister, Hawkins, and Kellas (1965a) conducted a more extensive study. This time a 1000-cps pure tone (presented at 25, 50, and 75 dB above threshold) was employed as the signal to respond. Normals and retardates received 36 test trials in three counterbalanced blocks representing the different intensity levels. Again, a significant interaction was found between intelligence groups and strength of RS. A more detailed analysis of order effects indicated that the interaction between intelligence and intensity was significant only for the orders 25, 50, and 75 dB and 50, 25, and 75 dB. That is, proceeding from weaker to more intense stimuli over the test session produced the interaction effect while the reverse did not. The authors speculated that the retardates were more alert in the context where the most intense stimuli appeared first and that this heightened arousal carried through the entire testing session to facilitate reactions to the weaker stimuli.

Another study (Baumeister, Hawkins, & Kellas, 1965b) in the sequence was a replication of the preceding experiment, but with RS tones of 5, 15, and 25 dB above threshold. It is well known that increments in the intensity of near-threshold stimuli have a greater effect on RT than those markedly above threshold. Although mean differences were in the same direction as the previous study, the interaction between intelligence group and intensity did not reach significance. Failure to turn up significance in this case may have been related, in part, to the small range of decibels sampled. As in the previous study, a significant interaction obtained between order and intensity. It was found to arise from relatively fast responses at 5 dB in those orders beginning with the strongest (25 dB) signal. These results occasioned another tentative hypothesis, namely, that the inferiority on the part of the retardate may stem from inappropriate response sets. In particular, the present authors speculated that the attention of the retardate is directed toward reception of stimuli rather than performance of the response, in spite of instructions designed to minimize such a set. Normals, on the other hand, may maintain a motor set beyond some minimal intensity value. As intensity approaches threshold values, normals are forced to attend more and more to reception of the signal, thus assuming, like the retardates, a sensory set. At higher intensities the two intelligence groups are performing under different response sets which would be differentially affected by signal intensity, resulting in the observed interaction. At lower intensities similar sets would be operative and no interaction would occur.

The present authors have completed another reaction signal intensity study in which the loudness of a pure-tone stimulus was varied (30, 60, or 90 dB re threshold) unpredictably from trial to trial as opposed to the trial-block procedures employed in the previous studies. In addition, a much wider range of preparatory intervals was used. A highly significant interaction was found ($p < .001$), again indicating that the retardates were differentially slow, relative to normals, at the lower intensities. This effect was most marked at the short PIs. The interactive effects of intelligence and intensity appear to be particularly pronounced under conditions designed to create maximum stimulus uncertainty.

Although the warning signal is usually regarded in relation to the temporal cues it provides, there is some evidence that under certain conditions high WS intensities have a detrimental effect on RT. Hawkins, Baumeister, and Holland (1965) reported an experiment in which three different intensities of visual WS were employed. The RS was also in the visual modality and exactly the same physical intensity as the most intense WS. The results indicated that increasing brightness of the WS produced slower RTs.

One interpretation of these findings is that the WS functions as part of the perceptual background against which the RS is presented. One may speculate that variations in WS intensities have their effects in terms of the perceptual changes they evoke in the RS. In other words, the effect is to reduce the perceived intensity of the RS. This would account for the finding that RTs of retardates are shorter when the WS and RS are in different sensory modalities (Hermelin, 1964). Nevertheless, a sensory interpretation is also feasible since both WS and RS were in the same modality. The different warning signals may have produced differentially pupillary changes.

In an effort to correct certain defects in the earlier experiment, Baumeister, Dugas, and Erdberg (1967) conducted another experiment with retardates in which RS and WS were both varied within the auditory modality, but with the WS presented to one ear and the RS to the other. Again, the results indicated that each increment in WS intensity produced reliably longer RTs. These findings lend credence to the perceptual interpretation made in relation to the results of Hawkins *et al.* It is difficult to imagine how changes in the sensory apparatus could have accounted for the WS effects found in the second experiment.

C. Stimulus Compounding

Related to the question of intensity effects are the results of studies in which the reaction or warning signals were presented as combinations of stimuli in different sensory modalities. There is some evidence to indicate that, with normal Ss, triple compound reaction stimuli will produce slightly faster RTs than single stimuli (Teichner, 1954).

Retardates do seem to perform better when the signals to react are simultaneously presented in three different modalities. Holden (1965) has shown that trimodal stimulation (auditory, visual, and cutaneous) yields significantly faster reactions than any of these stimuli presented singly. No comparisons were made with bimodal stimulation conditions. Holden attempted to rule out prestimulus attentional lag as an interpretation of his data by showing that a control group which received the three stimuli singly and randomly from trial to trial performed no better than the unimodal stimulus groups. Indeed, it is surprising that this control group did as well as the others in view of the finding that stimulus uncertainty of this type *detrimentally* affects RT in both normal and schizophrenic Ss (Sutton, Hakerem, Zubin, & Portnoy, 1961; Teichner, 1954). Greeson (1967), in fact, has recently obtained data showing that retardates and normals are both adversely affected when the RS is un-predictably changed from one modality to another.

Holden interpreted the results of his experiment as favoring the arousal deficiency hypothesis. He speculated that the effect of multiple stimulation was to increase the functional intensity of the reaction signal. These findings, together with those previously described, support the view that the consequence of increasing intensity, both inter- and intra-modal, is to facilitate a central alerting or preparatory process.

Compound warning stimuli (light and sound vs light) have been inves-tigated in normals and retardates (Baumeister, Hawkins, & Koenigs-knecht, 1965c). In one experiment, length of the interval separating warning and reaction signals were varied in an irregular (random) manner, and in a second study (involving retardates only) the interval was constant for a block of trials. In neither case was a reliable differ-ence found between the compound and single warning signal conditions.

Although the interpretation of nonsignificant results is a dubious procedure, it does appear that compounding of warning signals does not have the marked influence on RT as increasing warning signal intensity. The same is probably true of the RS.

D. Stimulus and Response Complexity

It is not unreasonable to expect that complexity as a variable will interact with intelligence to produce increasingly disparate performance between intelligence groups as the number of alternatives is increased. This consideration may be regarded as a special case of information processing. One of the hallmarks of mental retardation is often assumed to be an inability to manage complex demands made by an uncertain environment. This hypothesis has been investigated in a number of experimental contexts, including reaction time.

Stimulus complexity is usually defined in terms of the number of stimulus events to which the subject must respond. A simple RT implies complete event certainty. The subject knows what to expect, if not when. Choice RTs require the subject to first discriminate among the reaction stimuli. By subtracting an individual's performance under the simple RT situation from that of his choice RT, it is purportedly possible to infer the time S requires to process the additional data and arrive at a decision. It is generally held that RT increases with the number of al-ternatives or "bits" of information S must process (Hyman, 1953). However, as will be subsequently pointed out, there are exceptions to this rule.

The studies with retardates, involving a choice situation, have gen-erally required the subject to make different responses to the relevant reaction stimuli. Consequently, response complexity, in a sense, has been confounded with stimulus complexity.

The first, and in some ways, most thorough, study of an intelligence by complexity interaction was conducted by Scott (1940). He employed a series of four tasks ranging from a simple RT to a five-choice RT. High IQ subjects were faster than low IQ subjects at all levels of complexity. Although no tests of significance were employed, inspection of Scott's summary data hints that the differences between normals and retardates increased with more stimulus alternatives.

A series of RT studies by Berkson (1960a, 1960b) was designed to investigate systematically the interaction between task complexity and intelligence. Three different procedures were employed including a hand lift, simple button press, and choice button press. In the hand-lift situation, *S* was required to depress a button and release it upon presentation of a light. The simple button press measure consisted of the time required by *S* to release one button and depress another. The choice button press required *S* to release a button and then to push one of five buttons corresponding to one of five stimulus lights. Hand-lift speed was obtained from all three response classes. In the simple and choice button press a ballistic movement measure was also obtained by recording the time from the completion of the hand-lift response to the completion of the final response of both simple and choice button press.

Analyses of simple hand-lift scores and of ballistic movement times revealed that the more complex tasks produced slower responses than did the simpler tasks. However, no interactions were found involving intelligence. Although generally inferior, the retardates were not differentially disadvantaged by increased task complexity. Nevertheless, an examination of group means did indicate that the differences between intelligence groups were less for the hand-lift time than for the ballistic movement time, suggesting an interaction between intelligence and response complexity. This finding led to the hypothesis that IQ is related to a motor factor involving either initiation of the response or the performance of it.

Another study was conducted by Berkson (1960b) to test this notion. Normals and retardates were compared on two visual tasks in which both stimulus and response complexity were varied. In brief, it was found that IQ interacted with response complexity but not with stimulus complexity. On the basis of his series of studies, Berkson concluded that IQ is not relevant to making a choice or to planning a movement, but is related to the performance of that movement. Throne, Kasper, and Schulman (1964) concur with this conclusion, referring to defects in "performability." Nevertheless, in spite of Berkson's findings, there is some other evidence to implicate central factors in the retardates' relatively poor RT performance (e.g., the intensity effects mentioned earlier).

In view of the confounding introduced by increasing the number of responses along with the number of stimulus events, Hawkins, Baumeister, Koenigsknecht, & Kellas (1965b) compared college students and retardates on simple and choice RT tasks using a verbal reaction rather than a motor response. The subjects were instructed to respond by naming a color (either red or green) that appeared on a panel. Hawkins *et al.* predicted that augmenting complexity from one to two equally likely stimulus alternatives would be more deleterious to the performance of the retardates. Normals were faster than defectives, and both groups gave markedly slower choice RTs. But, as in the Berkson studies, no interaction between type of task and intelligence group was observed. This does not mean, however, that complexity is irrelevant to normal—retardate differences, rather, that further stimulus uncertainty in these experimental contexts did not produce differential effects.

It is necessary to make a clear distinction between the number of perceptual choices and the number of perceptually different events. Reaction time undoubtedly varies directly with degree of similarity between stimuli. If retardates suffer a discrimination deficit, they might be expected to be relatively disadvantaged in situations that require them to choose among highly similar alternatives before responding. Furthermore, it has been noted by others (e.g., Adams, 1964) that increased complexity appears to have greater consequences in situations involving low S—R compatibility. Considerable recent evidence shows that when the essential S—R sequences are greatly overlearned, RT does not depend on the number of stimulus alternatives. It may be argued that the responses "red" or "green" to red and green lights have a high degree of associative strength.

One other study is available which, although not designed specifically as a test of the S—R compatibility notion, did employ more abstract stimuli in choice and simple RT situations. As one phase of a sequential RT study, Baumeister and Kellas (1967) obtained verbal choice and simple RTs to a square or a cross projected on a stimulus panel. As in the previous cases, the main effects of intelligence and stimulus uncertainty were found to be significant. Again, the interaction between these factors was not significant, indicating that the retardates were able to manage the increased event uncertainty as effectively as college students.

All of the studies described in this section have employed procedures in which the probabilities of the various stimulus alternatives were equal. Such a stimulus code may not be sensitive to the subtle information-processing strategies utilized by the subject in choice reaction time situations. There is evidence that the rate of processing information is qualitatively and fundamentally different for equally likely and unequally likely stimulus occurrences (Lamb & Kaufman, 1965). Different sets of laws appear to apply in the two situations.

A study carried out by Stephen Wilcox under the direction of the senior author has shown that when the stimulus alternatives are not equally probable, the RTs of normal and mentally defective subjects may be differentially affected. Probability values of visual and auditory reaction stimuli ranged from 1.0 to .1. While both intelligence groups displayed increasing RTs with decreasing probability of RS occurrence, the retardates were especially slow on those trials in which the least likely stimulus was presented. However, this finding may be modality specific, since the interaction was significant only in relation to the sound stimuli.

E. Temporal Factors

1. Uncertainty

In most RT situations the only factor unknown to the subject is precisely *when* the RS will be presented. He knows what stimulus to expect and what to do when he observes it. Obviously, a significant source of variance in RTs must stem from temporal uncertainty. In fact, it may be stated that response speed of both normal and mentally retarded individuals is a direct function of the subject's uncertainty regarding the time of occurrence of the RS. There are two related sources of time uncertainty. One results from the objective variability in the interval separating WS and RS, and the other lies in the subject's covert time-keeping behaviors. The latter may have some special relevance for explaining intelligence group differences.

In most instances, statements made about WI apply equally to PI (see Fig. 1) since WS duration is usually a constant. In fact, most authors, when speaking of preparatory or warning period, are referring to the interval between onset of WS and onset of RS. Moreover, the experimental evidence reveals that the effective warning period begins with the onset of the warning stimulus for retardates as well as normals (Foley & Dewis, 1960; Kellas, 1967). Nevertheless, in the interests of clarity, the distinction between PI and WI will be maintained throughout this discussion.

The warning interval, defined as the time between cessation of the WS and onset of the RS, can be presented in one of two ways. In the *regular* method of presentation the same WI is given over successive trials. The *irregular* procedure, on the other hand, involves the random (or unpredictable) presentation of different WIs from trial to trial. Clearly, the former provides an additional cue to the onset of the RS by virtue of the constant interval. Under the regular procedure, S may be able to distinguish the time characteristics of the task and anticipate the onset of the RS. Temporal uncertainty, of course, is maximized with the irregular WIs.

Most researchers have used the irregular procedure in order to prevent the S from "jumping the gun" on the RS. The effects of a number of other variables on RTs are dependent upon whether the WIs are presented in a regular or irregular manner. The method of WI administration has been shown to interact with different factors.

2. LENGTH OF WARNING INTERVAL

Under conditions of constant WI presentation, beyond some minimal value, RT increases as a negatively accelerated function of WI. This conclusion seems to apply to both normal (Karlin, 1959; Klemmer, 1956) and retarded Ss (Baumeister & Hawkins, 1966; Baumeister *et al.*, 1965c; Hawkins & Baumeister, 1965; Hawkins et al., 1965a). One obvious explanation of this finding is that the S's ability to judge the interval decreases as the duration increases. The covert response of "attention" or "preparation" may be disruptive in its effects if its timing is inappropriate. It is well known that judgments of long intervals are less accurate than estimations of shorter periods of time. In view of the finding that retarded individuals are less accurate than normals at estimating longer intervals of time (Baumeister, 1964; McNutt & Melvin, 1968), one might expect an interaction between WI and intelligence. However, none of the studies employing the regular method of WI administration has yielded a significant interaction of this nature.

The relationship of WI and RT under the irregular procedure is more complex, and the results of studies with normals or retardates are contradictory. A number of factors affect RT at a particular WI. The context in which a given WI is presented appears to be critical. A short WI on a trial immediately following a long WI tends to yield slow RTs. The preparatory set produced by the temporal contingencies on one trial apparently carry over to the subsequent trials. Moreover, the range and the average value of the WIs appear to affect RT. Baumeister and Hawkins (1966) have speculated that the retardate develops a subjective notion of the central tendency of irregular WIs and assumes a preparatory set to respond to this average value.

Curves (from Baumeister & Hawkins, 1966) comparing RTs under regular and irregular procedures are shown in Fig. 3. It may be seen

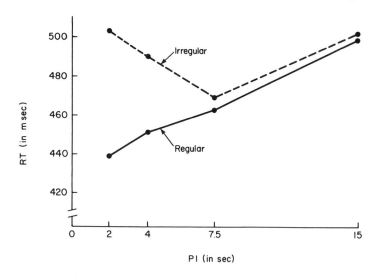

Fig. 3. Reaction time as a function of type of PI presentation and duration. These curves show mean RTs of retardates at four different PIs under both regular and irregular procedures. Since a constant WS (1.5 seconds) was employed on all trials, the PI values corresponded to WIs of .5, 2.5, 6.0, and 13.5 (from Baumeister & Hawkins, 1966).

that RT steadily increased across WIs in the regular condition. Clearly an interaction occurred when the irregular procedure was employed. Here the optimal WI was a middle value, which in this case also happened to be the average WI. Both very short and long intervals were associated with relatively poor performance. One may conclude, therefore, that the regular procedure produces faster responses than the irregular only at moderately short intervals. In fact, the authors have some recent unpublished data demonstrating that, under certain conditions involving long WIs, retardates respond significantly faster with the irregular presentation.

The results concerning the relationship of WI and intelligence under the irregular procedure are equivocal. Hermelin (1964) reported a significant interaction involving WI and IQ. In brief, she found that the differences between intelligence groups increased with progressive lengthening of the interval. These results were interpreted to mean that less intelligent subjects have difficulty in maintaining a set to perform the response. Terrell and Ellis (1964) likewise employed the irregular procedure with normals and retardates. They also found an interaction between intelligence and WI, but in this case the RT difference between normals and retardates *diminished* as the interval was lengthened. In short, these two studies lead to opposite conclusions, not only concerning the nature of a possible interaction between intelligence and WI but also with respect to the main effect of WI; that is, Hermelin reported a steady slowing of responses in retardates with increasing WI, whereas the Terrell and Ellis data indicate that RT improves with lengthened WI. The latter result appears to be more consistent with findings from other experiments.

The previously mentioned study by Baumeister and Hawkins (1966) revealed a nonlinear relationship between WI and RT under the irregular procedure. Figure 3 indicates that both relatively short and long irregular intervals are associated with slow responses in RTs. Further studies by Kellas (1967) have corroborated this result. In general, these data are in accord with the results of Terrell and Ellis (1964). If longer WIs had been employed, it is likely that their curves would have resembled those of Baumeister and Hawkins.

The explanation of this finding must be sought in contextual factors. In those trials where a short WI follows a longer WI, RT will be relatively slow. It is as if the subject has been led to "expect" a longer warning interval and is not ready to respond when the interval is brief. Baumeister and Hawkins proposed that the retardate's preparatory set derives not only from the conditions present on a particular trial but also from the temporal context in which the interval is presented. Although similar results have been reported for normals (Karlin, 1959; Klemmer, 1956), there is some suggestion from the Terrell and Ellis study and from Dickerson (1965) that this effect may be more pronounced among mentally deficient subjects.

3. PSYCHOLOGICAL REFRACTORY PERIOD

When a subject is asked to respond as quickly as he can to each of two successive stimuli, the speed of the second response is dependent on the interval separating the two stimuli. When this interval is very brief, the second RT usually is relatively slow. Apparently, the subject needs a period of time to recover from some inhibitory effects resulting from the first S − R sequence. This well-established phenomenon has usually been referred to as the "Psychological Refractory Period" (PRP).

Operationally, at least, one may view the PRP study as a special instance of the WS − RS relationship; that is, the first stimulus (and the accompanying overt response as well) may be regarded as a warning to prepare quickly for the second RS. Typically, of course, these signals are presented in close temporal contiguity.

Only one study (Baumeister & Kellas, 1967) has compared the PRPs of normals and retardates. In this experiment, the interval separating the two RT sequences ranged from .2 to 5.0 seconds. A voice RT was obtained to the first stimulus (visual) and a finger lift to the second stimulus (auditory). Both intelligence groups showed the PRP effect, but the retardates were more adversely affected by the short intervals. Furthermore, the retardates took longer to recover from the first S−R sequence; i.e., they had longer PRPs. A graph of these results is shown in Fig. 4. The interpretation given these data was that refractoriness stems from inappropriate response sets, which, in turn, arise from low expectations for short intervals. The less intelligent subjects may not have learned as well the statistically defined time relationships involved in this RT task. Baumeister and Kellas viewed the retardates as being more stimulus bound, with resultant difficulty in adjusting to rapidly changing environmental contingencies.

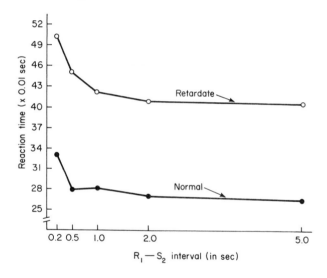

Fig. 4. Refractoriness in normals and retardates in relation to response−stimulus interval. These curves show RTs of normals and retardates as a function of the interval between the first response and a second signal to react (adapted from Baumeister & Kellas, 1967).

Considering the results of the Baumeister and Kellas PRP study together with those reported by Hermelin and her associates, one might suggest, quite tentatively, that retardates take longer to prepare for a response than normals and have greater difficulty in sustaining their preparation over long intervals. Unfortunately, the available data are not entirely consistent with this conclusion.

4. WARNING SIGNAL DURATION

Warning signal durations do not appear to have marked effects on RTs of normal individuals (Foley, 1959). There is some evidence that under certain conditions WS duration is related to RTs of mentally defective persons.

Terrell and Ellis (1964) compared normals and retardates under two conditions of WS duration. In one condition the WS appeared and remained on for the entire preparatory interval (filled condition). In a second condition (unfilled) the WS was presented for only 1.5 seconds of the PI. Four PIs (2, 4, 8, and 12 seconds) were varied under the irregular procedure. (Warning signal duration, WI, and proportion of PI filled are completely confounded in this design.) An interaction resulted in which normals were unaffected by WS duration, but the retardates were facilitated in the filled condition. The results were interpreted as indicating a short-term memory deficit (i.e., a fading WS trace in the retardates.

The opposite effect was obtained by Hawkins and Baumeister (1965), who attempted to extend the findings of Terrell and Ellis by using the regular procedure and thereby add a temporal cue to the RT context. In this case, the retardates performed better under the unfilled condition, exactly contrary to the results of the original study. Hawkins and Baumeister argued that the "trace" interpretation could not adequately account for the findings of either study and that an explanation should be sought in the preparatory sets which are associated with the particular temporal contingencies involved in the different RT situations.

Both of the above studies employed designs that confounded WS duration and WI. In order to separate these effects, Kellas (1967) conducted two experiments in which WI and WS durations were varied independently. The first experiment (with a regular procedure) revealed that WI, but not WS, duration was related to RTs of both normals and retardates. The second study, involving retardates only, was similar in design but used the irregular procedure. In this context WS duration was found to have an effect, but only in the condition where it filled the entire interval (O-WI); that is, when some blank interval followed the warning signal the duration of the signal was irrelevant to performance. In terms of the trace hypothesis advanced by Terrell and Ellis one would have expected longer WS durations to facilitate RTs. The results of these studies were viewed as inconsistent with the stimulus trace interpretation of warning signal effects. The present authors favor a "perceptual anticipation" notion (after Poulton, 1950) in which the subject comes to appreciate, more or less accurately, the regularities in stimuli and the temporal relations among them. The retardate is viewed as less able to internalize the relevant cues for responding.

F. Electroencephalogram Correlates

It is generally assumed that the WS in the RT task has an alerting effect on the subject. When this preparatory state is maximized, reactions should be particularly rapid. If desynchronization of the alpha rhythm into a fast, low voltage pattern is assumed to be a physiological index of alertness, one may predict that fastest RTs will occur at those instances in which the cortex is activated by an external stimulus. Thus, the WS may be viewed as effective to the extent that it produces an alpha block which persists until the RS is presented. If a particular WI exceeds the duration of the alpha block and the RS is presented at a point in which the alpha rhythm has resumed, one may predict that RT would be slow. This explanation, of course, would account for the fact that long WIs are associated with relatively slow reactions. Furthermore, since it has been shown that alpha blocks are shorter in defectives than normals (Baumeister, Spain, & Ellis, 1963; Berkson, Hermelin, & O'Connor, 1961), one may speculate that lack of electroencephalogram (EEG) responsivity is in some ways related to slowness in the RT situation. Moreover, there are data showing that reaction signals presented during the period of an alpha block are associated with faster RTs than reaction stimuli presented during a period of no block (Fedio, Mirsky, Smith & Parry, 1961; Lansing, Schwarts, & Lindsley, 1959). In view of these considerations, it is not unreasonable to ask whether retarded subjects whose alpha waves are particularly responsive to visual stimulation would also be rapid responders.

A recent study by Baumeister and Hawkins (1967) sought to answer this question. A group of 20 cultural familial retardates was tested on RT tasks involving regular and irregular modes of WI presentation and a wide range of WIs. Reactivity of the alpha rhythms to photic stimulation was measured in terms of alpha block latency, alpha block durations, and habituation. None of these measures correlated significantly with RT or with an index of preparatory set derived from RT differences between regular and irregular procedures. However, it should be added that the brighter *S*s in this sample displayed a significantly greater number of blocks and faster average responses. On the other hand, various alpha parameters did not seem to be related to the overall RT ability of the subject. In this study, RT and EEG tracings were not obtained at the same time. Consequently, the conclusions were based on average RTs in relation to average alpha blocks. A trial-by-trial analysis in which EEG recordings are made while the S is actually performing on the RT task might have revealed considerably different results.

A study of this nature was reported by Hermelin and Venables (1964). Visual warning stimuli of different durations were employed together with a wide WI range. Reaction times to a sound stimulus were obtained during periods of alpha or during alpha blocks. Reactions were found to be equally fast under the two EEG conditions, an outcome inconsistent with the results of Lansing et al. (1959) and Fedio et al. (1961). Whether the discrepancy is related to subject differences (normals vs retardates) or whether procedural factors must be implicated is not clear. In any case, the relationships of the various EEG parameters, intelligence, and RT would appear to be a research area of considerable promise.

G. Reinforcement Effects

Although the RT task appears to be particularly well suited for the investigation of the effects of motivation variables on performance, only a few studies with retardates have been undertaken in this regard. However, with the increased emphasis currently directed toward motivational constructs in relation to mental retardation (e.g., Cromwell, 1963; Zigler, 1966), it would not be surprising to see more studies involving timing behavior. Time-dependent measures seem to be most sensitive to motivational influences. In particular, recent reports suggest that RT may have a good deal to recommend it as a dependent measure in the study of incentive effects.

Wolfensberger (1960) has observed that verbal or social reinforcements might be more effective with retardates than material rewards. This speculation arose from Wolfensberger's finding that groups of retardates given reward or punishment, whether concrete or symbolic, did not differ from a control group in their RTs. Although his suggestion has considerable commonsense appeal, certain procedural factors in Wolfensberger's study probably worked to produce no differences between the various incentive conditions. He rewarded his Ss on a fixed ratio schedule—one out of every five trials—regardless of whether the S was slow or fast on that particular trial. Thus, speed was irrelevant to reward. Subsequent studies that have made reward contingent upon performance have shown that certain incentive conditions may exert considerable influence on RT.

Not surprisingly, money is one incentive that has a substantial effect on RT of retardates. Hawkins[1] paid his Ss a penny for each response which was faster than a preset value derived from an earlier unreinforced performance. He found rapid and marked improvement in RT under these reward conditions.

More extensive studies utilizing self-competitive procedures were undertaken by Baumeister and Ward (1967). In one experiment four different reward conditions were compared: money plus bell, praise, bell, and no objective reward. All of the incentives produced an improvement in RT. In fact, virtually every subject in the three reward conditions showed improvement as contrasted with a control period of no objective reward. The money-plus-bell and praise conditions were about equally efficacious. In spite of the great significance sometimes attributed to social reinforcers these retardates worked as hard, if not harder, for money than for a "good" from the experimenters. Although feedback cues were held constant for the bell and the money-plus-bell groups, the effect of the rewards resulted from something more than augmented feedback.

A second experiment conducted by Baumeister and Ward (1967) demonstrated clearly that RT performance can be influenced over a substantial period of time by rewards. The curves in Fig. 5 summarize the RT performance of two groups of retardates over 13 days and under different reward conditions. Group 2 was rewarded with pennies on Days 4 − 6, with nickels on Days 7 − 9, and with nothing on Days 10 − 13. Subjects in Group 1 were given no reward until Day 10, at which time they received two pennies for fast responses. It can readily be seen that Group 2 showed a steady improvement over days until the point where they were no longer rewarded, whereupon their performance deteriorated abruptly and markedly. The reaction speeds of Ss in Group 1, on the other hand, remained very constant across days. However, they improved considerably when reinforced for fast responses. These studies reveal very clearly that RT is governed by some of the same principles as other forms of instrumental behavior.

The consequences of reprimand, reward, and rest were compared by Holden (1966). The various treatment conditions were imposed midway through a simple RT task. The Ss in the reward group were told that if they did well from that point on, they would receive a dollar when they were finished. Both reward and reprimand were found to facilitate RT, with reward slightly more effective. This, of course, is a different reward contingency from that employed by Baumeister and Ward, who

---

[1]Personal communication from W. F. Hawkins, Department of Psychology, Central Michigan University.

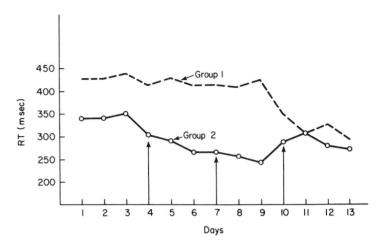

Fig. 5.   Mean RTs for Groups 1 and 2 plotted over 13 days. The arrows indicate the points at which reinforcement conditions were changed. For the first 3 days neither group received rewards. On Days 4, 5, and 6, Ss in Group 2 were given two pennies for each response faster than the median RT of the previous day. From Days 7–9 these Ss were rewarded with a nickel for each fast response. On Day 10 and thereafter the reinforcement conditions were reversed with Group 1 now receiving two pennies for fast reactions and Group 2 receiving nothing (from Baumeister & Ward, 1967).

reinforced specific responses. Holden concluded that part of the slowness in retardates is attributable to a depressed level of motivation, which, in turn, reflected in lowered prestimulus arousal. Although he did not have the data to conclusively demonstrate this type of interaction, it certainly does appear that retardates are capable of reacting much more rapidly than they actually do in many situations.

H.   Reaction Time Variability

A number of studies in which the RTs of retardates and normals have been compared have shown that the latter, as a group, are less variable. Tests of significance within these comparisons indicate that variances are larger for the retardates. Usually, there is a tendency to ignore this finding, except insofar as it poses problems for other statistical comparisons of the groups. However, it is possible that the concept of variability, particularly in relation to mental retardation, has as much theoretical relevance as measures of level of performance.

Whenever repeated measures are obtained on single individuals two fundamental sources of variability can be identified. One is attributable to *between-subject* differences. When reference is made to group differences in variability, it is usually in relation to these individual differences. A second source of variability, and one that may have considerable implications for a theoretical conceptualization of mental retardation, derives from trial-to-trial changes in the individual's performance. One may best regard this as *within-subject* variability. That this fluctuation in performance has implications for behavior theory is attested to by Hull's (1952) use of the concepts of *behavioral oscillation and reaction potential*. Nevertheless, we tend to overlook this variability by pooling scores over a number of trials to produce a single measure for a particular treatment condition. Most commonly these trial-to-trial deviations are regarded as random fluctuations and, consequently, as sources of unreliability in the task. However, some recent studies have indicated that not only are these within-subject fluctuations in RT scores reliable, but also they may have some implications for the understanding of behavioral retardation.

Berkson and Baumeister (1967), in examining variability in RTs of bright and dull *Ss*, found substantial correlations between medians and standard deviations. Retardates were not only slower, but variability between and within individuals was greater. This suggests that, in comparing normals and defectives on measures of speed, it is probably advisable to employ measures of dispersion as well as central tendency, since both are affected. Baumeister and Kellas (1968b) confirmed this finding, with respect to reaction time and extended it somewhat by showing that retardates also displayed more within-subject variability on a short-term memory task.

A thorough comparative investigation of variability was recently conducted in another study by Baumeister and Kellas (1968a). Six normals and six retardates were run for 900 trials on a simple serial RT task. The retardates were selected as typical responders from a large number of subnormal subjects who had been tested in previous RT studies. Frequency polygons on the last 600 trials for normals and retardates are presented in Fig. 6.

Some salient features of these curves should be emphasized. First, it is clear that the retardates displayed considerably more spread and skewness in their scores. Standard deviations computed on each individual showed no overlap between groups; that is, all normals had smaller standard deviations than any of the retardates. Another point that should be stressed is that the modal performance of the groups are more similar than mean performances.

It is obvious that the retardates were not able to maintain consistent performance. In fact, lack of consistency may be more descriptive of their inferiority than a particularly depressed level of performance.

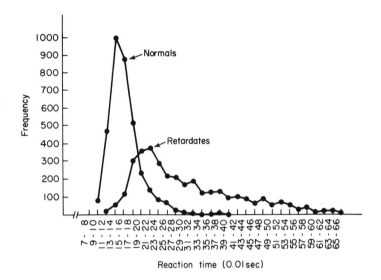

Reaction time (0.01 sec)

Fig. 6. Reaction time distributions of normals and retardates. These frequency polygons represent 600 responses for each of six normal and six retarded subjects.

Note that on some trials the retardates had a limit of speed that approached the best performance of the normals. The fundamental problem for the retardate was in staying near his optimal level of
performance.

One may speculate that the distributions shown in Fig. 6 represent
two qualitatively distinct populations of responses. Both groups of
subjects seem to be characterized by similar underlying RT distributions
of low variability. Furthermore, in each case, but particularly among the
retardates, there appears to be another highly variable response distribution that is particularly sensitive to attentional and motivational
fluctuations. These responses are not truly "reaction time" in that they
do not measure accurately S's ability to make a rapid response. Such
responses are products of psychological processes that are only minimally reflected in the "true" RT. This second distribution is assumed to
have greater prominence among the responses of the retarded. It is in
regard to this distribution that the conditions inherent in mental retardates manifest themselves most directly. In many situations the retarded individual may display an absolute level of performance that is
quite adequate in relation to the normal, but he is much less efficient in
consistently maintaining his optimal level.

The source of the greater intraindividual variability of the less intelligent subjects is not made clear by these studies. However, certain manipulations, such as increasing the intensity of the RS or adding an incentive, serve to reduce RT variability in the retardates. It must be assumed that changing internal characteristics of the individual are responsible for intrasubject variability and that such factors are more transient in the retardate. These subjects are unable to meet environmentally imposed demands in a consistent manner. One explanation may be that the defectives cannot sustain a preparatory set or state of alertness over many trials. It is clear that they "block" (defined as RTs 3.0 standard deviations beyond the individual's lower limit of performance) much more frequently than normals. Perhaps such blocks represent failures of attention. In any case, the identification of the correlates of these inhibitory factors may represent a significant increment to our understanding of behavioral pathology.

III. CONCLUSIONS AND SUMMARY

The literature does not reveal an overwhelming interest in the study of RT processes of mentally retarded individuals. Nevertheless, the research reviewed here is sufficient to bring focus on some areas that have implications for understanding the general behavioral inadequacies associated with mental retardation. In most ways, the RT adjustment of mental retardates to changing environmental exigencies is essentially the same as that of normal individuals. In fact, one may doubt that substantially unique sets of laws are required to account for timing behaviors at different levels of intelligence. On the other hand, this research suggests some subtle interactions in which normals and retardates are differentially affected by certain experimental manipulations.

Enough evidence has been presented to lead to the tentative conclusion that retardates suffer a prestimulus arousal deficiency or attentional lag. Although there are some marked individual differences, as a group, they appear to function under an impoverished perparatory set, both with respect to initial levels and in maintaining the set over lengthy warning intervals. The hypothetical concept of "homeostatic restraint," implying a tendency to organismic inertia, may be relevant to these considerations. In reviewing the literature on the autonomic nervous system functioning of mental defectives, Karrer (1966) arrived at the conclusion that many of these individuals display an abnormal resistance to change in certain autonomic states. Put less elegantly, it takes more to get them moving.

The source of this arousal deficiency has not been made entirely clear by the available research studies, but certain factors have been found to influence performance in such a way as to implicate an arousal mechanism. Obviously, some fundamental property of neural organization either has not been acquired or has been disrupted. This suggestion, of course, is not completely new, having been made by Lindsley (1957) and later by Berkson (1961) in relation to the functions of the ascending reticular activating system. The RT studies represent about the only systematic effort to experimentally explore this lack of responsiveness in the retarded and to relate it to observable stimulus events.

Another aspect of retarded RT performance that merits further experimentation concerns the process of information acquisition and utilization. Although studies specifically designed to examine intelligence group differences in choice RT situations have failed to turn up many meaningful interactions, it appears that retardates do not respond to the temporal aspects of the task in the same manner as normals. In particular, their subjective "expectancies" of certain stimulus events obviously differ from those of brighter individuals. The choice RT research reported so far has generally not employed the most effective procedures for probing information-processing factors. We need to explore more fully the independent and interactive roles of stimulus uncertainty, response uncertainty, temporal uncertainty, and stimulus-response compatibility.

The literature review presented in this article reflects the sensitivity and reliability of RT as a dependent measure. More importantly, the existing research indicates that RT is an especially effective method for probing a variety of complex relationships between mentally defective individuals and their environment.

The work outlined in this article provides support, in varying degrees, for the following conclusions:

(1) Intelligence is functionally related to RT within the defective population. Within the MA and CA ranges sampled, the function is best described as approximately linear.

(2) The intensity of the RS influences the retardates' response speed more than that of normals. As the intensity of the signal to respond increases, RT correspondingly decreases. However, at RS values near threshold, normals and retardates are similarly affected. The evidence for RT effects of WS intensity is not as conclusive. The only available research has employed warning and reaction signals within the same modality. As WS intensity is increased, there is a corresponding increase in reaction time. It is speculated that the WS serves as a part of the stimulus context against which the RS is perceived.

(3) Compound reaction stimuli appears to decrease RT in a manner similar to intensity. This effect may result from an increased state of arousal in the defective individual. Compounding of the WS has not been demonstrated to influence RT in this population.

(4) Response speed of normals and defectives are equally affected by RS's of increasing complexity. Response complexity, on the other hand, differentially affects intelligence groups. Retardates are relatively more disadvantaged by increasing response complexity than normals. The locus of the retardate deficit apparently involves both the motor and perceptual phases of the response.

(5) Temporal factors are related to the performance of mental defectives. Specifically, the uncertainty, length of the warning interval, psychological refractory period, and warning signal duration have all been implicated in varying degrees of importance.

(6) Attempts have been made to relate parameters of the alpha rhythm to RT of retardates. In contrast to research with normal individuals, no evidence has been found to indicate that any of the various EEG phenomena are directly related to RT. The origin of this discrepancy is unclear, and future research in this area is encouraged.

(7) Research concerning the effects of motivational variabies on retardate performance is meager. However, those studies which have been undertaken clearly indicate that certain incentive conditions exert considerable influence on speed. Reaction time is subject to some of the same contingencies as other forms of instrumental behavior.

(8) Finally, a number of studies have indicated the importance of within-subject variability for the understanding of behavioral retardation. It is suggested that greater variability may be a characteristic of the defective individual. The source of this variability is largely undetermined.

ACKNOWLEDGMENTS

Reproductions of Figures 3 and 5 published by permission of the editor of the *American Journal of Mental Deficiency*.

REFERENCES

Adams, J. A. Motor skills. *Annual Review of Psychology*, 1964, **15**, 181-202.
Baumeister, A. A. Time judgments by normals and retardates. Unpublished study, 1964.
Baumeister, A. A. Problems in comparative studies of mental retardates and normals. *American Journal of Mental Deficiency*, 1967, **71**, 869-875.
Baumeister, A. A., Dugas, J., & Erdberg, P. Effects of warning signal intensity, reaction signal intensity, preparatory interval, and temporal uncertainty on reaction times of mental defectives. *Psychological Record*, 1967, **17**, 503-507.

Baumeister, A. A. & Hawkins, W. F. Variations of the preparatory interval in relation to the reaction times of mental defectives. *American Journal of Mental Deficiency*, 1966, **70**, 689-694.

Baumeister, A. A., & Hawkins, W. F. Alpha responsiveness to photic stimulation in mental defectives. *American Journal of Mental Deficiency*, 1967, **71**, 783-786.

Baumeister, A. A., Hawkins, W. F., & Kellas G. The interactive effects of stimulus intensity and intelligence upon reaction time. *American Journal of Mental Deficiency*, 1965, **69**, 526-530. (a)

Baumeister, A. A., Hawkins, W. F., & Kellas, G. Reaction speed as a function of stimulus intensity in normals and retardates. *Perceptual and Motor Skills*, 1965, **20**, 649-652. (b)

Baumeister, A. A., Hawkins, W. F., & Koenigsknecht, R. Effects of variation in complexity of the warning signal upon reaction time. *American Journal of Mental Deficiency*, 1965, **69**, 860-864. (c)

Baumeister, A. A., & Kellas, G. Distributions of reaction times of retardates and normals. *American Journal of Mental Deficiency*, 1968, in press. (a)

Baumeister, A. A., & Kellas, G. Intrasubject response variability in relation to intelligence. *Journal of Abnormal Psychology*, 1968, in press. (b)

Baumeister, A. A., & Kellas, G. Refractoriness in the reaction times of normals and retardates as a function of response-stimulus interval. *Journal of Experimental Psychology*, 1967, **75**, 122-125.

Baumeister, A. A., Spain, C. J., & Ellis, N. R. A note on alpha block duration in normals and retardates. *American Journal of Mental Deficiency*, 1963, **67**, 723-725.

Baumeister, A. A., Urquhart, D., Beedle, R., & Smith, T. E. Reaction time of normals and retardates under different stimulus intensity changes. *American Journal of Mental Deficiency*, 1964, **69**, 126-130.

Baumeister, A. A., & Ward, L. C., III. Effects of rewards upon the reaction times of mental defectives. *American Journal of Mental Deficiency*, 1967, **71**, 801-805.

Bensberg, G. J., & Cantor, G. N. Reaction time in mental defectives with organic and familial etiology. *American Journal of Mental Deficiency*, 1957, **62**, 534-537.

Berkson, G. An analysis of reaction time in normal and mentally deficient young men. II. Variation of complexity in reaction time tasks. *Journal of Mental Deficiency Research*, 1960, **4**, 59-67. (a)

Berkson, G. An analysis of reaction times in normal and mentally deficient young men. III. Variation of stimulus and response complexity. *Journal of Mental Deficiency Research*, 1960, **4**, 69-77. (b)

Berkson, G. Responsiveness of the mentally deficient. *American Journal of Mental Deficiency*, 1961, **66**, 277-286.

Berkson, G., & Baumeister, A. A. Reaction time variability of mental defectives and normals. *American Journal of Mental Deficiency*, 1967, **72**, 262-266.

Berkson, G., Hermelin, B., & O'Connor, N. Physiological responses of normals and institutionalized mental defectives to repeated stimuli. *Journal of Mental Deficiency Research*, 1961, **5**, 30-39.

Bricker, P. D. Information measurement and reaction time. In H. Quastler (Ed.), *Information theory in psychology*. Glencoe, Ill.: Free Press, 1955. Pp. 350-359.

Cromwell, R. L. A social learning approach to mental retardation. In N. R. Ellis (Ed.), *Handbook of mental deficiency*. New York: McGraw-Hill, 1963. Pp. 41-91.

Dickerson, D. J. Effects of variations in warning interval duration on reaction time in normal and mentally defective subjects. *Journal of Abnormal and Social Psychology*, 1965, **1**, 392-396.

Dingman, H. F., & Silverstein, A. B. Intelligence, motor abilities, and reaction time in the mentally retarded. *Perceptual and Motor Skills*, 1964, **19**, 791-794.

Ellis, N. R., & Sloan, W. Relationship between intelligence and simple reaction time in mental defectives. *Perceptual and Motor Skills*, 1957, **7**, 65-67.

Fedio, P. M., Mirsky, A. F., Smith, W. J., & Parry, D. Reaction time and EEG activation in normal and schizophrenic subjects. *Electroencephalography and Clinical Neurophysiology*, 1961, **13**, 923-926.

Foley, P. J. The foreperiod and simple reaction time. *Canadian Journal of Psychology*, 1959, **13**, 20-22.

Foley, P. J., & Dewis, E. V. T. Pacing rate and ready signal in serial simple reaction time. *Canadian Journal of Psychology*, 1960, **14**, 7-12.

Greeson, J. M. The effects of stimulus complexity on the reaction times of mental retardates and normals. Unpublished Masters Thesis, University of Alabama, 1967.

Hawkins, W. F., & Baumeister, A. A. Effect of duration of warning signal on reaction times of mental defectives. *Perceptual and Motor Skills*, 1965, **21**, 179-182.

Hawkins, W. F., Baumeister, A. A., & Holland, J. M. Reaction time in retardates following variations in warning signal intensity and preparatory interval. *American Journal of Mental Deficiency*, 1965, **70**, 135-138. (a)

Hawkins, W. F., Baumeister, A. A., Koenigsknecht, R. A., & Kellas, G. Simple and disjunctive reaction times of normals and retardates. *American Journal of Mental Deficiency*, 1965, **69**, 536-540. (b)

Hermelin, B. Effects of variations in the warning signal on reaction times of severe subnormals. *Quarterly Journal of Experimental Psychology*, 1964, **16**, 241-249.

Hermelin, B., & Venables, P. H. Reaction time and alpha blocking in normal and severely subnormal subjects. *Journal of Experimental Psychology*, 1964, **67**, 365-372.

Holden, E. A., Jr. Reaction time during unimodal and trimodal stimulation in educable retardates. *Journal of Mental Deficiency Research*, 1965, **9**, 183-190.

Holden, E. A., Jr. The effects of rest, reprimand, and reward on simple reaction time in educable retardates. *American Journal of Mental Deficiency*, 1966, **71**, 427-432.

Hull, C. L. *A behavior system*. New Haven: Yale University Press, 1952.

Hyman, R. Stimulus information as a determinant of reaction time. *Journal of Experimental Psychology*, 1953, **45**, 188-196.

Karlin, L. Reaction time as a function of foreperiod duration and variability. *Journal of Experimental Psychology*, 1959, **58**, 185-191.

Karrer, R. Autonomic nervous system functions and behavior: A review of experimental studies with mental defectives. In N. R. Ellis (Ed.), *International review of research in mental retardation*. New York: Academic Press, 1966. Pp. 57-83.

Kellas, G. The effects of warning signal duration on the reaction times of mental defectives. Master's thesis, University of Alabama, 1967.

Klemmer, E. T. Time uncertainty in simple reaction time. *Journal of Experimental Psychology*, 1956, **51**, 179-184.

Lamb, J., & Kaufman, H. Information transmission with equally unlikely alternatives. *Perceptual and Motor Skills*, 1965, **21**, 255-259.

Lansing, R. W., Schwartz, E., & Lindsley, D. B. Reaction time and E.E.G. activation under alerted and non-alerted conditions. *Journal of Experimental Psychology*, 1959, **58**, 1-7.

Lindsley, D. B. Psychophysiology and motivation. In M. R. Jones (Ed.), *Nebraska symposium on motivation*. Lincoln, Nebr.: University of Nebraska Press, 1957. Pp. 44-105.

McNutt, T. H., & Melvin, K. B. Time estimation in normal and retarded subjects. *American Journal of Mental Deficiency*, 1968, in press.

Ordahl, L. E., & Ordahl, G. Qualitative Differences between levels of intelligence in feebleminded children. *Journal of Psycho-Asthenics Monograph Supplement*, 1915, **1**, 3-50.

Pascal, G. R. The effect of a disturbing noise on the reaction time of mental defectives. *American Journal of Mental Deficiency*, 1953, **57**, 691-699.

Poulton, E. C. Perceptual anticipation and reaction time. *Quarterly Journal of Experimental Psychology*, 1950, **2**, 99-112.

Scott, W. S. Reaction time in young intellectual deviates. *Archives of Psychology*, New York, 1940, No. 256, **36**, Pp. 1-64.

Sutton, S., Hakerem, G., Zubin, J., & Portnoy, M. The effect of shift of sensory modality on serial reaction-time: A comparison of schizophrenic and normals. *American Journal of Psychology*, 1961, **74**, 224-232.

Teichner, W. H. Recent studies in simple reaction time. *Psychological Bulletin*, 1954, **51**, 128-149.

Terrell, C., & Ellis, N. R. Reaction time in normal and defective subjects following varied warning conditions. *Journal of Abnormal and Social Psychology*, 1964, **69**, 449-452.

Throne, F. M., Kasper, J. G., & Schulman, J. L. Performance time and brain damage ratings. *American Journal of Mental Deficiency*, 1964, **68**, 656-659.

Wolfensberger, W. Differential rewards as motivating factors in mental deficiency research. *American Journal of Mental Deficiency*, 1960, **64**, 902-906.

Zigler, E. Research on personality structure in the retardate. In N. R. Ellis (Ed.), *International review of research in mental retardation*. New York: Academic Press, 1966. Pp. 77-108.

Mental Retardation in India:
A Review of Care, Training, Research, and
Rehabilitation Programs

J. P. DAS

UTKAL UNIVERSITY, BHUBANESWAR, INDIA[1]

I. INTRODUCTION

A review of work in the area of mental retardation in India may be premature at the present time. The country gained independence in 1947, and since then has been struggling to provide elementary school education to the ever-increasing group of school-age children. Policy-makers in education naturally felt that the problem of educating the retarded child can be postponed. Besides education, even medical care of the retardate has not become popular. This might be attributed to the relatively underdeveloped state of pediatrics in this country. On the other hand, people have not demanded facilities for the re-tardate, which might have prompted more governmental interest in this field. The disinterest in the education and care of the retardate resulted not so much from indifference to the retardate's problems but rather from a preoccupation with problems of national reconstruction soon after independence such as land reforms and reorganization of

---

[1] *Present address*: Centre for the Study of Mental Retardation, University of Alberta, Edmonton, Canada.

state boundaries, which were relatively more vital than mental retardation. Gradually, as some of the basic demands of the country are being fulfilled (e.g., flood control, electric power, and industries), both the government and the people are becoming increasingly aware of the problem of retardation. Therefore, 10 years from now, a reviewer might have some impressive progress to report instead of promises of progress.

Besides the general factors which have been adverse to the progress of retardation work, there are some specific factors. Chief among these is the variety of languages and dialects used in the country. Any standard test of intelligence cannot be constructed for the whole of India. The test must be regional, and it often has to use the local dialect if it is to be intelligible to young children. In many communities, certain dialects are used in the family and for day-to-day communication, but the school books might be written in one of the 16 recognized regional languages. Adaptations of well-known international tests into the regional languages have been attempted but it is difficult to assume that all have a uniform standard.

Any study on deviation must require a knowledge of the base line. For instance, an early detection of retardation would need norms for physical and mental development. These norms have to be separately established for many of the linguistic groups which differ from each other in racial characteristics. Recently, surveys for establishing developmental norms in some regions are in progress under the sponsorship of an agency of the federal government, the National Council of Educational Research and Training (see Appendix for details). Cultural differences, too, play a part in the development of a fair nationwide test of intelligence. An intelligence test may measure the speed and accuracy of response and the persistence of the subject but in certain regions these requirements may conflict with cultural values. For instance, in southern India speed is considered a virtue but in parts of northern India, persistence and not speed is valued. However, these general impressions await substantiation by appropriate studies. Projects directed at collecting such developmental norms and response patterns are some of the prerequisites for good research on retardation.

In spite of the underdeveloped state of work on retardation some good schools have been established which can compare favorably with some of the better institutions in the United States. These schools are in highly industrialized cities such as Bombay and Ahmedabad. This perhaps reflects the urban attitude toward mental retardation. With the rapid growth of industrialization, and hence urbanization, an increasingly large community of professionals and educated businessmen now inhabit the big cities. In cities, the enlightened newly rich as well as the overanxious professional parents have become aware of the need to train and educate the backward child. Educated mothers also play a key role in this. Thus, urbanization and its discontent would stimulate public support for work in retardation.

The federal government through its agencies has begun to take an interest in this area. The National Council of Educational Research and Training has established a unit for special education. In this unit as also in its unit for psychological research, projects relating to retardation are likely to be undertaken (see Appendix). The All India Institute of Medical Sciences at Delhi and the Indian Council of Medical Research are favorable to sponsoring projects of retardation. Thus a beginning has been made, and the future for care and training of the mentally retarded in India appears to be bright.

II. THE TYPICAL INSTITUTION FOR THE MENTALLY RETARDED

Institutions for the training and care of the mentally retarded have grown out of the personal efforts of either a dedicated individual or of a philanthropic organization. Not infrequently, the primary donors for a certain institution have in their family someone mentally defective. This is also true of a majority of social workers who have taken a keen interest in the growth of a retardate institution. The need to give and receive love has played an important part in procuring the selfless service of female workers in a typical retardate institution. The workers are either on a nominal salary or hold honorary appointments. Incidentally, most institutions are headed by women in addition to having other women employees who occupy many important positions. Of the 18 institutions for the retardate on the author's list, where names of those in charge are given, 15 are headed by women. According to personal interviews most of these women find the work satisfying and often ennobling, although quite challenging—as Nehru once described it, "a labor of love."

A majority of the institutions depend primarily on donations from the public, but they also receive assistance from state and federal governments. The government funds are made available through the welfare departments. Part of the grant may consist of payment toward expenses for maintaining the retarded orphans and destitute children sent from institutions under the direct management of the state government. For major expansion programs such as new buildings and equipment the government is usually asked for funds. Also, high government officers are often included among the patrons of the better institutions in the country (in Madras, the state governor and the chief of police are patrons of an institution).

The institutions for the retarded in India have both residential and day pupils. Many of these institutions were started in order to provide a boarding house for the retarded person, and they gradually expanded their programs to include scholastic as well as vocational education. Almost all the institutions have been established after the country gained independence in 1947. Besides training the retarded, some of the institutions have as their expressed objective the counseling of parents of the retarded child. The staff includes teachers, psychologists, and physicians. Some of the institutions are staffed only by physicians and psychiatrists, as are most of the mental hospitals in India.

A. General Work Program

In a typical institution, the work program may include diagnostic services, parent counseling, scholastic education, extracurricular and recreational activities, clinics, teacher training, occupational training, and vocational rehabilitation.

1. DIAGNOSTIC SERVICES

Diagnostic services are available both in residential as well as in day schools. Apart from the retardate schools, such services are also provided by a few child-guidance clinics whose sole concern is not retardation. Psychologists routinely administer tests for intellectual ability to new entrants following a medical checkup by the physician who may be only a part-time employee of the institution. The intelligence tests administered to determine the IQ of the new entrant are not always standardized instruments for application in India; most of the time form boards of one sort or another and translations of the Stanford-Binet are used. However, gradually indigenous norms are being worked out for these as well as for some other tests such as the Draw-a-Man Test and the Progressive Matrices.

Knowledge of an entrant's IQ aids in classification for the purpose of education and training. Only the bright retarded is accepted in certain institutions which are a part of a teacher's college or a clinic of a medical center. The residential homes usually accept any retarded child, but not many would admit an adult retardate. The latter can be placed in a mental hospital. The preferred age range for admission to the retardate schools in 8 to 16 years. A few schools however accept younger children who are taught simple habits of cleanliness and self-help (dressing, eating, etc.).

2. School Curriculum

For purposes of school instruction the retarded pupils are divided into the conventional categories of the educable and the trainable. Those who have lower capacities than the trainables are given appropriate sensory training and practice in muscular coordination. In a few schools elaborate curricula for this nontrainable group have been prescribed. The curricula include, in one instance, nine kinds of training such as habit training, sense training, self-help, vocabulary training, obedience, training to carry out instructions, playing with toys, resting, and table manners.

The educable group necessarily receives higher scholastic training than the trainable group. But except for a very few schools, the teaching program is application oriented. Greater importance is given to the learning of crafts and skills such as weaving, spinning, repairing cane furniture, and manual training for making toys and mats.

Thus, the emphasis is on learning crafts which contribute toward one's own maintenance rather than on mastering spelling or arithmetic. Significantly most schools for retardates in India aim at a second-grade education of their pupils, while in the United States it is usually a sixth-grade education. The pressure to give the retarded child a regular scholastic training comes from parents, who in the United States, might look down upon a purely vocational training. Such reactions are expected of urbanized and professional parents, a fact which may explain why the few retardate schools in India which give intensive school education are located in Bombay and Delhi.

In some schools, a definite syllabus is followed to teach the high-grade retardate. The teachers are usually trained persons having at least a B.A. degree and either a regular teaching diploma or a diploma for teaching retarded children. The latter are being increasingly employed. A few schools are staffed with teachers trained in the United Kingdom or the United States who have graduate degrees in special education. Considering the underdeveloped state of the mental retardation movement in India, the standard of teachers for the retardate institutions is very high indeed.

3. Physical Training and Recreational Programs

Training and recreational programs for the retarded exist in all institutions. The retarded pupils take part in outdoor and indoor games, go on field trips, and are enrolled in music and dance classes. The objectives here are the development of muscular coordination, learning how to adjust to both cooperative and competitive situations, and the development of a sense of rhythm.

4. TEACHER'S TRAINING

Teacher's training courses are given by three institutions. The training programs are meant for those who are otherwise qualified for school teaching but intend to specialize in teaching the retarded. In the oldest of such institutions (in Bombay), a 1-year diploma course is given to those who have at least a B.A. degree in psychology or education. The course consists of theoretical lectures and supervised practical work. The topics covered in lectures are the different branches of psychology (general, child, psychosomatics, etc.), mental testing, techniques of special education, counseling, and therapy. An institute for the retarded in Ahmedabad is planning a two-year course, with special emphasis on an internship in a retardate home or school. The diploma for special education awarded by the private institutions is usually recognized by the state governments. However, as the number of such institutions increase, some accrediting agency such as the local university nearest to the institution might have to approve the diplomas.

It now remains to briefly describe the occupational training given to the inmates of a retardate home and some details of clinical practice with regard to the retardates.

5. OCCUPATIONAL TRAINING

The program for occupational training in some institutions may only consist of including a craft class in the daily routine of teaching the three R's, while in a few others sheltered workshops are provided for the retardate whose manufactured articles may be sold and the retarded worker reimbursed for his labor. Many day schools can only afford to have a craft class because of lack of funds and facilities.

The vocational training classes must necessarily divide their trainable students according to age groups; the older age group is engaged in more strenuous jobs than the younger. Some of the articles manufactured by the retarded worker are hospital bandages, napkins and tablecloths, office stationery such as notebooks, cash vouchers, and folders, and for general use, doormats, wastepaper baskets, textile bags, embroidered dresses, and toys. These are usually sold on contract to local organizations.

6. CLINIC

Clinic and aftercare services are a part of many institutions in India. Both residential and day patients are treated in the clinics. In addition, counseling services for the parents of the retardate are also provided. Psychotherapy is given for children having anxiety, aggressiveness, stammering, and general excitability. Depending on the orientation of the therapist, the treatment might be psychoanalytical or ecletic in approach. Children in need of therapy are treated individually or in groups. Social maladjustments and defects owing to organic causes such as unstable temperament as a result of epilepsy might be suitable for group therapy, whereas tics and mannerisms might require individual therapy sessions. In addition to psychotherapy, many institutions provide some kind of speech and physiotherapy.

Counseling parents is entrusted to psychologists as well as to social workers. The latter provide scientific information on mental retardation to the parents, and they discuss in general the problems faced in bringing up the retarded child. Regular parent-teacher meetings feature in the programs of a few schools. Also, parents are encouraged to watch their children while interacting socially with other children during games. These opportunities aim at giving the parents confidence in handling their defective child as well as convincing them of the necessity of continuing the child's attendance in a special school.

III. RESEARCH

The research relating to mental retardation in India falls into three categories: (a) survey and rehabilitation projects, (b) psychological and educational research, and (c) medical research. The quantity or quality of research under any of these categories is not high. This is not without explanation, however. The majority of the retardate homes and schools are in an initial stage of development, and the administrators must concern themselves with the relatively pressing problems of providing adequate space and staff, and raising funds for their continued existence. An academic environment would be conducive to research, but universities and research institutes in the country have taken little interest in mental retardation.

A. Survey and Rehabilitation

The results of two surveys to determine the incidence of mental retardation in the junior school classes are now available. City-wide surveys in some areas are reported to be in progress; thus, in the next 5 years, the incidence of retardation in about a half-dozen cities would be known.

The two completed surveys were from the cities of Mysore in the south, and Calcutta in the east. The Mysore survey (Kuppuswamy, 1962) selected 10% of the students enrolled in the second-, third-, and fourth-year classes of all middle schools corresponding to the fifth, sixth, and seventh grades in the United States. The students thus selected for testing were 991 (589 boys and 402 girls). A verbal test of intelligence in the native language of the children was first administered to the students in groups of 15 or less. On the basis of these test scores, those who were under the fifth percentile were singled out for intensive testing. They numbered 56, with a mean age of 11.5 years.

The screening test of verbal intelligence is a timed test, requiring a maximum answering time of 18 minutes and a preliminary instruction period of 15 minutes. Its split-half reliability is reported to be 0.997, validity coefficient 0.612. For the purpose of intensive testing, two additional tests were administered to only those subjects whose scores were below the fifth percentile. These were the Seguin form board, and the Knox cube. If a subject had an IQ above 80, he was dropped from the potential sample for identifying retardates. The remaining subjects were administered two further tests, Raven's Progressive Matrices, and a regional adaptation of the Binet. Ultimately, 22 cases were identified: 8 between IQs of 70 and 79, 10 between 50 and 69, and 4 between 25 and 49. The percentage of true retardates in the school population surveyed was 1.68 (14 out of 834 subjects).

Before accepting the results of the survey, an important question regarding the validity of screening for potential retardation with the help of the verbal intelligence test should be raised. The test was employed to select the bottom 5% of the scorers who should be tested further for signs of mental deficiency. However, an examination of the scores of the 36 subjects for whom both the verbal intelligence scores and consolidated IQ scores (based on four further tests) are available (Appendix Table III, Kuppuswamy, 1962) reveals very little correspondence between the two. For instance, 20 subjects had scored more than 40 points in the screening test, and 16 subjects below 40 points. Of these 20 subjects, 10 had IQ scores above 80 (classified as normal in the survey report) and 10 below 80. The chi-square obtained from a fourfold table of screening test scores and IQ points was less than one. Thus one cannot rule out the possibility that cases of mental retardation might have been found among subjects who were screened as normal because they scored above the fifth percentile in the verbal intelligence test.

Some of the other findings of the survey were suggestive and might stimulate further work. A relatively higher incidence of retardation among the lower socioeconomic classes (based on 54 cases of retardates) was noticed. A breakdown of the retardates into their caste groups did not reveal any relationship between caste hierarchy and incidence of retardation. However, the highest caste, Brahmins, contributed 40% of the retardates to the small group of retardates detected by the survey. This was so, as the author of the survey report appropriately points out, because the number of Brahmin children in the school population was comparatively high. If cultural deprivation were a determinant of the incidence of retardation, an inverse relationship between higher caste and retardation would be expected.

The Calcutta survey (Ganguly, 1962) was much more modest in its objectives. The population of dull backward children was defined as those students of the sixth form (corresponding to the fifth grade in the United States) who had failed in three of their courses in the class examination. Although the author of the survey listed 75 schools under the criterion of "schools in and around Calcutta," he was given facilities for testing in only 39 of them. This, in itself, severely limits the scope and validity of the survey. A total of 251 students was located in those schools which met the criterion. They were given Raven's Progressive Matrices for children and also administered a test for simple reaction time. The reaction time would presumably demonstrate the characteristic slowness in the backward children, whereas the intelligence test was to reveal their poor ability for comprehension. But how did one locate the mentally retarded child with these two kinds of test scores neither of which has corresponding IQ norms for this sample? Perhaps the author's primary concern was to detect the dull backward children rather than the mentally retarded. Nevertheless, he concluded that of 70 dull-backward per one thousand children, "only 8 had been found to be mentally defective."

This figure is estimated as follows: Scores for the Progressive Matrices of each subject and his/her reaction time were combined. A frequency distribution of these combined scores was drawn up. The cumulative percent frequencies were obtained. The lowest class interval of this distribution had a .82% frequency, which upon rounding out, was eight per thousand. Perhaps, this figure is too low when compared to that given in the Mysore survey (1.68 per hundred in spite of the fact that the latter had children from higher classes (sixth and seventh grades besides the fifth grades).

But the difference in defining the two retarded samples precludes any comparison between them. It would appear that the Calcutta survey could have been improved with proper sampling and the assignment of IQ scores to subject's performance. (The author did not have sufficient grant money.)

The only major survey-cum-rehabilitation project exists in Nagpur and is financed by U. S. Public Health Service. This 5-year project (now in its second year) has for its objective a total rehabilitation of the retarded person, taking into account his psychological adjustment, vocational training, and placement.

As a first step, a sample survey of the population of Nagpur is being carried out. Information gathered from the survey will indicate the incidence of retardation, the total number of retarded persons who can be rehabilitated, and the potential and cultural loss to the community by failure to provide rehabilitation services. An important by-product would be the development of reliable tools and techniques for gathering the above data.

A prevocational occupational training class has already been started with 50 retarded persons as part of a demonstration program. This will form a part of a compact rehabilitation scheme providing sheltered workshops and residential facilities, which would make it easier to train the retarded under the project. Vocational training will be either a specific job training or will assist the retarded worker to adjust to general work demands. Ultimately, a placement program has to be started. Previous attempts at training and placement show that the retarded worker, under supervision, can earn the wages of a semiskilled laborer. The average age of the trainees at present is 17 years, and their mean IQ is 54. The project appears to be making good progress.

B. Psychological and Educational Research

Very little research has been done in India at the time of this report. Most institutions for the retardate, as previously indicated, did not have reports of completed research.

The author has largely depended on personal communication from the heads of different institutions and fellow psychologists in order to prepare this review of research. It is possible therefore that someone who might have a mimeographed paper on retardation was not contacted. But the probability of that being a major contribution to mental retardation research in India is small, since it would be relatively unknown to the community of research workers in this area.

Very few papers on mental retardation really qualify for serious consideration here. Some of these might be disqualified on the basis that although their authors are Indians, the research was conducted abroad. Thus, the author had the choice of either eliminating this section altogether, avoiding the presentation of research at a rudimentary stage, or of presenting a brief summary and then including a section on the possibility of worthwhile research which could take advantage of the peculiarities of Indian social and educational systems. The latter would include factors such as caste, cultural deprivation, and the multilingualism of the country. The author selected the more constructive choice.

Deb (1962) has a doctoral dissertation on the sensory discrimination of temperature, height, weight, and area. The study, based on 156 adolescent imbeciles, determined discrimination limens for the retarded sample. The hypotheses tested might not appear to be covering any new ground. Nevertheless, there was a need to demonstrate their validity with an Indian sample. The findings support the hypotheses that (a) sensorimotor discriminations of retardates are consistent enough to be measured, (b) the retardates' performance was poorer than that of normal CA controls, and (3) a direct relationship exists between sensory achievement and the level of mental retardation of the individual. A stable relationship between stimulus values and stimulus thresholds was found among the retardate subjects, as is usually obtained with normal subjects.

In another study, Deb (1964) compared the immediate memory span of 10 brain-injured and 10 familial imbeciles. Subjects were required to name familiar fruits whose models were exposed to them for 1 minute. Prior to this test, all subjects had been sufficiently trained to name the fruits when their models were presented. The memory span was four for both groups, revealing no difference between them.

The remaining four studies to be reviewed were on the verbal behavior of the retardates. Two of these studies were carried out in India, and two in the United States at the George Peabody College for Teachers.

J. P. Das (1961a), in an experiment on verbal conditioning, wanted to observe how efficiently the three grades of retardates use verbal concepts. The task involved an acquisition phase, followed by a reversal, which was itself followed by a reacquisition phase in a typical Pavlovian paradigm to test "lability" of nervous processes. It was assumed that the low-grade defective would be less labile because of a relatively inert verbal system. Three tasks of progressively difficult levels were given to the three retarded samples. Task I required that subject press a switch whenever a light appeared at the center of the display panel, Task II to do the same only when a pattern of lights (yellow, violet, red, and green) appeared on the right side of the panel, and not on the left side. In Task III, subject had to discriminate between two slightly different patterns of light appearing at the same place in the display panel, pressing the switch for one, and refraining from pressing for the other. For each task, subject had to learn the correct response through a conditioning model (cf. O'Connor & Das, 1959).

The results showed differences in performance of the three grades of defectives for the relatively difficult Tasks II and III. Reversals were not consistently faster or slower than acquisition. However, from previous studies on imbeciles (O'Connor & Hermelin, 1959) it was expected that reversal would be faster than acquisition in the imbecile group, but would become increasingly slower as one moved upward through morons to normal levels of intelligence. Because well-established verbal mediators at the acquisition phase would resist reversals, normals would have greater difficulty in reversal, requiring more trials to reverse than they needed for acquisition.

J. P. Das (1961), in another study, compared the body-sway suggestibility of the three grades of defectives. The body-sway test suggestions are verbal and use only a few words such as "you are falling forward," repetitively. A hypothesis has been advanced that these verbal stimuli act as conditioned stimuli and partly determine the amount of sway response; hence, the stronger these verbal habits, the greater the extent of sway. In regard to the three grades of defectives, one might suppose that the morons would have stronger verbal habits than the imbeciles, as the latter's verbal habits would be stronger than those of the idiots. A standard body-sway test was administered. The results show the idiots to be untestable since they failed to comprehend the meaning of the suggestions. They were either distracted by the suggestions, or took them literally, bending forward in real earnest. No difference between the average forward sway of morons and imbeciles was obtained. This may imply that for a simple suggestion, such as "you are falling forward," the verbal habit strengths of the two groups did not differ.

Of the two Peabody College studies, one concerned the effect of evaluative verbal labels (good, bad) on discrimination learning (J. P. Das, 1965), and the other on probability learning (G. Das, 1965).

In the discrimination learning test, 30 normal school children (CA = 17) and 30 institutionalized retardates (CA = 22, IQ = 50) were tested for acquisition and reversal of the key-pressing response. The apparatus was a simple display panel with two windows and two corresponding keys. The task for the subjects was to depress a key below the lighted window on forced trials, but when both windows were lighted (choice trial) to choose one of the two keys. Lighting of one of the windows was concurrent with the experimenter's saying "good," while the lighting of the other window was accompanied by "bad." Learning trials continued until, on choice trials, the "good" key was pressed. In the reversal phase which followed the learning phase in an uninterrupted sequence, the same procedure was used except that the previously "good" light was associated with "bad" and vice versa. Latencies of response to "good" and "bad" lights on forced trials and to "good" light on choice trials were obtained for each subject who had thus six scores (acquisition: "good," "bad"; reversal: "good," "bad"; choice trials: latencies for acquisition and reversal).

Did the verbal labels "good" and "bad" modify the subject's reaction time? The results show that mean latency for good trials was shorter than for bad trials. A further analysis revealed that this effect was clearly seen only with the retarded subjects but not with the normals. The retarded subjects appear to be more sensitive than normals to evaluative verbal labels. The other findings confirm well-known trends: The latencies for retardates were longer than those for normals, and the choice latencies were longer than forced latencies. Significantly, there was no difference between the two groups in learning trials, but the normals were faster to reverse than the retardates.

The other Peabody work was a dissertation of G. Das (1965). The study compared the retardates with normals in two-choice probability learning. The task was to predict the appearance of one of two alternative stimuli (box and cross) whose event probabilities were .80:.20; subjects were administered 200 trials a day on three consecutive days. The retardates had a mean IQ of 50, the normals were CA-matched college undergraduates. Prediction scores for blocks of 20 trials were computed separately for each day and reveal an interesting pattern. On the first day, the normals maximize (overshoot the event probability of .80) after 100 trials, gradually return to the event probability level on the second day, where they remain on the third day. In reverse, the retardates are below the event probability level on the first day, approach it on the second, and maximize on the third day. Appropriate analysis of variance confirmed that this disparate trend was significant. These results certainly do not show that the retardates maximize while the normals stabilize at the input probability level as reported in earlier studies. The maximization behavior of the retardates and normals turns out to be quite complex when one increases the trials to 600.

Another purpose of this experiment was to study the probability of prediction when the frequent event was presented consecutively for six to seven trials in a run. During runs, the probability of the prediction of the frequent event progressively decreases, producing a negative recency effect. The effect is at variance with any reinforcement theory in addition to being a deviation from probability matching behavior. One does not find this effect in children below the fourth grade (Bogartz, 1965). In older subjects, who show decreased anticipation of an event in a run, this response tendency is extinguished upon multiple experience of runs (J. P. Das & Nanda, 1963). Whether in such cases the biases resulting in negative recency effect are stamped out or those producing its opposite, the positive recency effect, are trained in is quite another matter (see Anderson, 1964). Our concern should be to verify whether the retardates in the present experiment do not show the negative recency effect, and whether our normals show this effect as anticipated from previous research. The results confirm these anticipations. Comparison of runs scores of normals and retardates for the second and third day (retardates had not completed learning on first day) can be made here. The performance on the middle trial blocks (trials 100 − 120) for the normals showed the negative recency effect for both days, while no such consistent tendency was noticed for the retardates. Mean percentage predictions for the frequent event on seven consecutive trials were 76, 92, 98, 92, 82, 76, and 70 for normals on the second day; corresponding scores for the retardates were 76, 71, 86, 71, 81, 74, and 81. Similar tendencies were seen in the third day's predictions.

In the field of *medical research*, the results of some surveys on the incidence of phenylketonuria (PKU) are now available. Krupanidhi and Punekar (1963) claim to have reported the first case of PKU in India. Another pioneer in the study of PKU is Centerwall, an American, whose completed report is published in the U.S. Public Health Reports. Punekar's paper (1966) presented at an international conference on inborn errors in metabolism summarized the recent work in this field, and might be reviewed here in brief. According to this report, only five cases of PKU have been detected so far in India. This contrasts strongly with a projected annual addition of 946 PKU babies to India's population. Punekar gives this figure from an estimation in the United States of 1 PKU among every 10,000 newborn babies. Obviously, then, no comprehensive surveys for the incidence of PKU have been undertaken. Centerwall limited his survey to the 26 retardate institutions and schools existing in India in 1965, and arrived at an estimate of .25%. Punekar (1966) screened 165 defective children between 1959 and 1961, of whom only 1 PKU was detected. His 1962 − 66 screening detected no case of PKU. As reported by Punekar, the combined estimate of incidence is .15%. Clearly, these figures cannot provide any basis for comparing the incidence of PKU in India with that in other countries. While a sample survey of 10.75 million newborn every year in India is an impossibility, confining one's survey to institutions for the retardate limits the generalizability of the findings. Because of the scarcity of such institutions (about 30 to serve 500 million Indians), a retarded individual might have very little chance of being admitted into one of these. In addition to retardate institutions, a survey should at least include screening the children's hospitals and children's wards in the general hospitals of the country. Sometimes, a clinician in a hurry might be tempted to base his figures of incidence on the patients he examines routinely from day to day in his clinic. This is incidental sampling and is a fallacious method according to statisticians.

The results of another medical survey are available which appear to be based on incidental sampling. Gupta and Virmani (1966) analyzed 200 cases of retardates who were referred to a neurological outpatient clinic. They could not establish any etiological diagnosis in 111 cases. In the rest of the sample, 52% had a history of cerebral seizures, and 18% showed hyperkinesia of varying degrees. Cerebral palsy was found in 25% of the cases. One mongol with trisomy at 21 was detected in the sample.

Several projects on the effects of nutritional deficiency are underway in the laboratory of Rajalaxmi who is studying both rats and children (Baroda University, 1967). Rats fed with protein-deficient diet showed poor performance in Hebb-William's maze and visual discrimination tasks. These animals also revealed impaired glutamic acid metabolism in the brain. In an attempt to test the effect of protein deficiency over three generations, she bred low and high protein-fed rats and compared them for biochemical and psychological reactions. The results suggest that postweaning nutrition is relatively more important for the offspring than the dietary history of the mother. Rajalaxmi now has supportive data from humans. Poor and rich mothers apparently have equally healthy babies for the first 6 months before weaning. Often the poor mother is superior in lactation to the rich, whose babies have to be put on supplementary diet even after the first 2 months. But differences between babies of the two classes are seen at the postweaning stage. Is it merely due to nutritional deficiency? Some longitudinal data on the psychological performance of poor and rich children suggest a slight superiority of the rich in intelligence test scores, but no noticeable retardation in other tests (discrimination, reversal, etc.). However, firm conclusions can only be drawn when the studies are published in detail.

IV. PROGRAMS FOR FUTURE RESEARCH PECULIAR TO INDIA

Mental retardation research should be promising in India if its uniqueness in social, cultural, and nutritional aspects is explored. Although most of its people are poor, not all are culturally deprived perhaps because of their belonging to high castes. The country has a variety of instructional systems: indigenous and Western. Does one system stimulate the child's curiosity and encourage him to be more vigilant than another? In some parts of India, consanguineous marriages are common. Does this result in an increase in certain types of mental defect? Finally, India provides varied nutritional habits which cut across socioeconomic strata: Some rich communities may have a poor protein diet, while a poor community may eat beef because it costs next to nothing. It should be interesting to explore the relationship between degree of intellectual growth and nutrition. Some specific suggestions for research arising from the above discussion are presented in this section.

A. Caste and Cultural Deprivation

In the United States cultural deprivation is predominantly noticeable in low socioeconomic groups, since contributing factors such as lack of stimulating environment and verbal intercourse with adults are a direct result of poverty. In India, birth in a high caste may compensate for poverty. For instance, the highest caste, Brahmin, has been traditionally engaged in intellectual pursuits though, in general, the traditional families among the Brahmins are poor. But in the past, people of this caste usually achieved eminence as scholars and interpreters of the ancient philosophical work. Even today, the number of senior professors, scientists, and judges who are Brahmins is grossly out of proportion with the ratio of Brahmins to non-Brahmins. The Brahmins, nevertheless, used to be poorer than many lower caste groups such as the business caste (*vaishya*). Maternity and child-care services are the same for all castes in a majority of villages; these services were almost absent 15 years ago. In food habits, the non-Brahmins were superior to Brahmins if protein intake is the criterion, since many Brahmins were vegetarians. In spite of similar environmental conditions for all castes outside one's family, the Brahmin achieved a superior intellectual status.

A specific study in this area could help to determine in what way economic level and caste together might be related to cultural deprivation. A beginning project might divide the experimental samples into four groups: the rich and high caste, the rich and low caste, the poor and high caste, and the poor and low caste. One of the primary objectives would be to demonstrate differences in intelligence and verbal ability for the four groups. If the general impressions were correct, then even the poor-high caste would be more resistant to cultural deprivation than the rich-low caste. A typical analysis of variance design will show whether the effects of caste and economic status separately contribute to the intellectual retardation of the subjects, and whether their interaction is significant. The latter effect is of special interest. If the high castes indeed resist cultural deprivation, subsequent projects should be directed at identifying the relevant factors which might be embedded in child rearing practices or early environmental experience. The knowledge thus obtained will help in planning intervention studies in poor, low caste communities whose financial resources will remain severely limited for many years to come.

The present author has started work on a beginning project as indicated above. Elementary school children between the ages of 8 and 10 years who fit into the four groups are administered the Progressive Matrices and the Peabody Picture Vocabulary Test (PPVT). They are also given the Stroop color−word conflict test (Jensen, 1965) which measures cognitive ability. The latter has recently been found to reflect the mental age of the subject: The first graders show little interference while naming the colors of color−names written in incongruous color (red written in green ink, green in red ink, etc.; S is to say the color in which the word is written). The interference becomes prominent in grades two and three, but decreases at the college level (Schiller, 1966). The test might show that the culturally deprived third grader has as little interference as the first graders.

As a subsequent stage of the project the firmly identified cases of culturally deprived will be given further tests of attention and verbal satiation (J. P. Das, 1964). Both tests relate to the cognitive aspects of the subject. The author has previously found that children cannot be easily satiated, the same expectation about retardates can therefore be extrapolated. Will the culturally deprived child be less vigilant than his normal counterpart? Or will the stimuli in the vigilance test remain relatively new for him thus evoking an orienting response?

If the latter happens to be the case, it will raise the number of false alarms, while the number of true signals detected might remain the same for the normal and the deprived subjects.

For those unfamiliar with the vigilance test, it is conducted as follows. In a typical auditory task, odd and even numbers between one and nine are randomly presented, usually played back from magnetic tape. When three successive odd numbers appear, it is a signal, and the subject is to detect it. Four kinds of scores in a standard half-hour test are recorded: detection of true signals (correct response), omission of true signals (error), false alarms or the detection of false signals (error), and nondetection of false signals (correct response).

B. Exposure to Boredom and Cognitive Function

Most cities of India have two kinds of elementary schools, Westernized schools managed by Christian missionaries (mostly British) where the medium of instruction is in English, and municipality schools where the teachers are from the local people and the medium of instruction is in the regional language. Recently, there has been a proliferation of government-sponsored public schools of high standard where the medium of instruction is in English, and the programs are similar to the

Westernized schools. Students in the missionary schools pay substantially high tuition and have a variety of curricular and extracurricular activities. The teachers are well trained (some have degrees from Oxford University, Cambridge University, and London University) and highly motivated. They teach bright and alert students. In contrast, the municipal schools are overcrowded because of free elementary education; increment in student enrollment far outstrips, in proportion, the increment in teaching staff. In the lower classes of the school, rote learning is emphasized. The student may repeat a word or a part of the multiplication table several times after the teacher, and perhaps have exposure to boredom unlike his counterparts in the missionary or public schools who are not subjected to such a tedious learning procedure. This contrast is readily noticeable in classes for the younger children (8 or 9 years).

Does early exposure to boredom contribute to a lowering of intellectual ability? It can do this by reducing the curiosity of the subject, and, consequently, making the student generally inattentive to verbal material. Perhaps the harmful effects of prolonged exposure to boredom in a scholastic milieu cannot be eliminated unless the young student is put under a preplanned corrective regimen.

The first phase of research, however, should examine whether a sample of children having considerable exposure to repetitive and passive school environment shows retardation in vigilance and accelerated satiation for verbal material. Previous research (J. P. Das, 1966) has indicated that the slow satiater is relatively superior in verbal conditioning to the fast satiater. Thus all three tests, vigilance, satiation, and verbal conditioning should be given to selected samples from the two kinds of school systems. If the author's guess about the effects of boredom is valid, the results will undoubtedly show a compelling need for the reform of elementary school education in India.

C. Surveys

(1) Sophisticated surveys regarding the acceptability of the retarded persons in rural versus urban communities have not been undertaken. It might appear to experts in developed countries that in largely agricultural and rural communities, the mentally retarded person is so well accepted that institutions for the retarded is not a pressing need. This might not be completely true. A number of retardates who are enrolled in the few overcrowded institutions might come from the families of farmers and, where communication is possible, from remote rural areas. A sociopsychological survey could determine the attitude of rural versus urban people toward the acceptance of the retarded individual

in the community when opportunity for admission into an institution is held to be the same for both samples. If the retarded person is gainfully employed in the rural areas, information on the nature of his vocation should be gathered. This would assist in rehabilitating the institutionalized urban retardate.

(2) Another survey of the relationship between dietary habits and incidence of subnormality can be profitably undertaken in India. There are many religious and caste groups who subsist on an eggless vegetarian diet. Some sects of vegetarians even avoid onion and garlic. The southern Indian Brahmins are vegetarians, who thrive on a very low protein diet. The main meal in a middle class home may consist of white polished rice, watery buttermilk, and very little vegetables, but extremely hot chillies. Yet many great scientists and lawyers come from this group. These may be exceptions. A proper survey should first show if the majority of people in this community are intellectually backward as might be predicted by nutritionists. On the other hand, if the community is found to be even on par (if not superior to) with nonvegetarian communities of the same geographic region, it will require careful reinterpretation of the relationship of intelligence to nutritional habits.

The research projects outlined above are related to cultural deprivation in one way or another and therefore directly bear upon the conditions which produce mild to moderate levels of retardation. With appropriate support from state and federal governments, such projects can not only determine the nature and extent of intellectual retardation, but also help in planning interventional studies to arrest and remove its causative factors. However, even if adequate funds were forthcoming, the ultimate success of the projects will depend on well-trained and highly motivated social scientists. This will require either a substantial rise in the standard of university instruction in the social sciences or special training centers for teaching the potential social scientist techniques for research, and, more importantly, methods of enforcing ethical standards in social research. The latter has assumed great importance now in India when literally hundreds of field investigators are collecting "data" for a large variety of social research projects.

APPENDIX

A Note on the National Council of Educational Research and Training

The future of research in mental retardation is likely to be determined by the programs of the National Council of Educational Research and Training (NCERT). It not only conducts research and trains teachers but also awards grants for psychological and educational research. Information given here includes a brief description of the organization and its projects which might be expanded to benefit mental retardation research.

The National Council of Educational Research and Training is an autonomous body established by the Ministry of Education, Government of India, in September, 1961 for the promotion of educational research and development in this country. It has five teachers colleges at Delhi, Bhubàneswar, Bhopal, Ajmer, and Mysore. These colleges are chiefly for the training of teachers for secondary schools and are affiliated with the universities in the area concerned. One of the main agencies for achieving the aims of NCERT is the National Institute of Education in Delhi.

The National Council of Educational Research and Training is engaged in developing a curriculum for schools (both primary and secondary) in all subjects, in publishing textbooks, and in producing audiovisual aids, laboratory equipment, etc. Its research is in the various areas of education, but it is largely concerned with applied problems. There is a Director and a Joint Director, who administer the Council and the National Institute of Education. A Faculty Committee and a Standing Research Committee advise the Board of Educational Studies on matters of policy concerning training, research, and other developmental activities to be pursued by the Council and its departments. The Board of Educational Studies reports to the governing body, which is presided over by the Union Minister of Education, who is president of the Council. Among members of the Council are all education ministers at the state level.

The National Institute of Education, an agency of the NCERT, has 12 departments, of which the Department of Psychological Foundations and special educational unit can develop projects relating to mental retardation.

The Department of Psychological Foundations was established in 1963 and works in the areas of child and adolescent psychology, learning, group dynamics, motivation, guidance, tests, and measurements. In addition to its own projects, it has undertaken others in cooperation with the U.S. State Department of Health, Education, and Welfare (HEW), which has sponsored nine projects of importance to education in which NCERT is cooperating; of these, three are with the Department of Psychological Foundations. These projects are on (a) the achievement motive in high school boys, (b) scholastic aptitude tests in Hindi, and (c) identification of talent in elementary and secondary schools. The Foundations' own projects, which would be of interest to mental retardation, is the Developmental Norms Project. Gesell's developmental scale, after suitable modifications, is being used to study the development of children between 2.5 and 5.5 years. Samples from seven centers scattered over India are included in this survey. Another project concerns the adaptation of programmed instruction for teaching science at the secondary school level. Because of the enormous problem of finding well-trained teachers, especially for the elementary schools, introduction of programmed instruction should be seriously considered. It may also help to fight cultural deprivation by providing a stimulating school program.

A Special Education Unit has been recently established. It is concerned with the education of the mentally retarded, the blind, the deaf, and the crippled children. This unit is expected to start some projects in the near future.

Thus, the Department of Psychological Foundations and the Special Education Unit are potential agencies for undertaking federally sponsored research in retardation. It is also possible that they will support research programs in this area initiated by individual researchers outside the organization.

REFERENCES

Anderson, N. H. An evaluation of stimulus sampling theory: Comments on Professor Estes' paper. In A. W. Melton (Ed.), *Categories of human learning*. New York: Academic Press, 1964. Pp. 129-144.

Baroda University: Annual Report (1966-1967) of Departments of Biochemistry & Foods & Nutrition, Baroda, India (mimeographed).

Bogartz, R. S. Sequential dependencies in children's probability learning. *Journal of Experimental Psychology*, 1965, **70**, 365-370.

Das, G. A comparison between retardates and normals in two-choice probability learning. Specialist in Education dissertation, George Peabody College for Teachers, 1965.

Das, J. P. Acquisition and extinction of verbal conditioned responses in mental defectives. *Psychologia*, 1961, **4**, 209-213. (a)

Das, J. P. Body-sway suggestibility in mental deficients. *International Journal of Clinical and Experimental Hypnosis*, 1961, **9**, 13-15. (b)

Das, J. P. Hypnosis, verbal satiation vigilance and personality factors: A correlational study. *Journal of Abnormal and Social Psychology*, 1964, **68**, 72-78.

Das, J. P. Discrimination learning in retardates and normals with the use of evaluative verbal cues. *Journal of Mental Deficiency Research*, 1965, **9**, 31-38.

Das, J. P. Relation between semantic satiation and verbal conditioning. *British Journal of Psychology*, *1966*, **57**, 87-91.

Das, J. P., & Nanda, P. C. Mediated transfer of attitudes. *Journal of Abnormal and Social Psychology*, 1963, **66**, 12-16.

Deb, S. An experimental investigation into some sensory discrimination of a group of severely mentally retarded adolescents. Doctoral dissertation, University of Calcutta, 1962.

Deb, S. Immediate memory-span: Brain injured and familial imbeciles. *Indian Journal of Psychology*, 1964, **39**, 91-94.

Ganguly, D. A limited survey for determining the rate of percolation of dull-backward children of secondary level of education in and around Calcutta. Report (type script) submitted to Ministry of Education, Government of India, 1962.

Gupta, P. C., & Virmani, V. Analysis of 200 cases of mental retardation. Paper presented to the XVI Annual Conference of Neurology Society of India, Bangalore, December, 1966.

Jensen, A. R. Scoring the Stroop Test. *Acta Psychologica*, 1965, **24**, 398-408.

Krupanidhi, I., & Punekar, B. D. A study of the incidence of phenylketonuria in India. *Indian Journal of Medical Research*, 1963, **51**, 1-7.

Kuppuswamy, B. A survey of mental retardation among children enrolled in middle schools of Mysore City. Available in mimeo from the author at India International Center, New Delhi, 1962.

O'Connor, N., & Das, J. P. Lability in schizophrenia. *British Journal of Psychology*, 1959, **50**, 334-337.

O'Connor, N., & Hermelin, B. Discrimination and reversal learning in imbeciles. *Journal of Abnormal and Social Psychology*, 1959, **59**, 409-413.

Punekar, B. A study of phenylketonuria in India. Paper presented to the International Conference on Inborn Errors of Metabolism, Dubrovnik, Yugoslavia, May 29 – June 3, 1966.

Schiller, P. H. Developmental study of color-word inference. *Journal of Experimental Psychology*, 1966, **72**, 105-108.

Educational Research in Mental Retardation

SAMUEL L. GUSKIN AND HOWARD H. SPICKER

INDIANA UNIVERSITY, BLOOMINGTON, INDIANA

I. INTRODUCTION

This review of educational research in mental retardation limits itself primarily to work reported between 1960 and 1967. Earlier work has been well covered in excellent reviews by Kirk (1964) and Quay (1963). Other valuable reviews of related literature have appeared by Blackman and Heintz (1966), Charney (1963), Dunn and Capobianco (1959), Heber (1963), and McCarthy and Scheerenberger (1966).

A.   Educational Research versus Learning Research

This review will not attempt to cover basic learning studies. Without attempting to ignore the large areas of overlap, there remain several characteristics which distinguish educational research from research on the psychology of learning. Whereas most learning research is carried out in a controlled laboratory setting, most educational research is carried out in a relatively uncontrolled natural school environment. Whereas most learning research attempts to answer relatively general questions about the learning process, most educational research poses questions about specific procedures to be employed in specific settings with specific subjects. And, finally, whereas most learning research involves no more than a couple of hours of each subject's time, educational research often involves hours of subject time weekly over a period of months. It is often assumed that basic research, in this case "learning" research, is more significant because it is likely to have implications for more situations. Yet, the specific complexities of many educational problems demand applied research to deal with the specific combinations of factors operating in the situation.

One of the reasons educators find little of applicability in learning theory and learning research is that learning theory presents merely a general format or language for dealing with the stuff or content of learning rather than a set of rules relating the various aspects of the content. If one wants to know how to teach arithmetic, learning theory suggests that he follow the appropriate response with immediate reinforcement, that the learning steps should be small, that the drive level of the student should be above a minimal level. It does not tell one in what sequence to put specific tasks, what learning will generalize to what, or which materials the student will be able to cope with at what stage.

Educational research also includes areas other than applied learning research. Studies of achievement motivation, peer acceptance, teacher—pupil relationships, and modifications in the social organization of the school also qualify as educational research. In fact, all studies concerned with schooling are included in this category. However, the authors do not include all studies using students as subjects since almost all psychological research employs that most available set of subjects, the student population.

B. Schooling and Mental Retardation

Before going on to discuss research on specific administrative arrangements for educating the retarded, specific academic learning deficits of the retarded, and specific techniques for teaching academic subjects, it would be well to raise the general question of the relevance and appropriateness of schooling for the retarded. Most of the known educable mentally retarded are identified upon referral for failure in school and labeled retarded upon "failure" on a test, the initial aim of which was to predict school failures. Thus, the requirement of schooling is intimately related both historically and currently to the very notion of higher levels of mental retardation and its measurement.

Dexter (1964) has argued that many of the educable mentally retarded would not be labeled "retarded" at all if we did not have compulsory universal schooling in our society and if we did not value academic achievement. That is, the presence of these persons would not constitute a social problem, and the individuals would not be identifiable as deviant. Dexter goes on to argue that their adjustment would likely be superior since society's current definition of them as retarded leads to further deviant behavior which fulfills others' expectations of incompetence. That is, we see ourselves as others see us, and we behave in accord with our own and others' "image" of us. The evidence for what might be termed "role determined deviant behavior," i.e., inadequate or unacceptable behavior determined by social definition of subnormality rather than by limited ability, will be discussed in greater detail in later sections.

It is clear that if society did not demand academic schooling and its results (e.g., ability to read, write, and add) there would be little need to identify the educable retarded or to provide special educational services for him. Since it is also clear that our society *does* demand both schooling and certain school-related competencies, then the educable retarded will be discriminable from others (in both school performance and on predictors of school performance), and he will require training in competencies required for survival and optimum adjustment in our society. The question remaining is: What sort of educational arrangements, teaching methods, and content should be provided for these individuals and should these provisions differ from those available for brighter children? Educational research in mental retardation has provided some useful clues for answering this question. Studies have attempted to evaluate the effectiveness of a variety of educational techniques with retarded children of all ages and levels of intellect.

II. THE PRESCHOOL PERIOD

One of the major trends in the education of mentally retarded children during the past decade has been the addition of preschool programs for such children. From the ground swell begun by Kirk's (1958) preschool study, the momentum for such programs has been greatly accelerated by the advent of Project Head Start in the summer of 1965. Although designed for economically deprived children, Head Start programs have the potential for providing preschool services to the majority of mildly retarded children since more than 90% of them have cultural-familial rather than organic etiologies (Dunn, 1963). It is not surprising, therefore, that such programs include as part of their objectives intellectual, language, and motor development as well as prevention of the progressive achievement decrements often exhibited by these children after school entrance.

How successful have preschool programs been in attaining these objectives? An attempt to answer this question will be made by reviewing some of the recent preschool investigations.

A. The Effects of Preschool Interventions on Intellectual Performance

Skeels, Updegraff, Wellman, and Williams (1938) were severely criticized for claiming to have increased the intelligence quotients of preschool orphanage children by providing them with a nursery school program. Critics pointed out that the gains were probably produced by such factors as violation of random sampling, Hawthorne effects, halo effects, statistical regression, and/or poor test reliability at the preschool level (McNemar, 1940).

So entrenched was the belief that IQ scores were unmodifiable, that no serious attempt to demonstrate otherwise was made until Kirk conducted his study in the middle 1950's. The intervention consisted of approximately two years of a general nursery school curriculum tailored to the mental level of the children and "clinical individual tutoring in areas of specific mental disabilities revealed by the diagnostic study for those children who needed such attention" (Kirk, 1958, p. 15). In addition, four of the children had been placed in foster homes during the study by the Division of Child Welfare because of neglect and inadequate environment. According to Kirk's (1958) report, the 28 community experimental children had made a mean gain of 11.2 points on the 1937 Stanford-Binet (72.5 − 83.7) and a mean gain of 8.7 points on the Kuhlmann (72.2 − 80.0). A contrast group of 26 community children who remained at home during the preschool period had lost .6 of a point on the Binet (75.8 − 75.2) and had gained 2.2 points on the Kuhlmann (72.4 – 74.6). The IQ gains made by the experimental group were significantly greater than those made by the contrast group on both measures. However, after the contrast group had attended special or regular classes for one year their mean IQs had increased to near that obtained by the experimental group (contrast – Binet: 82.7, Kuhlmann: 80.8; experimental – Binet: 84.2, Kuhlmann: 81.7).

A breakdown of these findings by case study analyses seemed to indicate that the major gains had been made by contrast children without organic etiologies who had come from adequate homes in which the parents were cooperative and interested in the welfare of their children. Children with organic involvements and those who had come from inadequate homes did not make significant IQ gains when school experiences had begun after CA 6. If one can have confidence in results based on a few case studies, the results suggest that community preschool education experiences, although desirable for all culturally deprived educable mentally retarded children, are essential only for those children who are also "psychosocially deprived," i.e., deprived of supportive family circumstances. It was further pointed out by Kirk that the four children who had been given a preschool experience and a change from an inadequate true home to an adequate foster home had made more progress than any other group. However, the small number of children constituting this group makes extremely tentative any recommendation based on this finding.

Also of interest are the somewhat different findings obtained by Kirk with an experimental and contrast institutional group of 15 and 12 children, respectively. After an average of 2 years of preschool, the experimental group had made a 12 point gain on the Binet (61.0 – 73.0) and an 11.2 point gain on the Kuhlmann (57.3 – 68.5). On the other hand, the institutional contrast group which received no formal preschool experiences had lost 7.2 points on the Binet (57.1 – 49.9) and 2.5 points on the Kuhlmann (54.3 – 51.8). The differences favoring the experimental group were significant. One year after both groups had completed a daily half-day special education program the mean IQ scores of the two groups had not changed significantly from the time of the last preschool testing. Thus, the significantly higher IQ scores of the experimental group were maintained one year after the preschool intervention.

One may speculate that institutionalized educable mental retardates (EMRs) gain much from preschool programs because they have the same type of inadequate history found in the psychosocially deprived child living in the community.

As a result of Kirk's investigation and the implementation of Project

Head Start in 1965, a large number of preschool studies with retarded and/or culturally disadvantaged children have been undertaken. A sample of these studies will be reviewed to indicate variations in research design, variations in intervention strategies, and the effect of these strategies on intellectual development.

One of the early replications of Kirk's study was conducted by Fouracre, Connor, and Goldberg (1962). The major goal of the investigation was to develop and evaluate a curriculum specifically designed for preschool educable mentally retarded children. The objectives of the curriculum included intellectual development, imagination and creative expression, social development, motor development, emotional development, manipulative development, and self-help. According to the investigators, "Language, in its broad sense, permeated every aspect of the curriculum and was considered as a cross-sectional emphasis" (Fouracre *et al.*, 1962, p. 64). Although the study was successful in producing a curriculum guide for preschool retarded children, the evaluation aspect of the study appears to have been far from successful. Originally designed to include experimental and at-home contrast groups, problems of case finding forced the investigators to eliminate the contrast groups and substitute 7-year-old EMR special class comparison groups.

Unfortunately, they made the mistake of seeking educable mentally retarded children primarily through medical referral agencies. Not only did this method of case finding restrict their sample size, but in addition, the children identified by this procedure tended to be a multiply handicapped, organically impaired, borderline trainable-educable group. This is evidenced by the fact that the 54 experimental subjects averaged more than two disabilities per child including defects of vision and hearing, mongolism, neurological impairments, convulsive disorders, and emotional disorders; in addition, the mean Binet IQ of the group was 59. It is not surprising that the 2-year preschool intervention produced no significant IQ changes (59-65) since similar negative results were obtained by Kirk with his organically impaired subgroup. It is also apparent that the curriculum developed by Fouracre *et al.*, if found to be effective, is more applicable for high trainable—low educable preschool mentally retarded children than for the more typical cultural-familial EMR children likely to be found in today's Head Start Programs.

Determined to overcome the case finding difficulties encountered by previous investigators, Blatt and Garfunkel (1967) used a unique method of case selection. The major criterion for selection ". . . was residence in a deprived area characterized by high delinquency rates, a considerable proportion of school dropouts and school failures, low-occupational status of parents, and run down homes" (p. 602). Furthermore, only those children without organic pathologies, whose parents consented to the child's project participation, whose residence was other than temporary in the area, and whose parents' education and occupation were usual for that area were included in the study. The initial mean Binet IQ for the 38 experimental 3-year-old children was 92.6 while that of the 21 nonexperimental children was 89.2. It was hypothesized that an enriched preschool curriculum coupled with a nonautomated "responsive environment" developed by Moore (1963) would significantly increase the intellectual level and social competence of the experimental children. It was also hypothesized that cultural deprivation would further depress the intellectual growth of the children remaining at home so that their intellectual functioning upon school entrance would be in the mentally retarded range. The results of the study indicated that neither hypothesis had been substantiated. Both the experimental groups and at-home group had made a mean gain of approximately 5 IQ points on the Binet. The investigators provided three alternative explanations for their negative findings: (a) ineffectiveness of the curriculum intervention, (b) failure of the instruments to adequately measure change, or (c) inability to maintain a true experimental design. However, as pointed out by the investigators, it is possible that no significant differences were obtained because the sample selected for the study was an atypical one. Whereas the turnover of children in urban, inner-city disadvantaged classrooms sometimes reaches 100% (Deutsch, 1965), subject attrition in the Blatt and Garfunkel study was negligible (one from an N of 60) over the 3-year period. The implication of this phenomenon is well stated by the investigators.

"Although the neighborhood was clearly lower lower class and the families in this neighborhood were classified as extremely impoverished and largely dependent on welfare assistance, the general nature of the community may have been such as to support the intellectual growth of the children. If this were true, one might expect that an experimental intervention, such as the one provided, would not produce any demonstrable results . . . The more deprived a child is, the more likely that he will respond to an intervention" (Blatt & Garfunkel, 1967, p. 607).

Not only did the atypical nature of their sample mitigate against significant IQ gains, but it also appears to have mitigated against any significant IQ losses. Evidence that such IQ losses do occur in a severely deprived population has been obtained in the Early Training Project of Gray and Klaus (1965). These investigators have demonstrated that severely deprived 3- and 4-year-old children testing in the dull-normal range of intelligence tend to drop in intelligence by the time they reach school age if they are not provided a preschool intervention program.

Since, according to Kirk, the psychosocially deprived children in his study appeared to be most in need of an enriched preschool program, Spicker, Hodges, and McCandless (1966) concentrated their research efforts on the development and evaluation of a specialized curriculum for that particular subgroup of disadvantaged children. This project included only 5-year-old children who scored between 50 and 85 on the 1960 Stanford-Binet L-M Intelligence Scale and came from families of the lowest socioeconomic class as determined by the Index of Status Characteristics (Warner, Meeker, & Eells, 1949). Children with organic pathologies, gross sensory impairments, and serious emotional problems were excluded from the study. The study was conducted in small communities (population 10,000 − 40,000) in southern Indiana, where the population meeting the criteria for inclusion in the project consisted primarily of Caucasian Appalachian children. In each of the 3 years of the study, children meeting the selection criteria were placed into either experimental preschool (EPS), kindergarten contrast (KC), or at-home contrast (AHC) groups, each with approximately 15 children. An experimental group received a structured curriculum designed to remedy specific diagnosed deficits of individual children in areas of language development, fine motor coordination, concept formation, and socialization. The diagnoses were made on the basis of standardized tests and direct observations by the teachers and project staff. A kindergarten contrast group received a traditional kindergarten curriculum. At-home contrast subjects remained home and received only the pre- and post-testing. During the first year of the study, two home contrast groups were employed, one in the community in which the experimental class was located and a second diffusion contrast group located in other communities. Since these two home contrast groups did not differ significantly at the end of the first year, only a single home contrast group was employed in the last 2 years of the study.

Subjects assigned to groups during the first 2 years of the study have now completed the first grade. Mean pretest, posttest, and end of first grade follow-up scores on the 1960 Stanford-Binet L-M are shown in Table I which combines the data from the first two sets of subjects.

Although all three groups had made reliable gains from pre- to posttesting, those made by the experimental group were significantly greater than those made by the kindergarten and at-home contrast groups. While the mean posttest IQ of the kindergarten group was relatively greater than that of the at-home contrast group, the differences were not statistically significant.

TABLE I

INDIANA PROJECT

STANFORD-BINET IQ MEANS FOR COMBINED

FIRST AND SECOND YEAR GROUPS

Group	N	Kindergarten pretest $\overline{X}$	Kindergarten posttest[a] $\overline{X}$	First grade follow-up[b] $\overline{X}$
Experimental preschool	28	75.8	92.4	91.3
Kindergarten contrast	29	74.1	83.2	82.9
At-home contrast	42	74.0	78.6	86.9

[a] EPS > KC; EPS > AHC; KC = AHC.
[b] EPS > KC; EPS = AHC; KC = AHC.

It should be noted that the at-home contrast group had made a significant mean IQ gain from pre- to posttesting rather than an IQ loss as obtained in the Early Training Project (Gray & Klaus, 1965) despite the fact that the children in the two studies were equally deprived. These seemingly paradoxical findings were probably the result of initial IQ differences of the children at the beginning of the projects. The use of an intelligence cutoff of 85 IQ in the Indiana Project as opposed to no intelligence criterion for inclusion in the Early Training Project undoubtedly produced some IQ gains owing to statistical regression in the former study and not in the latter.

After 1 year of regular first-grade experiences, the at-home contrast group made intellectual gains of sufficient magnitude to wash out the significant differences which had formerly existed between this group and the experimental group. These findings are consistent with the overall statistical findings reported by Kirk but are inconsistent with his case analyses which led him to conclude that psychosocially disadvantaged children, deprived of a preschool program, make only minimal intellectual gains following first-grade experiences. According to the Indiana Project, even psychosocially deprived children will make significant IQ gains once exposed to a formal school program. Whether these gains are the result of statistical regression and Hawthorne effects or are gains which will hold up in later grades after the initial novelty of school entrance wears off must await the results of further follow-up testing. However, it should be noted that the mean IQ of the contrast group which had received a traditional kindergarten program had not changed from the post to follow-up testing. Thus, by the end of the first grade, the kindergarten contrast group was still significantly below the experimental group in intelligence. It is possible that the novelty of school had worn off during kindergarten and that the first-grade teachers and/or the first-grade curriculum to which the kindergarten contrast children had been exposed were inadequate for producing continued intellectual gains.

Another study designed to provide data on the effectiveness of a preschool intervention on the intellectual development of culturally disadvantaged retarded children is the Perry Preschool Project directed by Weikart (1967a, 1967b, 1967c) at Ypsilanti, Michigan. The Perry Preschool Project differs from the Indiana Project in that it used Negro disadvantaged children and employed a multiple intervention approach. A cognitively oriented preschool curriculum for the children was provided during the mornings and a home intervention program with their mothers was provided during the afternoons. The emphasis of the morning school program was placed on structured group teaching, organized area teaching, and field trips.

The home-based afternoon program was used to involve the mother in the process of educating her child, to demonstrate teaching procedures, and to tutor the child. The home instruction was carried out by one of the teachers. Two types of afternoon activities were used: Cognitive skill training (including visual training, fine motor training, auditory training, premath training, and general science) and individual field trips for the child (and mother when possible).

A helpful summary of the entire treatment program is provided in Weikart, Kamii, and Radin (1964). It should be noted that later groups entering the project will be exposed to a somewhat different preschool program based on the theories set forth by Piaget (Weikart, 1967a).

Criteria for selection of the children included: (a) Residence within the attendance area of an all-Negro school, (b) date of birth, (c) cultural deprivation according to a formula which includes parents' education and occupation and degree of crowding in the home, and (c) IQs between 50 and 85 on the Stanford-Binet Intelligence Scale. Children who met these criteria were randomly assigned to an experimental and contrast group. New groups were constituted each year from 1962 through 1966 by the same selection procedure. These groups are referred to as Waves 1 through 5. Each of the five experimental groups received 2 years of nursery school prior to entering kindergarten. None of the contrast groups received nursery school treatment, but participated in the same testing program as the experimental children. In addition to the above five Waves, Wave 0 was selected in 1962 from among the available 4-year-olds. The Experimental half of Wave 0 received 1 year of special preschool before entering kindergarten while the remaining one-half remained at home as a contrast group. Each wave consisted of approximately 12 experimental and 12 contrast children.

Data on intelligence for Wave 0 children who have completed the second grade and are now in the third grade are shown in Table II. These experimental children had 1 year of nursery school and 1 year of kindergarten prior to completing grades one and two. As can be seen in Table II, there was no significant difference on Stanford-Binet Intelligence Test IQ scores between experimental and contrast children as they entered preschool, a significant difference at the end of preschool, and no significant differences at the end of kindergarten, grade one, or grade two. Weikart (1967a) reports that similar patterns hold for succeeding waves of children in the study.

TABLE II
THE PERRY PRESCHOOL PROJECT
STANFORD-BINET INTELLIGENCE SCALE
WAVE 0 DATA

Time of comparison	Experimental $N = 13$	Contrast $N = 15$	Differences
Fall, 1962—entrance into preschool	78.4	75.0	3.4
Spring, 1963—completion of 1 year of preschool	91.1	82.2	8.9[a]
Spring, 1964—completion of kindergarten	88.9	84.6	4.3
Spring, 1965—completion of first grade	90.7	84.6	6.1
Spring, 1966—completion of second grade	85.5	83.9	1.6

[a] Significant difference at the .01 level. All other comparisons were nonsignificant.

It should be noted that the preschool intervention program for the experimental group produced results quite similar to those of the Indiana study, a significant gain in intellectual level which was maintained until the end of the first grade. The relative drop in IQ at the end of second grade may be a function of greater emphasis on verbal content of the Stanford-Binet at the 7-year-old level. It is also possible that the curriculum or teaching strategies used at the second-grade level were less appropriate for these children. The major intellectual gains made by the contrast group were from pre- to posttesting with no intervening treatment. Following the posttesting, the intellectual level of the at-home contrast group remained relatively constant even after the children had been exposed to a traditional kindergarten program as their first school experience. This finding is contrary to that of the Indiana Project in which exposure to a traditional kindergarten as a first school experience for the kindergarten contrast group produced significant IQ gains. It is possible that these differences occurred because the traditional kindergarten class in the Indiana Project was specifically established as a contrast group for the study (in school systems without kindergartens), whereas the traditional kindergartens in the Perry Project were part of the regular school program rather than part of the study. Therefore, it is probable that a Hawthorne effect influenced the results for the Indiana kindergarten contrast group. In addition, increased test sophistication and statistical regression would occur largely during the kindergarten year for the Indiana Project and during the preschool year for the Weikart project, producing the difference in favor of the Indiana Project kindergarten group.

B. The Effects of Preschool Interventions on Language Development

One of the major cognitive deficits accounting for the below average general intellectual functioning of cultural-familial EMR children is in the area of language behavior. It is, therefore, not surprising that all preschool projects with these children have emphasized language development as a major curriculum goal. Although the need for improving the language functioning of retarded children is well recognized, specific intervention strategies and measurement tools for assessing language changes are only beginning to emerge. Some of these emerging language intervention strategies include verbal bombardment (Weikart, 1967c), pattern drill (Bereiter & Engelmann, 1966), diagnostic teaching (Spicker et al., 1966), and programmed instruction (Keislar & Stern, 1966). Techniques for assessing language changes have included the use of such standardized instruments as the Peabody Picture Vocabulary Test (PPVT) and the Illinois Test of Psycholinguistic Abilities (ITPA), as well as the application of various linguistic approaches for analyzing language samples of children.

Although the language approaches developed by Bereiter, and those being developed by Keislar and Stern appear to be quite promising, data as to their effectiveness are not yet available. Data are available on both the Indiana and Perry Projects.

During the first year of the Indiana Project, described earlier, Stearns (1966) developed 67 language lessons which were implemented by the experimental class teacher during the second half of the year. During the first half of the year, the teacher had been given no diagnostic information concerning the language strengths and weaknesses of the children so that a base-line rate of language change without a specific diagnostic treatment could be determined. The lessons were designed to develop the children's elaborative language and were built upon the children's level of language skill as diagnosed by the ITPA. In addition, they were programmed for complexity according to the development shown by the children, as judged by the teacher.

The effectiveness of Stearns' language lessons was assessed by administering the ITPA to the experimental group, to a kindergarten group receiving a traditional preschool curriculum, and to an out-of-school contrast group. The test was administered at the beginning of the school year, at midyear prior to the implementation of the language lessons, and at the end of the year.

During the treatment period (midyear to end of year) the mean total language age scores of all three groups had increased. The experimental group had gained 9.6 months, the KC group 6.3 months, and the AHC group 5.4 months. The differences were not statistically significant. However, analysis of the language gains of the three groups over the entire year indicated that the 19.4-month gain made by the EPS group was significantly greater than the 12.6- and 12.2-month gains made by the KC and AHC groups, respectively. The failure of the kindergarten contrast group, which was receiving a traditional middle-class-oriented preschool curriculum, to make significantly greater gains than the at-home contrast group raises the question as to the adequacy of the traditional preschool curriculum for meeting the language needs of disadvantaged retarded children.

The follow-up data collected at the end of first grade indicated that the rate of language development for all groups during first grade is less than one-half that made during the previous year. This seems to indicate that language development occurs more readily during the preschool years and/or implies a need for a continued oral language development program during the early school years.

In addition to the ITPA, the children in the Indiana Project were administered the PPVT to assess experiential or recognition vocabulary. The results from the combined first- and second-year groups shown in Table III indicate that although the scores of the three groups were not reliably different from one another on the pretest administered at the beginning of kindergarten, the PPVT scores of the experimental group were significantly greater than the scores of all contrast groups by the end of kindergarten.

The PPVT first-grade follow-up data are quite similar to the Binet IQ follow-up data. Again, the at-home contrast group made substantial IQ gains during first grade while the kindergarten contrast group remained relatively unchanged. The five-point regression by the EPS group coupled with the gains of AHC and KC groups washed out the significant differences which had existed among the groups at the end of the treatment period. The regression in particular further points out

TABLE III
INDIANA PROJECT
PPVT MEAN IQs FOR COMBINED
FIRST- AND SECOND-YEAR GROUPS

Group	N	Kindergarten pretest $\overline{X}$	Kindergarten posttest[a] $\overline{X}$	First grade follow-up[b] $\overline{X}$
Experimental preschool	28	65.1	94.7	89.5
Kindergarten contrast	29	66.4	79.1	82.1
At-home contrast	42	65.9	76.8	84.5

[a] EPS > KC; EPS > AHC; KC = AHC.
[b] EPS = KC = AHC.

the need for continued stress on language development in the elementary grades.

Both the ITPA and PPVT results seem to indicate that factors other than the language lessons were producing increased language performance of the experimental children over the year. At least two explanations seem feasible at this time. The first is the teacher variable. The experimental class teacher spent a considerable amount of time eliciting language from the children whenever the opportunity presented itself. On the other hand, the kindergarten class contrast teacher tended to "talk at" the children, giving them little opportunity to express themselves. The second factor which may account for the differences is the manner in which language was brought into every aspect of the experimental curriculum. Whereas snack time, lunch periods, art, music, physical education, structured field trips, and story telling were used as vehicles for eliciting and developing language in the experimental class, these activities were used as ends in themselves in the kindergarten contrast class. For example, in the experimental class a wooden puzzle of a farm scene would be used to teach the concepts of color, position, size, shape, quantity, texture, and function. In the kindergarten class, the same puzzle would be used only to teach the child to put the correct pieces together.

The approach used to develop language in the Perry Preschool Project, termed "verbal bombardment," is described by Weikart (1967a) as follows:

"In this method, the teacher maintains a steady stream of questions and comments to draw the child's attention to critical aspects of his environment. This *bombardment* does not necessarily demand answers from the child. It is continued when rewarding a child for a good performance, when disciplining him, and when presenting academic material. The complexity of the language is increased as the child's verbal ability develops" (p. 173).

Every activity in the curriculum was used as an opportunity to develop language by the "verbal bombardment" technique.

The Illinois Test of Psycholinguistic Abilities data are reported by Weikart *et al.* (1964) for Wave 0 at the completion of kindergarten and for Wave 1 at completion of 2 years of preschool. In neither wave was the difference in mean total language ages between the experimental and contrast groups statistically significant. Since no pretest or yearly ITPA tests were administered to the Perry groups, it is impossible to compare the language gain rates of the Perry Project children with those of the Indiana Project children.

Analysis of the Perry Project PPVT data indicate that the initial mean PPVT IQ score of 70.2 for the Wave 0 experimental group was relatively higher than the initial mean IQ of 65.1 obtained by the combined first- and second-year experimental groups from the Indiana Project. Although no definitive statement can be made about the comparability of the Perry and Indiana groups with regard to their initial total language abilities, it appears that the groups were at least comparable in initial experiential vocabulary. However, the mean Perry Project PPVT IQ of 74.7 for Wave 0 experimental children after 1 year of preschool plus 1 year of traditional kindergarten and of 84.6 for Wave 1 experimental children after 2 years of preschool as compared to a mean Indiana Project PPVT IQ of 94.7 after 1 year of experimental kindergarten appears to indicate that the language strategies used in the Indiana Project were more successful in increasing experiential or recognition vocabulary than were the strategies employed in the Perry Project.

C. The Effects of Preschool Interventions on Motor Skills

A survey of the literature indicates that the motor skills of educable mentally retarded children are significantly less well developed than those of middle class children of normal intelligence (Francis & Rarick, 1959; Malpass, 1960; Sloan, 1951).

One of the few attempts to study the effects of a sequential motor development program for EMR preschool children was made by Lillie (1966) as a substudy of the Indiana Project.

To determine the exact nature of the motor deficits exhibited by the children, it was first necessary for Lillie to determine the specific factors that make up motor proficiency. Guilford (1958) had successfully accomplished this by factor analyzing existing motor proficiency tests. His analysis revealed that motor skills consist of two major factors—fine and gross. The fine motor factor includes finger speed, arm steadiness, arm and hand precision, and hand and finger dexterity; included in the gross motor factor are static balance, dynamic precision, gross body coordination, and flexibility. Lillie applied these findings to the Lincoln-Oseretsky Motor Development Scale (Sloan, 1955) and classified each item as either fine or gross motor. The Scale was then used to divide his subjects into two instructional groups of approximately 8 children each on the basis of whether they scored high or low on the fine or gross motor portion of the Scale.

The treatment for the experimental group consisted of 65 diagnostic motor lessons. Although many of the kinds of activities found in good preschool and kindergarten classes were incorporated in the lessons, specific attention in lesson construction was given to the fine and gross motor proficiency levels of the children, the interest level of the lesson, and the sequential position of the motor experience (Lillie, 1967). The effectiveness of the motor development program was determined by comparing the motor proficiencies of the experimental group after treatment with contrast groups of similar children who had received either a traditional preschool curriculum or had remained at home.

The posttest results indicated that although all three groups had made significant gains in the *gross* motor items of the Lincoln-Oseretsky Motor Development Scale, the differences among the three groups were not statistically significant. This finding is especially interesting because the two school groups had been exposed to a regularly scheduled physical education period each day. It appears that the running, jumping, balancing, and climbing opportunities available in the home and neighborhood are sufficient for developing gross motor skills. However, the posttest results indicated that only the experimental and kindergarten contrast groups had made significant gains in *fine* motor development, with the experimental group significantly superior to the kindergarten contrast group. It, therefore, appears that although a traditional preschool curriculum is effective for improving the fine motor proficiency of cultural-familial EMR children, even more effective results can be obtained by using techniques similar to those developed by Lillie.

D.   The Effects of Preschool Interventions on Academic Achievement

The previous sections have dealt with the effects of intervention on intelligence, language, and fine motor skills. While the effects on these variables are certainly important in their own right, the major purpose of most intervention projects has been to offset the progressive achievement decrement so often noted for retarded disadvantaged children after school entrance.

Data on the academic achievement of retarded children who have been the subjects in experimental preschool intervention projects are just becoming available. Weikart (1967a) reports California Achievement Test mean percentile ranks and comparisons of the contrast and experimental children of Wave 0 through the completion of second grade (see Table IV). In evaluating these results it is important to remember that the mean IQs of the experimental and contrast children just prior to school entrance were 88.9 and 84.6, respectively. The difference between these mean IQs was not statistically significant, but the differences between achievement test mean percentiles were statistically significant as can be seen in Table IV. It appears that the experimental children were, at least, able to profit from the first 2 years of school, whereas the contrast children who had not been exposed to the special preschool did not appear to profit from school at all. As a matter of fact, the consistently low mean percentiles of the contrast group are indicative of minimal performance on these achievement tests. It is also apparent that the achievement of the experimental children in comparison with test norms indicates they also have trouble with traditional curricula and teaching strategies. It is important to remember that the experimental children in Wave 0 received only one year of preschool and a traditional kindergarten experience. Later waves of the Perry Project will have had 2 years of preschool before entering

TABLE IV
PERRY PRESCHOOL PROJECT
CALIFORNIA ACHIEVEMENT TEST
MEAN PERCENTILE RANKS
WAVE 0

	End of first grade		End of second grade	
	Experimental	Contrast[a]	Experimental	Contrast[a]
Reading	30	8	23	4
Arithmetic	10	3	17	5
Language skills	39	16	20	3
Total	22	5	18	3

[a]These differences between experimental and contrast mean percentile ranks were significant at the .05 level.

kindergarten. One may conjecture that the earlier and longer intervention programs for subsequent waves of children will produce more adequate school achievement than that demonstrated by this first experimental group.

III. EDUCATIONAL ARRANGEMENTS FOR THE SCHOOL AGE EDUCABLE MENTALLY RETARDED

A. Special Classes

The major educational arrangements in our society for children with IQs in the 50–80 range have been special classes in the public schools. Despite the prevalence of such classes, a large proportion of children with IQs in the 65–80 range are educated in regular classes (Dunn, 1963) and many of those with IQs in the 50-65 range are not provided for at all in the public schools (Dunn, 1963). The interest in, and expansion of, special class programs since 1945 has led to a number of studies attempting to determine the efficacy of such programs. Most of these investigations have been summarized and critically evaluated by Kirk (1964) and Quay (1963). In general, these studies suggest poorer academic achievement in special classes and poorer social adjustment in regular classes. However, these investigations are open to a number of serious methodological criticisms.

Inappropriate or biased sample selection has been one of the major inadequacies in previous attempts to compare special and regular classes. Educable mentally retarded children found in special classes have been compared with EMR children who remain in regular classes. This amounts to a comparison of poorer with better EMR students since assignment to special classes in any school system is not random within an IQ range, but is usually based on initial referral by teachers for poor classroom performance.

A study in Chicago by Mullen and Itkin (1961) handled the selection problems by matching educable mentally retarded (IQ 50–74) children in special classes individually on several variables with retarded children on waiting lists for special classes. The matching variables included: age, IQ, sex, community socioeconomic ratings, reading achievement, location of previous school attendance, foreign language spoken in the home, adjustment appraisal by teachers and research staff, and presence or absence of recorded brain injury. Pretests were given and then comparisons were made of gains in achievement and adjustment for 140 matched pairs who were retested after 1 year and 64 pairs retested after a 2-year interval. The only statistically significant achievement difference between regular and special class children was in first year arithmetic achievement gain, the regular class children showing superiority.

The regular class children also showed a higher gain in ratings of over-all classroom work over the 2-year period and a greater 2-year gain in reading (which only approached significance).

The authors explain that despite their care in matching, a selective factor seemed to bias their results in favor of the regular class group. The regular class group seemed to be brighter as measured by their Chicago Test of General Information and General Comprehension. They also noted that those on the waiting list who were placed during the course of the study seemed to be those who were more "in need of placement."

A critical examination of the matching procedures employed in their study suggests weaknesses which may have biased the results in either direction. First, it must be remembered that the authors matched on initial reading achievement and initial adjustment. "Initial" here means at the beginning of the study, not upon entrance to special class. Since most of these special class children had probably been in special classes for at least a year, these pretest scores may already reflect changes which have previously occurred. If the average child in a special class de-creased his rate of improvement in reading and arithmetic during the years prior to the study as a function of the special class curriculum and the average retarded child in a regular class maintained his rate of im-provement, then to match children at the beginning of this study a child *above* average in achievement for the special class would have to be matched with an educable child of average achievement in the regu-lar class. The opposite is also possible, i.e., a higher rate of progress for special class children during the years preceding the study. Both of these possible effects could be washed out by the matching procedure.

A second matching problem results from the error present in any individual's score. If we choose any person from the group whose score is atypical for the group on that occasion, we may expect that on a re-testing, his score would be less atypical, i.e., it would "regress" toward the group mean since part of the deviation from the mean is a result of measurement error. Since special class EMRs as a group have a lower mean IQ than regular class EMRs, matching individuals from the two groups would involve selecting more of those who deviate on the high end from the special class group and more of those who deviate on the low end from the regular class retarded group. On retesting, those from the special class group would be expected to score lower (closer to their own group mean) and those in the regular class group would be ex-pected to score higher. The results of a comparison of these matched pairs would then favor the regular class group. This is borne out by the data on the Chicago test.

A third result of matching is that the final comparison of matched groups cannot be generalized to the original unmatched populations; that is, these are atypical special class children and atypical regular class retarded children. Thus, if the matched sample includes mostly children in the 70−74 IQ range and the regular class group does somewhat better, the appropriate generalization might be that children with IQs of 70−74 do at least as well in regular as in special classes. Very few children with IQs of 50−59 are likely to be included in the matched-pair sample since they are rarely found in regular classes. Therefore, the study cannot tell us about how well this lower IQ group does.

If comparing unmatched regular and special class children is inappropriate because of referral of poorer academic performers for special class placement and comparing matched samples is inappropriate for the reasons just discussed, what method is appropriate?

A recent study in Illinois by Goldstein, Moss, and Jordan (1965) was carefully designed to overcome the methodological problems of previous studies. The Illinois study coped with this sampling problem by creating new special classes in areas not previously having them at the primary level, and then assigning children at random to either regular classes or the newly created special classes. Thus, in the Illinois study, the children in both regular and special classes have been drawn in an unbiased manner from the same population. The authors of the Illinois study were also concerned about the effect of prior failure experiences in regular classes on those assigned to special classes; that is, any inadequacy found in special class children might reflect reduced motivation and adjustment problems which were created by their prior educational history in regular classes. The Illinois study handled this by assigning children to special classes during the first grade, before a poor history could be created.

Goldstein et al. (1965) further criticized previous studies for failing to determine whether any special program was established in the special classes or whether specially trained or competent teachers taught these classes. The Illinois study employed a carefully constructed curriculum guide and specially trained and supervised teachers.

Finally, previous studies were criticized by Goldstein, Moss, and Jordan for failing to use evaluation instruments appropriate to the goals of the special class which may emphasize training in social and occupational skills at least as much as academic skills. In addition to the usual intelligence and achievement measures, the Illinois study employed measures of social knowledge, parental perception of their child, relationships with neighborhood peers, response to success and failure experiences, and productive thinking.

The specific selection and placement procedures were as follows: All

1938 children entering the first grade in 20 cooperating school districts were administered the Primary Mental Abilities (PMA) Test, primary battery, at the beginning of the school year. Those children scoring an IQ of 85 or below on the PMA were administered the Stanford-Binet scale (1937 Form L) and those who also obtained an IQ of 85 or below on the Binet were the subjects for the study. Fifty-seven of these children were selected at random from the larger group and assigned to one of four newly created special classes; the remaining 69 children remained in their regular classes as controls. All of these children were then examined periodically, 93 remaining in the study for 4 years.

The findings of the Illinois Study were as follows:

(1) *Both experimental (special class) and control (regular class) groups gained significantly in IQ* (from a mean of about 75 on the Binet pretest to about 82 at the end of the first year and ending up with a mean IQ of about 83 at the end of their fourth year). *The groups did not differ significantly in their IQ gains.*

(2) At the end of the first 2 years, the control group was markedly superior in reading skills, but this difference disappeared by the end of the fourth year. The authors explain these results on the basis of an extended reading readiness program in the special classes. The control group was also significantly superior in word discrimination (test given only in the fourth year), and in first-year arithmetic achievement (but not in later years). No other significant differences on standardized achievement tests were reported.

(3) On the specially developed Test of Basic Information (social knowledge) there were no significant differences between experimental and control groups.

(4) More mothers of special class children thought their child was doing pretty well at academic work compared with other children.

(5) Children in special classes seemed less ready to interact with neighborhood peers than those in regular classes.

(6) Children in special classes in one county scored significantly higher than controls on verbal tests of originality, fluency, and flexibility of thought. Special class children also tried to answer a greater number of difficult questions on an orally administered questionnaire.

The authors also reported findings based on a secondary analysis which separates results for those with terminal IQ below and above 80. Since by the end of the first year over 50% of the children scored above 80 on the Binet, the authors decided to analyze the data separately for the group with a final (average third- and fourth-year Binet) IQ above 80 and those with IQs of 80 and below. They reasoned that it is only the latter group which "were considered to be mentally retarded in the usual sense," i.e., might be legally assigned to special classes. Their post hoc analysis suggested that those with terminal IQs above 80 showed greater achievement in regular classes, whereas those with terminal IQs of 80 or below achieved better in special classes. The authors' interpretations of their findings were as follows:

"The results of this study suggest that the probability of a rise in intellectual functioning following school entrance is greater among children above 75 IQ (Binet) than among those with lower IQs. Children with an IQ above 75 are also more likely to sustain any gain in intellectual functioning, as indicated by tests at the end of the fourth year. Hence, there appears to be some justification for children with a Binet IQ below 75 being placed in a special class at the beginning of their school career and for children with scores of 75 or above entering the regular school program" (Goldstein *et al*, 1965, p. 106).

These statements cannot be justified by the methods and findings of the study, because of the following weaknesses:

(1) The division into lower and higher IQ groups was *not* made on the basis of initial IQ but on the basis of terminal IQ which is influenced by schooling.[1] Thus, one can only say that those who *ended up* with an IQ of 75 or higher rose more in intellectual status. How then can one decide, on the basis of these data, that children with IQs below 75 *at the beginning* of their career should be placed in special classes?

(2) The initial selection criterion was an IQ less than 85 so that those closest to the cutoff are statistically more likely to gain since they include more children whose scores were reduced on the pretest by error factors. (Those of similar IQ whose scores were "accidentally" raised are excluded by the cutoff and therefore cannot show the downward movement on the second occasion to balance the upward movement of those included.)

(3) The initial random assignment was not carried out within IQ levels.

(4) There were only 12 children in special classes and 13 in regular classes with a terminal IQ of 75 or below, representing only about one-fourth of the children in the study. Thus, even if one assumed that these low IQ children had gained in achievement from the special class, one would be hesitant to generalize since there were so few children involved and since any gain might have resulted from the presence of the higher IQ children in their special classes.

It is clear, then, that the findings based on this secondary analysis into (terminal) low and high IQ groups must be discounted.

---

[1]A personal communication from Moss justifies the use of later measures on the basis of the instability of first-year scores.

In his preface to the report, Kirk states, "The methodology used in this study and the results should tend to obviate the necessity for further studies which compare the gross progress of mentally retarded children in special classes with that of similar children remaining in regular grades. A more fruitful area for research may be found in the investigation of the processes by which mentally retarded children can develop mentally, socially, and academically" (Goldstein et al., 1965, p. iv).

This statement implies that the Illinois study has demonstrated something conclusively because of the fine methodology. The strong points of the study's original design have been presented and only the weakness of the secondary analyses suggested, but it is necessary to examine certain basic design limitations which prevent the conclusion that the crucial study has been done.

(1) In dealing with primary special classes initiated for 6-year-olds, the Illinois study revealed little about the more common special class for children beyond the age of 8.

(2) In selecting children solely on the basis of IQ rather than classroom learning problems, it revealed little about the effectiveness of special classes for children who have been selected by teachers for demonstrated difficulties.

(3) Since only four special classrooms and 10 carefully selected teachers were involved in the study, one has no idea about the specificity of the findings to the peculiar motivation, competence, and training of these teachers or the adequacy of the classroom setting.

Now it may be argued that this is what all the other efficacy studies have examined and that this investigation was an attempt to test ideal arrangements rather than commonly existing arrangements. Unfortunately, the previous studies have been seriously flawed in evaluating existing arrangements primarily because of the lack of appropriate comparison groups. There is as yet no reported study which has selected children referred for school failure and then randomly assigned one group to special classes and the other to control classes. What the study has indicated is that it is not promising to select children for special classes when they enter first grade solely on the basis of IQ scores. Children with IQs of about 75 or 80 at age 6 are likely to have IQ scores above 80 by the age of 7 or 8. Children with IQs in the 60's will probably still score 75 or below a year or two later but this will differ little whether the child has been initially placed in a regular or special class.

If we are to agree with Kirk that what we need to study are learning and developmental processes rather than administrative arrangements, the same argument could have been just as legitimately made before carrying out the study. If we demand evidence for the effectiveness of special class arrangements, this study may be the best we have so far, but it is far from decisive.

Educational administrators should be given evidence about the effectiveness of various learning arrangements they are considering. It seems, then, that the only real reason for dropping research on this topic is that few administrators are faced with this choice any more. An "enlightened" school system makes provisions for its needy pupils if it can. The retarded seem to need help. Funds are available. Therefore, special services are provided.

Perhaps research should be aimed at examining alternative possibilities for improving the educational lot of the mentally retarded. One possibility is to provide separate arrangements for lower and higher level EMRs. A study comparing "single-track" and "two-track" plans for EMRs in New York City was reported by Wrightstone, Forlano, Lepkowski, Sontag, and Edelstein (1959). The evaluation included 147 classes in 1957−58 and 165 classes in 1958−59. Numerous standardized tests and study developed measures were administered. Few significant differences were found. The few statistically significant comparisons on standardized achievement tests mostly favored the contrast (heterogeneous) classes and the few statistically significant differences on teacher ratings (peer acceptance and health habits) favored the experimental low educable over the contrast low educable group. In response to a questionnaire, teachers of the reorganized classes preferred the new homogeneous arrangements to the heterogeneous approach. As the authors indicate, the evidence in favor of the new placement is hardly strong enough at this point to consider homogeneous grouping of EMRs a success.

Other interesting comparisons possible are: (a) comparisons of high school work-study programs with 100% classroom or prevocational programs, (b) comparisons of academic or readiness preschool programs with 100% playroom or home visit programs for preschoolers, (c) comparison of consultant or itinerant teacher (tutor) programs with special class programs. If such studies are to be carried out, the research worker must be more aware than he has been that this is applied research for administrative decision making. Such decisions must be based on relative cost, efficiency, and important educational gains provided by competing administrative arrangements. A statistically significant but small difference in achievement places greater decision weight on cost factors. Since we have had so little success in demonstrating the superiority in educational achievement of new (and costly) arrangements, the acceptance of special classes must be a function of other factors, e.g., reduction of pressure on teachers and administrators by removal of problem children from regular classes. Here, the payoff is in teacher and administrator satisfaction. Perhaps another outcome is superior performance by those children who remain after the source of distress is removed. Certainly the local administrator's decision is based on whether his district must pay for the special services. There seem to be no studies of why special classes have been instituted, as opposed to statements giving the public rationale for such decisions.

If we are to carry out other studies comparing administrative arrangements, it would be well to consider costs and outcomes other than achievement and adjustment gains for the mentally retarded.

B. Institutional Educational Programs

Although residential centers for the retarded began as educational or training centers and frequently are labeled "school," the major function of most residential institutions is custodial, i.e., the maintenance and protection of the inmates. Nevertheless, most institutions have educational programs for educable and trainable school age children and two recent studies have attempted to compare such programs with public school programs.

Reynolds and Stunkard (1960) compared 173 educable children in public school special classes with 158 pupils of comparable age (10 − 15 years) in a state school for EMRs on several measures.

The sampling weaknesses discussed in the section on efficacy studies are even more applicable to this study. There is obviously a considerable selectivity entering into admission to a residential school as opposed to a special class. The Reynolds and Stunkard study finds what one would suspect, that EMRs in the residential school have lower mean IQ and academic achievement than the noninstitutionalized EMRs.

Stanton and Cassidy (1961) added a residential school comparison group to their earlier study which compared public school regular and special class programs for the retarded (Cassidy & Stanton, 1959; reviewed by Kirk, 1964, and Quay, 1963). Subjects in all three groups had to have: (a) an IQ between 50 and 75, (b) a CA between 12 years and 14 years 11 months, and (c) been in that educational setting for at least 2 years. Further, based on the distribution of IQs in the state's special class population, each sample was stratified by IQ levels (50 − 54, 55 − 59, etc.). The final samples included 100 children in special classes in 16 school systems, 94 in regular classes in 20 school systems, and 47 in one residential school with its population drawn from the entire state. Several measures were obtained on all three samples.

Obviously, the Stanton and Cassidy study made a considerable effort to overcome sampling bias by stratifying on IQ. The result is a very small and unrepresentative sample of the institutionalized educable population. Furthermore, by matching samples on IQ, it is likely that any major educational difference between settings has been matched away. What are left are profile differences: residential pupils higher on WISC block design and lower on coding, higher on the Progressive Matrices and lower on the Stanford Achievement Test, higher on the Test of Personality and lower on the Draw-A-Man Test. While the data are difficult to interpret, the most expected finding is the achievement test difference favoring the regular class and the least expected finding is the personality test differences favoring the institutional group. However, the latter finding is open to question because of the unknown validity of the 30-item test (see Gardner, 1966, on this point). It is also somewhat surprising that there was not a more marked regression to the group mean on the intellectual measures following initial stratification on this variable. The one final surprise was the lack of correlation of IQ with the achievement test and with the WISC block design and coding scores for the regular class group. It is hard to make sense out of this even as an artifact of small sample size, or matching procedures.

C. Curriculum Practices

Although the present authors have criticized Kirk's eagerness to drop the study of the effectiveness of special classes, they agree with his other conclusion. To the extent that one must contend with a given administrative arrangement such as special classes, the problem arises of providing maximum effective learning within that setting: What are the best materials, techniques, sequences, and content for effective learning?

In a recent survey of special classes in the state of Indiana (Bauer, 1967) it was noted that the overwhelming majority of teachers were still using the watered-down curriculum described by Inskeep (1926). This approach uses content similar to that employed in the regular grades but is presented to retarded children in more simplified language at a slower pace with endless repetition to enhance overlearning. It was further noted that in rare instances attempts were made to apply tool subject skills to prevocational and work-study experiences. Such practices as programmed instruction and diagnostic teaching were seldom observed. Unfortunately, the use of the watered-down curriculum is probably the rule rather than the exception in the majority of special classes throughout the United States. Therefore, it is not too surprising that EMR children are little benefited by special education programs as they exist today.

1. Traditional Methods and Arithmetic Achievement

The ineffectiveness of the watered-down approach to teaching arithmetic is exemplified in the Finley (1962) study. To determine whether the context in which an arithmetic problem is presented influences the ability of EMR children to solve it, special class EMR and regular class normal children equated for MA (8 years) were presented arithmetic problems in three different forms—concrete (problems illustrated by real money and objects fastened to a board), pictorial (problems illustrated by pictures of money and objects), and symbolic (arithmetic computation problems). Contrary to expectation the retarded Ss tended to do least well on the concrete test but performed significantly better than the normal Ss on the symbolic test. These findings indicate that retarded children are able to memorize abstract symbols required for arithmetic computation but are apparently unable to apply them to functional problem solving involving money and objects. This suggests that the traditional approach to teaching arithmetic, wherein emphasis is placed on the manipulation of arithmetic symbols, does not necessarily produce arithmetical understanding. To insure understanding, it is necessary to provide retarded children with opportunities for applying arithmetic computation skills to such problems as purchasing, cooking, household budgeting, and checkbook balancing.

2. Traditional Methods and Reading Achievement

The ineffectiveness of traditional methods of teaching reading to retardates is adequately documented in Kirk's (1964) comprehensive review of the literature on that topic. In general, retarded children tend to read one or more years below their mental age expectancy. With our society becoming more and more complex, it is quite likely that literacy will become increasingly more essential for economic self-sufficiency in adulthood. Therefore, it is readily apparent that more effective procedures than those presently being used must be developed to teach EMR children how to read.

The results of the U. S. Office of Education first-grade reading studies summarized in the May, 1966 issue of *The Reading Teacher* provide some promising strategies for improving the teaching of reading to cultural familial EMR children. In general, innovative approaches such as initial teaching alphabet (i t a), linguistic readers, language experience charts, and audiovisual methods were equal to basal reader series in their effectiveness in teaching reading to middle class children. This finding supports the generally held view that the majority of children will learn to read by any method or even despite the method used. However, any one of the innovative approaches mentioned above tended to produce better reading achievement results than basal readers in those studies where disadvantaged children or poor readers were used as subjects. Although it is easy to dismiss these findings as owing to a Hawthorne effect resulting from additional attention, it is possible that such an effect provides the motivational thrust to both teachers and children to try harder. It is also possible that the reading materials supplied with the newer approaches are themselves more interesting than basal readers and thus more motivating to children with reading disabilities.

3. CURRICULUM INNOVATIONS AND THEIR EFFECTIVENESS

The procedures most often advocated, but least often implemented, with retarded children are individualized instruction and diagnostic teaching.

a. The Individualized Approach. The individualized instruction approach has received its greatest impetus from advocators of programmed instruction techniques. Studies on the effectiveness of these techniques have been thoroughly reviewed by Greene (1966) in a previous volume of this series.

Greene's review indicated that when programmed instruction was compared to traditional classroom methods, essentially no achievement differences between the two methods were obtained in the majority of studies. In one study where the machine-instructed groups performed significantly better on reading and spelling than the traditionally instructed group the differences were eliminated after the latter group was tutored individually over the same material.

It seems reasonable to conclude that programmed instruction techniques, to date, have been far from successful in producing achievement gains superior to those obtained by traditional methods. Where programmed instruction is found to be superior, it appears that individualized attention played a more important role in enhancing achievement than the program used. Since programs designed for large groups of children appear to be relatively ineffective, it remains to be demonstrated whether or not individualized programs based on the individual differences among the children would be more effective.

In the absence of studies on the effectiveness of a nonprogrammed individualized instruction approach with retarded children, a study by Spencer (1966) comparing the effectiveness of an individualized with a basal reading approach using typical groups of first graders in rural communities will be used to illustrate this approach. Twenty-two combination first and second grade classes participated in the study. Twelve of the classes were taught by the individualized reading approach and 10 were taught by the Scott-Foresman basal reader program. Pupils were randomly assigned to the classes. Only "above-average" experienced teachers were selected for the project. Teacher preference governed whether she taught by the individualized or by the basal reader approach. Although both groups of teachers received in-service training, those teachers using the individualized approach received 3 weeks of instruction and weekly visits by the project director, while those teaching by the basal reader approach received 2 days of instruction and infrequent visits by the project staff. The individualized program was divided into two parts: intensive systematic phonetic instruction and motivated varied story reading. The program was presented to the children by the teacher using "...a variety of grouping patterns from individuals working alone to a whole-class teacher-directed group" (Spencer, 1966, p. 596). Following the teacher instruction period, independent oral practice was provided by a pupil-team technique.

"Some teams were of equal ability, and some teams were effective with unequal ability, allowing a weaker pupil to receive help from the more able learner . . . The pupil-team technique was essential to free the teacher to work with individuals" (Spencer, 1966, p. 596).

After 140 days of instruction the individualized reading group performed significantly better than the basal reader group on the Stanford Achievement Test, Gates Word Recognition, and Gates Pronunciation Tests. Although this study appears to demonstrate the superiority of an individualized approach to teaching reading, the findings must be viewed with extreme caution. The greater interaction of project staff with teachers using the individualized approach may have produced a substantial Hawthorne effect in favor of the individualized instruction groups. More serious, however, is the contamination of curriculum content with teaching method. The individualized instruction groups were taught by a phonetic method using Durrell and Murphy's *Speech to Print Phonics*, while the nonindividualized instruction groups were taught by the multiple methods prescribed in the Scott-Foresman basal reader series. It is, therefore, impossible to determine whether the significant differences in favor of the experimental groups were the result of the individualized instruction or the result of the particular materials employed.

b. The Diagnostic Method. The diagnostic approach to teaching refers to the procedure of identifying the specific learning disabilities of a given child or group of children and then applying methods specifically designed to remedy those disabilities. This approach is best illustrated by the Strauss and Lehtinen (1947) techniques designed for "brain-

injured" children exhibiting behavioral symptoms such as distracti-
bility, perceptual disturbances, and/or thinking disorders, with or
without accompanying neurological evidence of organic brain damage.
This rather unorthodox definition of brain injury has produced considerable confusion in the research literature, especially in those instances
where the Strauss-Lehtinen techniques were applied to brain-injured
children selected on the basis of neurological tests without regard to behavioral symptoms. The nonsuperiority of the Strauss-Lehtinen techniques over traditional methods when applied to both organically and
nonorganically impaired hyperactive children was demonstrated by
Cruickshank, Bentzen, Ratzeburg, and Tannahauser (1961).

The only attempt to assess the effectiveness of the Strauss-Lehtinen
techniques for organically brain-injured children who also exhibited
specific perceptual deficits was made by Frey (1961). A group of children
displaying perceptual problems on psychological tests and then confirmed to be brain-injured by a neurological examination were compared on reading abilities to a group of nonbrain-injured children
matched for mean IQ (79), MA (8 years 2 months), and CA (10 years
4 months). The brain-injured group had been taught by the Strauss-
Lehtinen method for an average of $2\frac{1}{2}$ years while the nonbrain-
injured group had been taught by traditional methods in regular or
special classes. The findings indicated that the reading performance
of the brain-injured group was significantly superior to that of the
nonbrain-injured group on the Gates Primary Reading Test, Gray Oral
Reading Test, Iota Word Recognition Test, Monroe Sound Blending
Test, and four of the reading error types on the Monroe Diagnostic
Reading Test.

Thus, on the basis of the Frey (1961) and Cruickshank *et al.* (1961)
results, it appears that the Strauss-Lehtinen method is effective when
used with organically impaired children who in addition exhibit common perceptual disturbances. This finding dramatically demonstrates
the importance of making behavioral diagnoses rather than medical
diagnoses when attempting to group children for educational purposes.

4. PERSONAL AND SOCIAL ADJUSTMENT

Although it is a widely held belief (e.g., Robinson & Robinson, 1965)
that mentally retarded school children are less well adjusted than
nonretarded children and that adjustment of the retarded is better in
special classes than in regular classes, both assumptions have only
weak evidence to support them (Gardner, 1966). Perhaps the beliefs
are so widely held because they mesh nicely with two popular "tra-

ditional strategies or rationales for teaching the retarded:" "training for social competence" and "strengthening motivation and self-esteem" (Lynch, 1967). Just what reliable evidence is there on (a) the inferiority of educable mentally retarded children in personal and social adjustment; (b) the gains in personal and social adjustment induced by special classes; (c) the adequacy of special techniques for improving personal and social adjustment; and (d) the social adjustment of the mentally retarded after they leave school?

a. The Adjustment of Educable Mentally Retarded School Children. One consistent finding has been the positive moderate (.25 – .50) correlation between intelligence and peer acceptance found within regular classes, special classes, and institutional populations. Most of these studies have been reviewed by Dentler and Mackler (1962). A study by Meyerowitz (1965, pp. 215-222) suggests that neighborhood acceptance as well as classroom acceptance is reduced by retardation.

Aside from peer acceptance measures, investigations have employed projective techniques, teacher checklists and ratings, and personality inventories (Gardner, 1966). The validity of such measures is difficult to demonstrate, and the projective tests and personality inventories which depend so heavily on verbal skill and response styles are particularly open to question with the retarded.

b. The Effect of Special Classes on Social Adjustment. The consistent positive correlation between ability and sociometric status suggests that the retarded child will gain in peer acceptance by classmates when he moves from a regular class with children of higher intelligence than his to a special class in which he is about average in intelligence. Data to support this finding are provided by Johnson (1961), using the Syracuse Scale of Social Relations. The 16 retarded subjects in special classes were better accepted by their classmates than the 16 retarded children in regular classes. The retarded children in special classes obtained about the same ratings as the total sample of regular class children, most of whom were normal in intelligence. Six of the regular class retarded children were later shifted to special classes, showing a significant gain in peer acceptance. In a related finding, Milazzo (1963) reported that retarded children who were most recently admitted to special classes were rated lowest in social effectiveness by their special classmates and those who had been in special classes from the earliest age were rated lowest in aggression by their special class peers. Milazzo's interpretation is that the longer they stay in special classes, the better the adjustment. An alternative explanation is that earlier referrals are for gross developmental lag, later referrals for disturbing classroom behavior.

Social and personal adjustment data were also obtained in the efficacy studies of Ainsworth (1959), Blatt (1958), Cassidy and Stanton (1959), Ellenbogen (1957), Goldstein *et al.* (1965), Mullen and Itkin (1961), and Thurstone (1959). Most of their findings are reviewed in Gardner (1966), Kirk (1964), and Quay (1963). In brief, those studies where teacher ratings of adjustment or personality inventories were employed found either superiority of special class children or no differences. The teacher ratings may be criticized on the grounds that a teacher will develop a frame of reference based on the group she has to work with. The special class teacher may rate her retarded children in comparison with the other retarded children in her class, whereas the regular class teacher will compare her retarded pupil with the other children of normal intelligence in her regular class. This criticism also holds for sociometric ratings by classmates.

There are two methods of evaluating the special class child's adjustment which do not depend on ratings of their special class peers or teacher. One approach is to obtain social preference measures from neighborhood peers rather than classmates. The other method is to employ self descriptive measures, tests answered by the subject himself.

Neighborhood peer acceptance studies are difficult to carry out as may be seen in a study by Meyerowitz (1965, pp. 215-222). Beginning with the basic Illinois study sample of 120 7-year-old children with Binet IQs of 50−85, half of whom were assigned to a newly created special class at age 6 and half of whom remained in regular classes, and a comparison sample of 60 normal classmates (IQ 95−110) of the regular class children, the requirements of a neighborhood peer acceptance study reduced the sample to 10 special class pupils, 12 regular class retarded children, and 11 normal control children. The reduction in sample size occurred as follows: (a) from 180 to 90 by dealing only with the urban half of the sample; and (b) from 90 to 33, requiring each subject to have lived at the same address for at least 6 weeks, and to have at least five children of the same age (plus or minus one school grade) living on the same street within a reasonable distance and that the child know at least one of the five neighborhood children. Having identified five neighborhood children for each subject, all six were interviewed to determine how many of the other five children they knew and how many knew them; how many of the others they said they played with and how many of the others said they played with them; how many of the others they did not like and how many did not like them; how many of the others they thought were "dumb" at play, slow learners, different, and unpopular and how many of the others thought this of them. There were no discernible differences between the reactions of others to experimental (special class) and to control (regular class) retarded subjects. Both retarded groups were more often known, less often played with, less often rejected as companions, and less often attributed negative traits than were the normal comparison subjects. In brief, the retarded children, whether in regular or special class, were more likely to be known but less likely to be interacted with, either positively or negatively, than normal children.

Although the two retarded groups did not differ in the degree to which normal children knew them or reacted to them, the regular class children knew more of their normal neighbors, reported playing with more of them, and more often attributed negative traits to them than did the special class retarded children. The authors interpreted this to mean that the special class reduced "the extent to which the retarded child attempted to interact with age peers in the neighborhood" (Goldstein et al., 1965, p. 221). Unfortunately, the briefness of the available report of this substudy makes it difficult to evaluate since the authors report neither the degree of equivalence of these small specially selected samples nor any tests of statistical significance on the findings. If one assumes the differences reported above to be true differences, the study implies not only that the special class does not improve the retarded child's neighborhood peer acceptance but also that it reduces the readiness of the retarded child to interact with his neighborhood peers.

Several studies have used self-report measures to get at the adjustment of the retarded child. Most of these studies have employed standardized personality inventories, particularly the California Test of Personality. The personality inventory findings, using this test, have been criticized by Gardner (1966) for use of unreliable subtest scores and for the questionable validity of the entire instrument with the retarded.

Two recent studies have employed measures of self-evaluation. As part of the Illinois study discussed earlier (Goldstein et al., 1965), Meyerowitz (1962, 1966) had measures of self-derogation administered to experimental retarded (special class), control retarded (regular class), and nonretarded children at the end of the first year of schooling, the beginning of the second year, and at the end of the second year. The instrument required a subject to choose one statement out of each of several pairs of statements read orally to him. Choice of one statement in each pair was self-derogatory, the other was a socially desirable self-description. At the end of the first year, the special class (experimental) children chose more self-derogatory remarks than did the retarded regular class group, which, in turn, chose more self-derogatory remarks than the nonretarded regular class children. At the beginning of the second year, on a revised instrument, the three groups did not differ.

At the end of the second year, on a third form of the self-derogation test, the experimental group again showed more self-derogation than either of the other two groups but this time the retarded and nonretarded children in regular classes did not differ from one another. Perhaps this can be explained by Milazzo's (1963) finding that most special class children wished they could be in regular classes despite enjoying special classes more. Also, Willey (1966) found that regular class children hold a relatively negative stereotype of children in special classes. The low status of the special class may influence the child's self-perception. However, other evidence in Willey's (1966) study suggests that the special class child does not describe those in his class in negative terms but instead describes his classmates much as the regular class pupil describes his peers. The notion that we see ourselves as others see us requires that we specify who the relevant "others" are.

Mayer (1966) examined the effect of length of stay in special class upon two self-concept measures in a group of junior high educable mentally retarded pupils. He predicted that the earlier the placement, the more positive the self-concept, but he found no significant effects of time of placement on the self-concept measures. This is in contrast to Milazzo's finding that reputation among peers in special classes was more positive among those placed earlier than among those placed later. Both of these studies hoped to provide information on the changes which occur in children as a result of length of time they have been in the special class, yet the investigators were limited to comparing different children who were placed in special classes at different ages. A more desirable approach is to trace the same children over time. Such a study was reported by Towne, Joiner, and Schurr (1967). The experimenters identified 62 pupils aged 7 to 15 years, who were about to be placed in special classes and administered a measure of their "self-concept of ability" prior to students' knowledge of their selection. Four subsequent measures were obtained on the same instrument over the first year in which the pupils were in special classes. The self-concept of ability measure includes eight items which ask subjects how well they think they do in school. The authors had predicted that self-concept of ability would drop as the child was placed into special classes as a result of his interpreting the placement as a sign of his failure. His self-concept of ability would then gradually improve as he adapts to his new circumstances and undergoes a "redefinition of self."

The findings of the study are shown in Fig. 1. The results are contrary to the hypothesis. Self-concept of ability rises upon entry into special class and continues to rise until the end of the first year when it begins to drop. The investigators believe that their results may be ex-

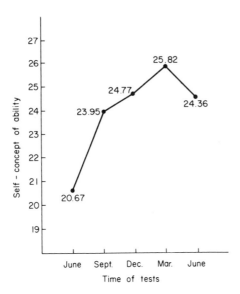

FIG. 1. Changes in self-concept of the EMR upon moving from regular classes (June) to special classes (Sept., Dec., Mar., June).

plained by a change in reference group from the regular class to the special class group. Two of the items on the test require that the pupil compare himself with others in his class. Presumably after placement he will compare himself with special class pupils on these items rather than with regular class pupils, seeing himself as relatively more competent when compared with his new group. Other questions deal with how well he is doing in his school work and he presumably would be doing better on the less demanding work of the special class. These factors would tend to enhance the self-concept of the pupil as measured by this test. By the end of the year, however, he may be accumulating experiences with others who are comparing him with those outside and are defining him as retarded. This might explain the drop in self-concept of ability at the end of the year.

Although special classes have been widely recommended as a way of reducing the poor personal and social adjustment of the educable retarded, it can be seen that there is little definitive evidence either that these children are seriously maladjusted outside of special classes or that special classes have a consistently favorable effect on adjustment of the retarded. The first point is difficult to demonstrate because of the difficulty of obtaining reliable and valid measures of retarded children's adjustment. The question of evaluating the efficacy of special classes adds all the special problems of that type of study. Most important of all, the special class treatment is rarely homogeneous with regard to techniques used by different special class teachers to improve social and personal adjustment. It seems that three things are generally meant by teaching social adjustment. One is "socialization" or teaching the child the standards of the group, in this case, the school or classroom rules, but perhaps also the rules of his peer group. Another meaning of teaching social adjustment seems to be the more permissive approach to academics, that is, weakening the special demands of the classroom so that it simplifies the adjustment problem of the child. A third approach is to teach about social adjustment, e.g., how to get along on a date and how to behave courteously. The difference between this and the first definition is that here the pupil is getting information about a future situation, whereas in direct "socialization" he is immediately rewarded or punished for behaving appropriately or inappropriately in the classroom.

Which of these techniques, if any, or which combination of them, or what other approaches were used in the classes sampled by each efficacy study? In most of the studies, the authors had no control over the curriculum or selection and training of teachers for the special class, nor did they systematically observe or report what was going on in regular or special classes. The Illinois study is an exception, the special class teachers being specially selected and trained, and employing a standard curriculum manual (Goldstein & Seigle, 1958). However, even this study fails to provide any description of teachers or procedures employed in regular classes nor does it report systematic observational measures of the events going on in the classroom.

c. *Techniques for Improving Social Adjustment.* Though it has not been demonstrated that mentally retarded children as a group are more poorly adjusted than the nonretarded nor that special classes in general improve the adjustment of mentally retarded children, it is likely that there are many maladjusted mentally retarded individuals both in special classes and in regular classes in those school districts where no provisions have been made for special classes. Given this problem, what techniques are available for improving the adjustment of these individuals?

Though it is difficult to find studies which have identified children in regular classes as both retarded and poorly adjusted and then sought to develop a remedial program for them, there are studies in regular classes which attempt to reduce the number of isolates in the class (Gronlund, 1959). One technique involves placing an isolated child in a work group with more popular children (Atkinson, 1949). Another assigns leadership or other responsible roles in organized activities to rejected pupils (McLelland & Ratliff, 1941). Most studies of this sort have been carried out with a single class and are thus difficult to evaluate.

If there are few good studies demonstrating improvements in the social status of poorly accepted children in regular classes, it is hard to find *any* studies at all which demonstrate techniques for working with isolates or rejected children in special classes. A recent study by Chaires (1966) has done much to reduce the void in this area. She identified the four least accepted children in each of eight intermediate and eight junior high school classes for EMRs. Half of the classes were assigned to an experimental condition and half to a control condition. Within each experimental class, two of the four lowest status children were randomly assigned to a special treatment condition consisting of 5 weeks of twice-weekly, 15-minute group activities shared with the two highest status pupils in the class. During these sessions, one of the experimenters removed these children from the class and together they rehearsed a skit which was presented in the last session. Another experimenter administered pre- and postsociometric tests to the class as a whole. The major findings were: (a) the low status children who participated in the treatment increased significantly in peer acceptance; (b) the participants also increased their estimate of how others accepted them; and (c) these improvements for the experimental subjects were greater than any improvement for the control subjects, i.e., those who did not participate. This study thus suggests the usefulness of the sociometric measure as a diagnostic and evaluative procedure and the value of providing specially devised group experiences for lower status mentally retarded children in special classes. However, there is no evidence provided for the long-term stability of this change in peer acceptance, nor can one easily identify which aspects of the intervention were responsible for the observed improvement in sociometric status.

5. LANGUAGE DEVELOPMENT

It is evident from the previous sections that the criterion measures for evaluating special education administrative and curriculum practices for EMR school-aged children have been reading, arithmetic, and social adjustment. In recent years a number of investigators have included measures of language development and productive thinking as supplements to these criteria. The sections which follow will review some of these studies, to determine their effectiveness in increasing language development and productive thinking; if found to be effective, further analyses will be made to determine the extent to which these variables contribute to success in academic achievement.

One of the earliest efforts to improve the language abilities of a group of children enrolled in special classes for the educable mentally retarded was made by J. O. Smith (1962). Thirty-three language lessons based on the language model of the ITPA were presented to two groups of eight special class EMR children between the ages of 7 and 10. The instruction period consisted of three 45-minute sessions a week for 3 months. At the conclusion of the treatment period, the posttest ITPA total language age scores indicated that the 16 experimental subjects had made a mean gain of about 7 months. A control group of 16 children, matched with the experimental group on CA (mean = 9 years) and IQ (mean Binet IQ = 68), without the benefit of the language lessons, had regressed about ½ month in language age. The difference between the groups was statistically significant.

A 1-year follow-up of the Smith study by Mueller and Smith (1964) indicated that the mean language age for the experimental group was no longer significantly greater than that of the control group. It is interesting to note that the 8 months language gain of the control group from posttest to follow-up testing was almost twice that of the gain made by the experimental group for the same period of time. Mueller and Smith suggest that the effects of the language program might have been more lasting if the treatment period had been of longer duration. However, it is just as plausible to suggest that the treatment language gains made by the experimental group were produced by a Hawthorne effect which dissipated after the experimental children were no longer taken from their special class and given special attention from an adult other than their teacher.

The effects of small group tutoring on a specific psycholinguistic disability of EMR children was investigated by Blessing (1964). A group of 40 children ranging in CA from 8 to 15 and in IQ from 50 to 80 with vocal encoding (verbal expressiveness) age scores at least 1 year below MA expectancy were randomly divided into an experimental and a control group. The experimental subjects were given 45 1-hour language tutoring sessions designed to develop vocal encoding, three times a week for approximately 4 months. These sessions were administered to groups of two to four children by one of six language clinicians. The control group received the same curriculum as the experimental group with the exception of the language sessions. Analyses of the pre- to posttest gains on ITPA total language ages indicated that the mean gain of 11 months made by the experimental group was not statistically greater than the mean gain of 9 months made by the control group. Analysis of gains on Binet vocabulary scores also failed to produce a significant difference between the groups. However, significant differences in gain scores favoring the experimental group were obtained on the vocal encoding subtest of the ITPA, and for total word count, mean sentence length, and the mean of the five longest remarks obtained from exposure to one of the Children's Apperception Test cards. A 4-month follow-up of the experimental and control groups indicated that the language behavior of the experimental children continued to exceed that of the control children on the latter three measures. The vocal encoding subtest had not been used for the follow-up.

A comparison of the total language ITPA results from the Smith and Blessing studies reveals an interesting paradox. Whereas the language gains made by Blessing's experimental Ss were substantially greater than those made by Smith's Ss (11 months vs 7 months), Blessing's gains were not significantly greater than those made by his control group while Smith's gains were. It is apparent that the paradox occurred because the control Ss in Smith's study regressed slightly while those in Blessing's study gained substantially. Whereas the language gains of Blessing's control group are comparable to those made by Smith's control group the following year and by the control groups in similar investigations (Dunn & Mueller, 1966; Stearns, 1966), the poor language performance of Smith's control group during the intervention period must be viewed as atypical.

The findings from the school (Blessing, 1964; Smith, 1962) and preschool (Stearns, 1966; Weikart, 1967c) language intervention studies demonstrate that a formal language period added to a traditional school curriculum is not significantly more effective in improving the language development of EMR children as measured by the ITPA than a traditional school curriculum by itself. However, as demonstrated by the Indiana Preschool Project (Spicker et al., 1966), a formal language period coupled with a curriculum which stresses language development throughout the day may significantly improve overall language development.

Since it is often assumed that adequate oral language development is essential for successful school achievement (especially reading), the accuracy of this assumption needs to be examined. As may be recalled from the Indiana Project, at the completion of kindergarten in May, the mean ITPA total language age of the experimental group was 5 − 8 while that of the kindergarten contrast group was 5 − 2. However, despite the 6-month language advantage of the experimental group, there were no significant academic achievement differences between the groups at the completion of first or second grade.

A possible explanation for these discouraging results seems to appear in the findings of the Dunn and Mueller (1966) study in which the effectiveness of the Peabody Language Development Kit (PLDK) and the i t a with disadvantaged (mean Binet IQ = 84) first-grade children was investigated. At the completion of first grade the investigators found that the PLDK groups had made significantly greater gains than the non-PLDK groups in mean language age as measured by the ITPA. However, the PLDK groups learning to read by traditional methods performed significantly poorer on the word knowledge, word discrimination, and reading comprehension subtests of the Metropolitan Achievement Test, than groups learning to read by the i t a method without PLDK. In fact, reading achievement of the PLDK groups was no better than that of the control group receiving a traditional reading program without the PLDK. It, therefore, appears that an innovative approach to teaching reading produces significantly better reading achievement scores than a traditional approach to teaching reading even when coupled with an intensive language development program. However, since the reading achievement scores of the groups receiving i t a plus PLDK were relatively (although not statistically) greater than those of the groups receiving i t a alone, the possibility that a combined program of language instruction and innovative reading instruction will be more effective in enhancing reading achievement than either program by itself cannot be dismissed until further follow-up results are available.

6. PRODUCTIVE THINKING

Following Guilford's (1959) paper on the structure of intellect, several major investigations (Getzels & Jackson, 1962; Torrance, 1962; Wallach & Kogan, 1965) have explored the factor he called divergent or productive thinking. One of the most interesting findings reported by Getzels and Jackson indicated that children scoring high on measures of creativity[2] and relatively lower on intelligence (mean IQ = 127) performed as well on achievement tests as children scoring high on intelligence (mean IQ = 150) but relatively lower on measures of creativity. Torrance obtained similar results but found that the equal achievement phenomenon no longer held when high creativity was coupled with IQs below 115.

It appears that three questions regarding productive thinking in retarded children need to be investigated: (a) To what extent do re-

---

[2] The term "creativity" is used to denote high scores on measures of divergent or productive thinking abilities.

tarded children exhibit productive thinking abilities? (b) Can the productive thinking abilities of retarded children be increased? (c) To what extent does productive thinking of retarded children enhance their academic achievement or creative abilities?

One of the most extensive investigations of the creative thinking abilities of EMR children was conducted by R. M. Smith (1967). Forty-eight EMR children enrolled in regular classes were matched with 48 intellectually normal children on the basis of sex, race, socioeconomic status, school and classroom settings. They were then compared on eight tests of creative thinking ability. Since these tests could be scored along several dimensions, comparisons were made on 18 separate creativity factors, three subtotal creativity scores, and one grand total score. The comparisons indicated that the normal Ss significantly exceeded the retarded Ss on 12 of the 14 verbal creativity factors. There were no significant differences between the two groups on the seven nonverbal creativity factors. On the basis of these findings it appears that only the verbal productive thinking abilities of retarded children are significantly poorer than those of normal children.

The question as to whether the productive thinking abilities of retarded children can be enhanced was investigated by Tisdall (1962) and Rouse (1965).

As a substudy of the Goldstein *et al.* (1965) study discussed previously, Tisdall (1962) compared a group of EMR children in special classes with a group of EMR children in regular classes on three verbal and three nonverbal measures of creativity developed by Torrance. The special class children had been exposed to a curriculum which among other things used the discovery method to teach inductive reasoning. Tisdall found that the special class retardates performed significantly better than the regular class retardates on verbal fluency, flexibility, and originality. The groups did not differ significantly on the nonverbal measures of creativity. Since no tests of creativity had been administered prior to treatment, it is impossible to determine whether the differences on verbal creativity tests had existed prior to the treatment or were produced by the treatment. It should also be noted that the verbal creativity scores of the special class EMR children were not significantly different from those of a group of intellectually normal children of the same CA.

A direct attempt to increase the productive thinking abilities of a group of EMR children was made by Rouse (1965). Thirty lessons designed to foster creative thinking ability were presented to 47 EMR special class children between the ages of 7 years and 5 months and 16 years on a daily 30-minute basis for 6 consecutive weeks. One verbal and one nonverbal test of creativity developed by Torrance was used to make pre- to posttest comparisons between the treatment group and a control group comparable in IQ, MA, and CA. On both measures of creativity, the pre- to posttest gains made by the experimental group were significantly greater than those made by the control group. However, a comparison of the Rouse findings with those of R. M. Smith (1967) indicated that even after treatment the creativity scores of the retarded children were only comparable to those of normal children who were more than 2 years younger than the retarded children. Therefore, although Rouse has demonstrated that the productive thinking abilities of retarded children can be substantially improved by direct intervention, the level of productivity reached by them is still significantly below that of intellectually normal children. It remains to be demonstrated whether a longer treatment period would eventually close the productive thinking gap between retarded and normal children. Further research is also needed to determine whether the productive thinking gains made as a result of an intervention program will be retained when the intervention program ceases.

The extent to which increased productive thinking in retarded children enhances academic achievement or such creative endeavors as artistic expression and creative writing cannot be adequately determined at this time because of the limited research evidence available on this topic. The fact that the academic achievement of the high productive thinking special class retarded group in the Goldstein *et al.* (1965) study did not exceed that of the low productive thinking regular class retarded group seems to indicate that the productive thinking abilities of retarded children are either inadequate or nonfunctional for enhancing academic achievement. Whether productive thinking enhances other aspects of behavior must await further research.

D.   General Factors Influencing School Performance

Research has examined several factors held to be related to the general school performance of retarded children. These factors may be classified into family background factors, teacher characteristics, and classroom characteristics.

1.   FAMILY BACKGROUND FACTORS

a. Socioeconomic Status: a Control Variable and a Correlate of Mental Retardation. The positive correlations between socioeconomic status and intelligence and socioeconomic status and academic achievement have been demonstrated in numerous studies (Sarason & Gladwin, 1958).

Similarly, it has been found that the nonorganic educable mentally retarded are most frequently found in the lowest social strata (Sarason &
Gladwin, 1958). Both genetic and environmental factors (McCandless,
1964) have been used as explanations of the relationship. Thus, any
study which compares the performance in school of retarded and nonretarded children is likely to be comparing children of different family
and subcultural backgrounds unless the variable is taken into consideration. The problems involved in controlling on this variable may be seen
in Meyerowitz and Farber's (1966) investigation of the family background of the children in the Illinois study. The families of the 120
mentally retarded first graders (IQ 50−85) were compared with the
families of the 60 children of normal IQ (95−115) who were in the same
classes as the control retarded children. The normal group was selected
to be comparable to the retarded on parents' occupation, total family
income, and neighborhood. Descriptive data indicate that matching was
fairly close on these variables, suggesting that socioeconomic status was
well controlled. However, when a detailed interview was obtained with
the mother or surrogate in these families, it was found that the families
of the retarded children had: (a) a lower educational level for parents,
(b) a lower income per family member, (c) somewhat greater reliance on
welfare, (d) more frequent lack of telephones in the home, (e) poorer
health of mother, (f) less frequent movie going, (g) less frequent regular
receipt of newspapers and magazines in the home, (h) greater residential
mobility, (i) less participation in voluntary associations, (j) less church
attendance, (k) less contact with friends and neighbors, (l) more frequent
remarriage, (m) greater likelihood of mother having been a teenager
when retarded child was born, (n) more frequent crowdedness in the
home, and (o) retarded child less likely to be oldest or youngest child.
These differences indicate that the normal and retarded groups did not
come from the same socioeconomic and subcultural background, that
despite initial matching on occupation, family income and neighborhood, the home of the retarded child was on the average lower in
socioeconomic status.

   Given these differences in family background, it is difficult to interpret the remaining findings comparing the normal and retarded school
child. Are they related to retardation or to family social status? The
remaining differences between the mothers were: (a) the retarded child
was more likely to be seen by his mother as causing problems, and (b)
lower educational expectations were held for the retarded child by
his mother.

   b. *Parental Beliefs and Attitudes.* Although it is often implied that the
beliefs and expectations of parents have a great impact on a child's

school performance, one cannot find data which convincingly demonstrate this point. However, there are studies which show that parents of normal and retarded children hold different beliefs and expectations regarding the competencies of their children. Meyerowitz (1967) studied the beliefs of parents of the 60 experimental and 60 control EMR children in the Goldstein et al. (1965) study as well as parents of 60 normal comparison children. Parents were interviewed about 1 month after the child began school, at the end of the first school year, and at the end of the second school year. Judges made "blind" evaluations of whether parents were aware or unaware of deficiencies in their child. Judgments were based on answers to two interview questions, "How has your child been growing up in comparison with (your) other children?" and "What do you think (he) is getting out of school?" Only three of the 60 families of normal children were judged "aware" of deficiencies in their child, whereas 18 of 60 families in the control EMR group and 27 of 60 in the experimental (special class) EMR group were judged aware of deficiencies in their child. The difference between the two EMR groups did not reach statistical significance ($.05 < p < .10$) but the EMR groups differed significantly from normals on awareness. A related finding in this study was that parents of these EMR children had lower educational expectations for the retarded child than did parents of nonretarded subjects. Nevertheless, only about 10% of the parents of the EMR children thought their child could not graduate from high school. Meyerowitz also reported that in the second and third interviews parents of normal children accepted fewer derogatory statements about their children than parents of retarded children. Further, in the second year, more derogatory statements were made about experimental than control children. (Statistical analyses were not presented in the report.)

Any interpretation of Meyerowitz's findings must recognize two problems: (a) the finding of Goldstein et al. (1965) that by the end of the first year of their study, over half of the "retarded" sample obtained IQ scores above 80; and (b) the finding of Meyerowitz and Farber (1966) that the families of the "retarded" children apparently came from a lower status subcultural group than did the families of normal children. On the latter point, it has already been noted how intertwined are socioeconomic status and higher levels of mental retardation. It would thus be naive to focus on parents' stated beliefs about their child's competencies and attribute lower intelligence and therefore probable poor academic performance to these beliefs and expectations. One would be tempted to interpret the data as realistic response to observed incompetency but, as we have seen, the sample of "retarded" children in fact seems to show little measurable retardation. There is, however, a substantial difference in mean IQ between the retarded and normal samples and this may justify the latter interpretation.

2. TEACHER CHARACTERISTICS

a. Teacher Expectations: Can They "Create" or "Cure" Mental Retardation? Rosenthal (1967) has carried out many studies which demonstrate that experimenter expectations about probable results can have a significant effect upon the results of experimental studies. In a recent investigation (Rosenthal & Jacobson, 1966), this approach was extended to an examination of the effect of teachers' expectations upon their pupils' measured intelligence. All children in the 18 first- through sixth-grade classrooms of one school were administered Flanagan's Tests of General Ability at the beginning of a school year. The test was disguised as a predictor of intellectual gains. The names of about 20% of the children in each class were *randomly* selected and presented to the teacher as a list of children who would show unusual intellectual gains during the school year. At the end of the year, the tests were readministered. The findings are shown in Table V. When all grade levels were combined, the mean IQ gains were significantly higher for experimental (E) subjects (those "predicted" to gain) than control (C) subjects. When data were broken down by grade level, it was found that the effect only occurred in the first two grades. The differences were most dramatic in the first grade where experimental subjects gained a mean of 27 IQ points, 15 points higher than the gain for

TABLE V
ROSENTHAL AND JACOBSON STUDY
MEAN GAINS IN IQ
FLANAGAN'S TEST OF GENERAL ABILITY[a]

Grade	Controls	Experimentals	E−C
1	12.0	27.4	15.4[b]
2	7.0	16.5	9.5[c]
3	5.0	5.0	0.0
4	2.2	5.6	3.4
5	17.5	17.4	−0.1
6	10.7	10.0	−0.7
Weighted Mean	8.4	12.2	3.8[c]

[a] Taken from Rosenthal and Jacobson (1966).
[b] *t* is significant at the .002 level.
[c] *t* is significant at the .02 level.

controls. The investigators suggest various reasons why the effect occurred only in the first two grades. Among these reasons were that
older children's competencies are too well known for the experimental
prediction to be credible and that younger children may be more
malleable in the hands of the teacher.

The method and findings are intriguing but hardly conclusive.
Weaknesses include the instrument used, the lack of adequate control
of test administration, and the few teachers involved in the classes
which showed gains. This would be an exciting study to replicate with
first-grade children in a large school system. An inexpensive screening
device could be used at the beginning of first grade to identify at least
25 classes with two possibly retarded children. In each of these classes,
one of the two children would be identified to the teacher as highly
likely to show marked intellectual and achievement gains during the
year. The other child would remain a control subject. At the end of
the year a reliable individual intelligence test could be given to both
of the subjects. Would one of the children end up "retarded" and the
other "normal"?

The implications of such a study could be enormous. If Rosenthal's
findings are substantiated in a well-designed study with children of
low intelligence, it would suggest that some kind of Hawthorne effect
can have a crucial impact on their educational development. Perhaps
we have been attending to curriculum development and to teaching
techniques when we should have been working on teacher motivation
and expectations. Furthermore, it would suggest that special classes
are not seen as "special" by teachers in the sense of an experimental
program since research has shown no advantage to accrue to participation in this treatment. What would happen if children identified
as retarded by early screening were randomly assigned to one of two
types of newly instituted classes, (a) special classes for the retarded or
(b) "experimental" classes for poorly performing children who are
expected to gain enough to return to regular classes? Suppose that
the curriculum materials were left completely open to teachers. What
would happen?

One point should be made clear. We are not hypothesizing that any
normal child can be made retarded or any retarded child normal,
only that there are many children whose educational history and
diagnostic label can be altered drastically by the expectations of teachers
such that in one case they would end up being labeled retarded with
all that this implies for them in school and in the other case this would
not occur.

b. Teacher and Prospective Teacher Attitudes. Given the above discussion of the possible importance of teacher expectations to pupil performance, one might ask what evidence is available on the attitudes and beliefs of teachers regarding retarded children and their orientation toward their role as teacher of the retarded. Jones (1966) has reviewed several studies on preference for teaching handicapped children. There is some suggestion in the research that teaching the retarded is a highly valued position, particularly among those interested in teaching younger children and those who believe that the retarded child has a great need for sympathetic understanding. These findings suggest that teacher orientation to the retarded child is likely to be maternal and not achievement-focused, fostering dependency rather than expecting and demanding performance improvement. This would seem to maximize rather than minimize educational retardation.

A related finding is described by Bergan and Smith (1966) who reported that teachers anticipate that lower socioeconomic status children will have fewer skills and do more poorly than other children.

c. Teacher Behavior. A great gap in research is in the area of teacher behavior. It is one thing to say that teachers of the retarded have different self-reported attitudes toward their pupils than do other teachers. It is quite something else to demonstrate that these teachers do, in fact, behave differently in the classroom from other teachers.

Two pieces of research reported in their preliminary phases are attempting to compare teacher – pupil interaction in the special class with interaction in the regular class. Preliminary findings by Semmel, Herzog, and Jorgenson (1965), using Flanders' (1960) procedures suggested that special classroom teachers used more frequent praise or encouragement of student action, more frequently accepted or used student ideas, less frequently gave directions, and more frequently talked. The greatest difference between types of class was the greater frequency of student-initiated response in the special class.

A proposed study by Hirsch (1966) will examine the cognitive aspects of teacher-pupil verbal interaction in special classes for EMR's. Observational procedures developed for an investigation of productive thinking in gifted children (Gallagher, 1965) will be applied to determine the effectiveness of an attempt by Goldstein (1963) to train special class teachers in the use of an inductive teaching method. The observational study will enable evaluation of the extent to which divergent thinking is actually fostered by the classroom teacher.

Although observational studies of natural behavior of teachers in special classrooms may provide us with important findings, such investigations cannot evaluate the extent to which such teacher behavior is determined by teacher attitudes and expectations or by differences in such factors as classroom size, pupil characteristics, and teacher characteristics. On the other hand, while the findings reported by Rosenthal and Jacobson (1966) were intriguing in their demonstration that teacher expectations influence pupil performance, the study provides no information on teacher behavior. What did these teachers do differently with pupils expected to gain markedly in intellect than they did with those expected to show no gains? Beez (1968) has examined this problem in a more controlled tutorial situation. Immediately prior to working with a child, teachers were given a psychological report describing the child as being expected to do either well or poorly in school. Sixty 5- and 6-year-old Head Start preschool pupils were randomly assigned to low or high expectancy conditions. Similarly 60 students in Master's level education courses were randomly assigned to one of these two conditions. Each of these subjects was asked to teach one pupil, supposedly to see how well Head Start children would perform on a series of learning tasks. The first task was to teach the child to recognize a series of words on cards (e.g. "Stop," "Walk," "Boys"). Twenty words were provided and the teacher was instructed to teach as many words as she could to this child within a 10 minute period, using whatever techniques or strategy she wished. An observer recorded various aspects of teacher behavior, including the number of words covered by the teacher. Later the child was independently tested for recognition of the words.

The findings were dramatic. Teachers working with pupils who were expected to do poorly covered a mean of 5.66 words. Those teaching pupils who were expected to do well covered 10.43 words. There was little overlap in groups (t=6.97). Whereas 24 of the 30 with high expectancies covered 9 or more words, only 1 of 30 with low expectancies covered 9 or more words. The results for pupil learning were comparable. The low expectancy group learned 3.07 words, the high expectancy group 5.90 words. Again the difference was clearly a statistically significant one (t=7.12). In terms of overlap, 23 of 30 in the high expectancy group obtained 5 or more words correct when tested, whereas only 4 of 30 in the low expectancy group scored that high. The performance of teachers was unrelated to the number of years teaching experience and the performance of pupils was unrelated to their vocabulary level (PPVT).

These findings by Beez demonstrate that teacher expectancies very strongly influence their teaching behavior and, as a consequence, pupil performance. In this particular case, the effect is to reduce teaching rate or volume of material covered and thus to reduce learning rate or volume of material learned. This may help explain those studies in which regular class EMR pupils do better on standardized achievement tests than special class pupils. Although this study is an important one, it cannot be readily generalized to the typical classroom situation. First of all, this was a one-to-one tutorial situation. Secondly, the psychological report was presented immediately prior to the first exposure of the teacher to the pupil and teaching had to be initiated immediately. This gave the teacher little other information to rely on in choosing her strategy. More typically, the teacher's expectations can be continuously shaped by exposure over a long period of time to pupil performance in learning situations.

Though the study is limited in these respects, the findings conclusively show that in certain teaching situations, biasing information can have a dramatic impact on teacher behavior and pupil performance.

3. Classroom Characteristics

Economic feasibility is perhaps the point of greatest interest to administrators making decisions about educational programs for the retarded, yet there is very little research upon which they can base such decisions. A recently initiated study by Blessing (1966) suggests the directions such research can take. Blessing is systematically varying teacher–pupil ratio in special classes by manipulating class size and by employing teacher aides in half of the classes. Aside from obtaining various standardized achievement measures on the pupils, and obtaining videotaped time samples of classroom behavior, cost analyses will be conducted to determine economic and instructional efficiency. From the administrator's point of view the study also has the advantage of having built-in procedures for disseminating the findings of the study.

IV. POSTSCHOOL ADJUSTMENT OF THE EDUCABLE MENTALLY RETARDED

The rationale for special class programs for the retarded is largely that these arrangements will maximize the likelihood of the retarded child developing into a well-adjusted, productive, nondependent adult, and that without such programs the retarded adult is likely to become a problem to both himself and his community. Goldstein (1964) has reviewed the literature on the social and occupational adjustment of the mentally retarded and summarized it as finding that: (a) the large majority of adult retardates living in the community have made a succesful adjustment, (b) on most criteria of community adjustment as adults the mentally retarded were inferior to their normal schoolmates, and (c) most retarded adults hold jobs below the "skilled" level.

Baller, Charles, and Miller (1966) tried to locate 206 mentally retarded ex-special class students (1916 Stanford-Binet under 70), 209 "dull subjects" (IQ 70–90), and 206 normal controls (Terman group IQ 100–120) who had been studied earlier by Baller (1936). The sample of survivors located resembled the original subjects sought in terms of sex, age, and original IQ. The study found that the mentally retarded group differed from the brighter group on several adjustment criteria. Nevertheless, the great majority of the mentally retarded group were regularly employed, entirely self-supporting, and had few law violations.

Peck and Stephens (1964) studied five groups, each with 25 males, aged 18–26, IQ 50–75 (Stanford-Binet Form LM or Wechsler Scales) who were randomly selected from graduates of four special programs for education or rehabilitation of the mentally retarded and from regular classes in school districts without special classes. Over 200 measures were obtained for all 125 subjects based on about 5 hours of structured interviewing of the subjects, 2 hours of parent interviewing, a half-hour employer questionnaire, and credit ratings. The continuous measures were divided into predictors and criteria, and these were separately factor-analyzed. Multiple regression was then employed to predict from all continuous predictor measures to each criterion measure and from all predictive factors to each criterion factor. Finally, the 100 subjects in special programs were compared with the 25 control subjects on all predictor and criterion measures and factors. Although the term "predictor" and "criterion" are appropriate to describe the way the variables were entered into the multiple regression analysis, these were not predictors in a temporal sense. All measures, both predictor and criterion, were obtained at about the same time.

The regular class EMRs (controls) reliably surpassed the special program Ss (experimentals) on such predictors as intelligence, divergent thinking, social maturity, and mental health. This raises the question of whether any further comparisons on criterion measures are appropriate. Nevertheless, the control group did not surpass the experimentals on all variables. In general, control subjects showed superiority in their social and recreational life and had more often established a family or residence of their own, whereas experimental subjects were much more job oriented and seemed to obtain more satisfactions in this area. This study is marred by the lack of a comparable control group and the absence of a clear description of the experimental subjects and programs.

It hardly seems necessary to do further research to demonstrate that the average educable mentally retarded adult does more poorly economically and socially than does the nonretarded adult. Nor is there much point in continuing to demonstrate that the typical retarded individual makes a somewhat satisfactory adjustment to adult life and that few mentally retarded are a serious threat to the community. The problems in obtaining equivalent samples of children in regular and special classes and making appropriate comparisons have been discussed extensively. Is there any value, then, in continuing follow-up studies of adults who have been through special programs for the mentally retarded? A study by Dinger (1961) of 100 adults who had been in special classes in one city illustrates that an investigation of postschool adjustment can be carried out to provide suggestions for curriculum revision in a specific community. Thus, among Dinger's findings and recommendations were:

(1) Most current employers of ex-special class students in the city he studied would not hire persons under 18, therefore, schooling for the retarded should continue to that age.

(2) Only low-level reading, writing, and arithmetic skills were required for the great majority of jobs held by his subjects; therefore, the curriculum should not focus on academic learning but on learning specific information and skills relevant to their most likely adult roles as employee, spouse, and parent.

(3) Most of the eligible males had been in the armed forces where they had performed adequately; therefore, the high school training program should help prepare the student for military service.

(4) Most of the interviewed subjects felt that a high school diploma would have aided them in job hunting; therefore, it was suggested that the schools provide a respectable diploma to special class graduates.

While the suggestions may not be agreed upon by other readers or by the administrators in the school system involved, the information collected is directly relevant to decision making regarding curriculum for the mentally retarded and to further follow-up studies evaluating curricular changes.

V. THE TRAINABLE MENTALLY RETARDED

Educational research with trainable mentally retarded children (TMRs) has received very little attention in recent years. The major body of research with this population has been in the area of basic learning. Since these studies have been comprehensively reviewed in the previous volumes of this series, they will not be included in this chapter. The few studies that appear applicable to this section are those which have investigated the effectiveness of special classes for TMR children and those which have evaluated the sheltered workshop performance of TMR adults.

A. School Arrangements for the Trainable Mentally Retarded

The impetus for the remarkable growth of special classes for trainable children in the last decade is largely the result of the influence exerted by the National Association for Retarded Children which was formed in 1949. Public day school services for the TMR increased 260% from 1953 to 1958 (Mackie & Robbins, 1961). Past efforts to evaluate the effectiveness of these classes have geen greatly hindered by the lack of reliable instruments for measuring the small and sometimes subtle improvements which TMR children are likely to make during a given school year (Goldstein, 1956; Hottel, 1958; Johnson & Capobianco, 1957). To overcome this major obstacle, Cain and Levine (1963) developed and standardized a social competency scale (Cain, Levine, & Elzey, 1963) designed to measure the self-help, initiative, social skills, and communication status of TMR children. This instrument was then used to evaluate the performance of TMR children. The Cain-Levine (1963) study compared school children with nonschool children living at home, and compared school and nonschool children living in an institution. Experimental groups were equated with control groups on CA, MA, IQ, and initial social competency scores. None of the Ss had prior school experience. Social competency comparisons among the four groups and parent adaptability comparisons between the community groups were made over a 2-year period. No special curriculum or teaching strategies were developed for the study. The social competency findings were as follows:

(1) Both the school and nonschool groups living at home made significant gains in social competency; however, there were no significant differences between the two groups.

(2) Both the school and nonschool institutionalized groups substantially *decreased* in social competency (relative to the standardization sample) with no significant differences between the groups.

(3) The school *and* nonschool community groups made significantly greater social competency gains than *either* the school or nonschool institutionalized groups.

The lack of significant differences in the social competency gains between community children attending or not attending special classes for the trainable substantiates the results obtained by Hottel (1958) in a similar controlled experiment. Since Cain and Levine did not compare the gains of high and low IQ children, it is not possible to substantiate or refute Hottel's finding that special class attendance was significantly more beneficial than nonattendance for TMR children with IQs of 40 or above.

To some extent, the institutional results are even more disturbing than the community results. While community living increases social competency skills, institutional living impairs the development of these skills. Since the need for a social development program is so much greater in an institutional setting, it is apparent that more effective special educational practices than those presently used in institutions will have to be developed.

To further investigate the finding that TMR children attending special classes performed no better than similar children not attending classes, Cain and Levine developed an observation schedule for obtaining data on the curriculum content and instructional procedures used in the special classes. It was found that "Approximately 44% of the community classroom time was categorized as instructional and 56% was categorized noninstructional. Of the instructional time, approximately 25% was considered to be instructional-social competence, half of which was judged 'low adequacy' and half judged 'high adequacy.' Seventy-five percent of the instructional time was categorized as instructional-general. Of the total institutional classroom time, 35% was categorized as instructional and 65% as noninstructional. Of the instructional time, approximately 25% was categorized instructional-social competence, all of which was judged as 'low adequacy'" (Cain & Levine, 1963, p. 45).

On the basis of the above findings, it is reasonable to conclude that two of the major reasons why special education programs for the TMR have not been shown to facilitate social competency are inadequacy of curriculum content and poor teaching. The need for drastic improvements in the training of teachers of the trainable appears to be the most important implication of these findings.

It is often argued that although special classes for the TMR may not directly benefit the children, they may indirectly benefit the parents. Because of parent contacts with professional personnel in the school system Cain and Levine predicted that the parents of children who attended special classes would increase in adaptability. No significant differences in adaptability between parents of children attending and not attending special classes were found. The investigators suggest that these negative findings "...may be due to the lack of parent-teacher contacts as well as the inadequacy of those contacts when they occurred" (Cain & Levine, 1963, p. 50).

It must, therefore, be concluded that special classes for the trainable as presently constituted cannot be defended on the basis of benefit to the parents.

B. Postschool Arrangements for the Trainable Mentally Retarded

In his excellent review of research on sheltered workshops for the trainable mentally retarded, Huddle (1967a) pointed out that the sheltered workshop is not the appropriate postschool program for all trainable retarded individuals, that other organized community activity programs should be developed for those who cannot meet the objectives of the sheltered workshop. Huddle emphasized that the objective of the sheltered workshop is at least partial economic self-sufficiency. He reported evidence suggesting that: (a) "trainable subjects can satisfactorily perform some kinds of regular industrial tasks and meet industrial standards" (p. 66); (b) certain grouping methods and monetary incentives improve work performance and only minimal supervision seems required; and (c) "training procedures may be standardized which would be applicable to a broad range of trainable subjects" (p. 68). As an illustration of this last point, Huddle cited his own research (Huddle, 1967b) in which "a structured training procedure . . . achieved the goal of enabling almost all of the subjects (mean $IQ = 42$), in groups of 12 to 15 each, to successfully complete a 17-sequence, five component task at the end of one 45-minute training period" (Huddle, 1967a, p.68). These subjects ranged in IQ from 29 to 58.

Huddle added a final comment regarding schooling. "The school curriculum for trainable individuals should probably be revised so that the trainable individual who truly belongs in a sheltered workshop program may be identified sooner (in relation to his vocational prognosis) and be introduced to a presheltered workshop program sooner" (Huddle, 1967a, pp. 68 and 69).

VI. CURRENT RESEARCH TRENDS AND FUTURE RESEARCH POSSIBILITIES

Though the body of educational research in mental retardation is expanding rapidly, there is a tendency for research to follow the existing pattern of investigations rather than to break new ground. Most studies fall into one of the following categories: (a) correlating intelligence measures with indices of academic achievement, (b) comparing constituted groups of educable (or trainable) retarded children with groups of normal children of equal CA or MA on measures of achievement and adjustment, (c) comparing EMR children in special classes with EMR children in regular classes (and institutional groups) on achievement and adjustment, and (d) comparing EMR special class groups exposed to different teaching methods. This seems, at first, to exhaust the research possibilities. Some alternative educational research approaches are discussed here.

A. The Educational Career of Typical Educable Mentally Retarded Children

In the same way that we may examine a sequence of employment experiences as the occupational career of an individual, we may also note the sequence of experiences of any child in school. The reason for such an analysis is that most theoretical, empirical, and experimental studies in education are cross sectional or at best studies of behavior at two points in time or over a 1-year period. They do not trace the history of the child in the school setting. Certain possible career patterns are clear even in the absence of systematic data collection:

(1) A child has not done well in school and also scored in the retarded range on a group intelligence test during the school years. However, he has done sufficiently well so that he has not been referred for any special services, he has been promoted with his peers, and stays on in school until his peers also drop out. His career differs from that of his more intelligent peers only in his having greater difficulty doing school work and his obtaining poorer grades on examinations and on report cards.

(2) A child is unable to master first-grade reading, writing, and numerical skills, repeats first grade once; repeats second grade once; he is referred for possible placement in special classes, "flunks" the IQ test, is placed in special class at 10 years of age, remains in special classes until age 16 when he leaves school because of an absence of further special class provisions.

(3) A child in a large urban school does poorly in the first two grades and is placed in the lowest stream where he continues through eighth grade always falling toward the bottom of the class in grades but never different enough to require special services. He is then placed in a high school work study program which prepares him for employment and actually places him on a full time job during the last year in school. His employer is quite satisfied with his work.

(4) A child is in an experimental school with an "ungraded" program, having primary (grades 1−3), intermediate (4−6), and junior high divisions (7−9). He remains in the lowest primary reading group for 2 years, the middle group for 2 years, and the upper group for 1 year. At age 11 he enters the intermediate division where he remains until age 15 when he is moved to a special high school work study program.

It would be valuable to have a good description of the variety of patterns which occur and their relative frequency in different states and communities. But, more important, it seems necessary to examine the consequences of different patterns. Studies have compared special classes and regular class placement and some have examined the correlates of length of stay in special class (e.g., Mayer, 1966; Milazzo, 1963). These hardly account for the many variations possible. It would seem valuable to determine the average academic skill and vocational success found with each of the educational careers described. Another approach would be to examine the "moral career" (Goffman, 1961) paralleling the academic career, i.e., to examine the changes in self-esteem or self-evaluation which occur during each of these stages in the educational career. One could focus on the changes which follow upon receiving poor grades, being "left back," being placed in a special class, remaining in special classes, flunking out of school, etc. The study by Towne *et al.* (1967) discussed earlier, which examines the changes in a child's self-concept of his ability when he enters a special class, is a move in this direction.

This type of study is ecological in that it examines the frequency and sequence of events in the natural setting. It is longitudinal in that the same subjects are followed and measured over an extended period of time. It examines the patterns of individual data rather than grouping data first and then looking for patterns. Each of these characteristics is rare by itself in the literature. Taken together, the method has not been reported at all.

B. The Effect of the Presence of a Retarded Child on the Teaching, Achievement, and Adjustment of Nonretarded Children

Although the official rationale for special classes emphasizes the gains in adjustment and functional learning for the retarded child, it is well known that referral of a child to special classes serves to reduce the tension for the regular class teacher caused by having to cope with difficult learning and management problems. Occasionally, a public rationale justifying this procedure implies that teacher and student morale and performance is improved by the removal of the retarded child since it reduces the heterogeneity of the class. Yet there seem to be no studies of the impact on the normal class members of the presence, removal, or absence of a retarded child. The design of this kind of study is parallel to that of an efficacy study, comparing regular classes in which the retarded child is present with classes in which the child has been removed. To avoid most of the sampling problems of efficacy studies, a longitudinal design would be desirable observing changes in the same regular class before and after placement of the retarded child.

C. Conclusion

There are undoubtedly many more promising approaches to educational research in mental retardation. It is to be hoped that a review of this field in 1980 would find many investigations which go far beyond the current style of research, which, as yet, has contributed pitifully little that is of value for the educational practitioner.

ACKNOWLEDGMENT

We are grateful to Nettie Rose Bartel, our graduate assistant, both for her excellent bibliographic work and her critical reading of our manuscript.

REFERENCES

Ainsworth, S. H. An exploratory study of educational, social and emotional factors in the education of mentally retarded children in Georgia public schools. Cooperative Research Project No. 171, 1959, U. S. Office of Education, Washington, D.C.

Atkinson, G. The sociogram as an instrument in social studies teaching and evaluation. *Elementary School Journal*, 1949, **50**, 74-85.

Baller, W. R. A study of the present social status of a group of adults who, when they were in elementary schools, were classified as mentally deficient. *Genetic Psychology Monographs*, 1936, **18**, 165-244.

Baller, W. R., Charles, O. C., & Miller, E. L. Mid-life attainment of the mentally retarded: A longitudinal study. University of Nebraska, 1966.

Bauer, E. E. Suggested curriculum for educable mentally retarded children. Unpublished paper, Indiana University, 1967.

Beez, W. V. Influence of biased psychological reports on teacher behavior and pupil performance. Unpublished doctoral dissertation, Indiana University, 1968.

Bereiter, C., & Engelmann, S. *Teaching disadvantaged children in the preschool.* Englewood Cliffs, N. J.: Prentice-Hall, 1966.

Bergan, J. R., & Smith, J. O. Effects of socio-economic status and sex on prospective teachers' judgments. *Mental Retardation*, 1966, **4**, 13-15.

Blackman, L. S., & Heintz, P. The mentally retarded. *Review of Educational Research*, 1966, **36**, 5-36.

Blatt, B. The physical, personality, and academic status of children who are mentally retarded attending special classes as compared with children who are mentally retarded attending regular classes. *American Journal of Mental Deficiency*, 1958, **62**, 810-818.

Blatt, B., & Garfunkel, F. Educating intelligence: Determinants of school behavior of disadvantaged children. *Exceptional Children*, 1967, **33**, 601-608.

Blessing, K. R. An investigation of a psycholinguistic deficit in educable mentally retarded children: Detection, remediation, and related variables. Unpublished doctoral dissertation, University of Wisconsin, 1964.

Blessing, K. R. Class size and teacher aides as factors in the achievement of the educable mentally retarded. Proposal for research and/or related activities submitted to the U. S. Commissioner of Education for support through authorization of the Bureau of Research, 1966.

Cain, L. F., & Levine, S. Effects of community and institutional school programs on trainable mentally retarded children. *CEC Research Monograph*, 1963, Series B, No. B-1.

Cain, L. F., Levine, S., & Elzey, F. F. *Manual for the Cain-Levine social competency scale.* Palo Alto, Calif.: Consulting Psychologists Press, 1963.

Cassidy, V. M., & Stanton, J. E. An investigation of factors involved in the educational placement of mentally retarded children: A study of differences between children in special and regular classes in Ohio. Cooperative Research Project No. 043, 1959, Ohio State University, Columbus, Ohio.

Chaires, M. C. Improving the social acceptance of educable mentally retarded pupils in special classes. Unpublished doctoral dissertation, Indiana University, 1966.

Charney, L. The trainable mentally retarded. In S. A. Kirk & B. B. Weiner (Eds.), *Behavioral research on exceptional children.* Washington, D.C.: Council for Exceptional Children, NEA, 1963, Pp. 90-114.

Cruickshank, W. M., Bentzen, F. A., Ratzeburg, F. E., and Tannahauser, M. T. *A teaching method for brain-injured hyperactive children.* Syracuse, N.Y.: Syracuse University Press, 1961.

Dentler, R. A., & Mackler, B. Ability and sociometric status among normal and retarded children: A review of the literature. *Psychological Bulletin,* 1962, **59,** 273-283.

Deutsch, M. Annual Report, 1965, Institute for Developmental Studies, New York Medical College, New York.

Dexter, L. A. *The tyranny of schooling.* New York: Basic Books, 1964.

Dinger, J. Post school adjustment of former educable retarded pupils. *Exceptional Children,* 1961, **27,** 353-360.

Dunn, L. M. Educable mentally retarded children. In L. M. Dunn (Ed.), *Exceptional children in the schools.* New York: Holt, 1963. Pp. 53-127.

Dunn, L. M., & Capobianco, R. J. Mental retardation. *Review of Educational Research,* 1959, **29,** 451-470.

Dunn, L. M., & Mueller, M. W. The effectiveness of the Peabody Language Development Kits and the initial teaching alphabet with disadvantaged children in the primary grades: After one year. Institute on Mental Retardation and Intellectual Development (IMRID) Science Monograph, 1966, No. 2, George Peabody College for Teachers, Nashville, Tennessee.

Ellenbogen, M. L. A comparative study of some aspects of academic and social adjustment of two groups of mentally retarded children in special classes and in regular grades. Unpublished doctoral dissertation, Northwestern University, 1957.

Finley, C. J. Arithmetic achievement in mentally retarded children: The effects of presenting the problem in different contexts. *American Journal of Mental Deficiency,* 1962, **67,** 281-286.

Flanders, N. A. *Interaction analysis in the classroom: A manual for observers.* Ann Arbor, Mich.: School of Education, University of Michigan, 1960.

Fouracre, M., Connor, F. P., & Goldberg, I. The effects of a preschool program upon young educable mentally retarded children. Cooperative Research Project No. 167, 1962, U. S. Office of Education, Washington, D.C.

Francis, R. J., & Rarick, G. L. Motor characteristics of the mentally retarded. *American Journal of Mental Deficiency,* 1959, **63,** 292-311.

Frey, R. M. Reading behavior of public school brain injured and non-brain injured children of average and retarded mental development. Unpublished doctoral dissertation, University of Illinois, 1961.

Gallagher, J. J. Productive thinking in gifted children. Cooperative Research Project No. 965, 1965, Institute for Research on Exceptional Children, University of Illinois, Urbana, Illinois.

Gardner, W. I. Social and emotional adjustment of mildly retarded children and adolescents: Critical review. *Exceptional Children,* 1966, **33,** 97-105.

Getzels, J. W., & Jackson, P. W. *Creativity and intelligence.* New York: Wiley, 1962.

Goffman, E. *Asylums: Essays on the social situation of mental patients and other inmates.* Garden City, N. Y.: Anchor Books, Doubleday & Co., 1961.

Goldstein, H. Study projects for trainable mentally handicapped children. Report No. 2, 1956, Superintendent of Public Instruction, State of Illinois, Springfield, Illinois.

Goldstein, H. A demonstration-research project in curriculum and methods of instruction for elementary level mentally retarded children. Demonstration application abstract, FOE D-016, 1963, Yeshiva University, New York.

Goldstein, H. Social and occupational adjustment. In H. A. Stevens & R. Heber (Eds.), *Mental retardation: A review of research.* Chicago: University of Chicago Press, 1964, Pp. 214-258.

Goldstein, H., Moss, J. W., & Jordan, L. J. The efficacy of special class training on the development of mentally retarded children. Cooperative Research Project No. 619, 1965, U. S. Office of Education, Washington, D.C.

Goldstein, H., & Seigle, D. The Illinois plan for special education of exceptional children: A curriculum guide for teachers of the educable mentally handicapped. Circular Series B-3, No. 12, 1958, Office of the Superintendent of Public Instruction, Interstate Printers & Publishers, Danville, Illinois.

Gray, S. W., & Klaus, R. A. An experimental preschool program for culturally deprived children. *Child Development,* 1965, **36**, 887-898.

Greene, F. M. Programmed instruction techniques for the mentally retarded. In N. R. Ellis (Ed.), *International review of research in mental retardation,* Vol. 2, New York: Academic Press, 1966. Pp. 209-239.

Gronlund, N. E. *Sociometry in the classroom.* New York: Harper, 1959.

Guilford, J. P. A system of psychomotor abilities. *American Journal of Psychology* 1958, **71**, 146-147.

Guilford, J. P. Three faces of intellect. *American Psychologist,* 1959, **14**, 469-479.

Heber, R. F. The educable mentally retarded. In S. A. Kirk & B. B. Weiner (Eds.), *Behavioral research on exceptional children.* Washington, D.C.: Council for Exceptional Children, NEA, 1963. Pp. 54-89.

Hirsch, E. An analysis of the teacher-pupil interaction in special classes for the mentally retarded. Research proposal submitted to U. S. Commissioner of Education, Yeshiva University, New York, 1966.

Hottel, J. V. *An evaluation of Tennessee's day class program for severely mentally retarded children.* Nashville: George Peabody College for Teachers, 1958.

Huddle, D. D. Sheltered workshops for the trainable mentally retarded: Research implications. *Education and Training of the Mentally Retarded,* 1967, **2**, 65-69. (a)

Huddle, D. D. Work performance of trainable adults as influenced by competition, cooperation, and monetary reward. *American Journal of Mental Deficiency,* 1967, **72**, 198-211. (b)

Inskeep, A. D. *Teaching dull and retarded children.* New York: Macmillan, 1926.

Johnson, G. O. A comparative study of the personal and social adjustment of mentally handicapped children placed in special classes with mentally handicapped children who remain in regular classes. Syracuse University, Syracuse, New York, 1961.

Johnson, G. O., & Capobianco, R. J. Research project on severely retarded children. New York State Interdepartmental Health Resources Board, Albany, New York, 1957.

Jones, R. L. Research on the special education teacher and special education teaching. *Exceptional Children,* 1966, **33**, 251-257.

Keislar, E., & Stern, C. *Improving language performance of young children from low-income homes.* Los Angeles: University of California, 1966. (Mimeographed)

Kirk, S. A. *Early education of the mentally retarded.* Urbana, Ill.: University of Illinois Press, 1958.

Kirk, S. A. Research in education. In H. A. Stevens & R. Heber (Eds.), *Mental retardation: A review of research.* Chicago: University of Chicago Press, 1964, Pp. 57-99.

Lillie, D. L. The effects of motor development lessons on the motor proficiency of preschool culturally deprived children. Unpublished doctoral dissertation, Indiana University, 1966.

Lillie, D. L. The development of motor proficiency of educable mentally retarded children. *Education and Training of the Mentally Retarded,* 1967, **2**, 29-32.

Lynch, W. W. Instructional objectives and the mentally retarded child. *Bulletin of the School of Education, Indiana University,* 1967, **43**, No. 2.

Mackie, R. P., & Robbins, P. P. Exceptional children and youth: A chart book of special education enrollments in public day schools of the United States. U. S. Office of Education, Bulletin, OE-35019, 1961, Gov. Printing Office, Washington, D.C.

Malpass, L. F. Motor proficiency in institutionalized and non-institutionalized retarded children and normal children. *American Journal of Mental Deficiency,* 1960, **64**, 1012-1015.

Mayer, C. L. The relationship of early special class placement and the self-concepts of mentally handicapped children. *Exceptional Children,* 1966, **33**, 77-81.

McCandless, B. R. Relation of environmental factors to intellectual functioning. In H. A. Stevens & R. Heber (Eds.), *Mental retardation: A review of research.* Chicago: University of Chicago Press, 1964, Pp. 175-213.

McCarthy, J. J., & Scheerenberger, R. C. A decade of research on the education of the mentally retarded. *Mental Retardation Abstracts,* 1966, **3**, 481-501.

McLelland, F. M., & Ratliff, J. A. The use of sociometry as an aid in promoting social adjustment in a ninth grade homeroom. *Sociometry,* 1941, **10**, 147-153.

McNemar, Q. A critical examination of the University of Iowa studies of environmental influences upon the I.Q. *Psychological Bulletin,* 1940, **37**, 63-92.

Meyerowitz, J. H. Self derogations in young retardates and special class placement. *Child Development,* 1962, **33**, 443-451.

Meyerowitz, J. H. The neighborhood sociometric. Appendix F of Goldstein, H., Moss, J. W., and Jordan, L. J. The efficacy of special class training on the development of mentally retarded children. Cooperative Research Project No. 619, 1965, University of Illinois, Urbana, Illinois.

Meyerowitz, J. H. Self-derogation and special classes. Unpublished manuscript, 1966, Department of Psychiatry, Baylor University College of Medicine, Houston, Texas.

Meyerowitz, J. H. Parental awareness of retardation. *American Journal of Mental Deficiency,*

Meyerowitz, J. H., & Farber, B. Family background of educable mentally retarded children. In B. Farber (Ed.), *Kinship and family organization.* New York: Wiley, 1966. Pp. 388-398.

Milazzo, T. C. School progress of educable mental retardates as a function of age at special class placement. Unpublished doctoral dissertation, George Peabody College, Nashville, Tennessee, 1963.

Moore, O. K. Orthographic symbols and the preschool child—a new approach. *Proceedings of the Third Minnesota Conference on Gifted Children.* Minneapolis: University of Minnesota Press, 1963.

Mueller, M. W., & Smith, J. O. The stability of language age modifications. *American Journal of Mental Deficiency,* 1964, **63**, 537-539.

Mullen, F. A., & Itkin, W. Achievement and adjustment of educable mentally handicapped children. Cooperative Research Project SAE 6529, 1961, Board of Education, City of Chicago, Chicago, Illinois.

Peck, J. R., & Stephens, W. B. Success of young adult male retardates. Cooperative Research Project No. 1533, 1964, University of Texas, Austin, Texas.

Quay, L. C. Academic skills. In N. R. Ellis (Ed.), *Handbook of mental deficiency.* New York: McGraw-Hill, 1963, Pp. 664-690.

Reynolds, M., & Stunkard, C. A comparative study of day class versus institutionalized educable retardates. Cooperative Research Project No. 192, 1960, University of Minnesota, Minneapolis, Minnesota.

Robinson, H. B., & Robinson, N. M. *The mentally retarded child: A psychological approach.* New York: McGraw-Hill, 1965.

Rosenthal, R. *Experimenter effects in behavioral research.* New York: Appleton, 1967.

Rosenthal, R., & Jacobson, L. Teachers' expectancies: Determinants of pupils' IQ gains. *Psychological Reports,* 1966, **19**, 115-118.

Rouse, S. T. Effects of a training program on the productive thinking of educable mental retardates. *American Journal of Mental Deficiency,* 1965, **69**, 666-673.

Sarason, S. B., & Gladwin, T. Psychological and cultural problems in mental subnormality: A review of research. *Genetic Psychology Monographs,* 1958, **57**, 1-284.

Semmel, M. I., Herzog, B., & Jorgenson, F. A pilot study of the verbal interaction of regular elementary classes and special classes for the educable mentally retarded. In H. L. Lane (Ed.), *Studies in language and language behavior.* Vol. I. Ann Arbor, Mich.: Center for Research on Language and Language Behavior, 1965.

Skeels, H. M., Updegraff, R., Wellman, B. L., & Williams, H. M. A study of environmental stimulation, an orphanage preschool project. *University of Iowa Studies of Child Welfare,* 1938, **15**, 129-145.

Sloan, W. Motor proficiency and intelligence. *American Journal of Mental Deficiency,* 1951, **55**, 394-406.

Sloan, W. The Lincoln-Oseretsky motor development scale. *Genetic Psychology Monographs,* 1955, **51**, 183-252.

Smith, J. O. Effects of a group language development program upon the psycholinguistic abilities of educable mental retardates. *Peabody College Special Education Monograph Series,* 1962, No. 1.

Smith, R. M. Creative thinking abilities of educable mentally handicapped children in the regular grades. *American Journal of Mental Deficiency,* 1967, **71**, 571-575.

Spencer, D. U. Individualized first grade reading versus a basal reader program in rural communities. *The Reading Teacher,* 1966, **19**, 595-600.

Spicker, H. H., Hodges, W. L., & McCandless, B. R. A diagnostically based curriculum for psycho-socially deprived preschool mentally retarded children. *Exceptional Children,* 1966, **33**, 215-220.

Stanton, J. E., & Cassidy, V. M. An additional phase of an investigation of factors involved in the educational placement of mentally retarded children: A study of differences between children in residential school classes and special and regular classes in Ohio. Columbus, Ohio, 1961.

Stearns, K. E. Experimental group language development for psychosocially deprived preschool children. Unpublished doctoral dissertation, Indiana University, 1966.

Strauss, A. A., and Lehtinen, L. E. *Psychopathology and education of the brain-injured child.* New York: Grune & Stratton, 1947.

Thurstone, T. G. An evaluation of educating mentally handicapped children in special classes and in regular grades. Cooperative Research Project No. 168, 1959, University of North Carolina, Chapel Hill, North Carolina.

Tisdall, W. J. Productive thinking in retarded children. *Exceptional Children,* 1962, **29**, 36-41.

Torrance, E. P. *Guiding creative talent.* Englewood Cliffs, N.J.: Prentice-Hall, 1962.

Towne, R. C., Joiner, L. M. & Schurr, T. The effects of special classes on the self-concepts of academic ability of the educable mentally retarded: A time series experiment. Paper read at the 45th Annual Council for Exceptional Children Convention, St. Louis, 1967.

Wallach, M. A., & Kogan, N. *Modes of thinking in young children.* New York: Holt, 1965.

Warner, W. L., Meeker, M., & Eells, K. *Social class in America.* Chicago: Science Research Associates, Inc., 1949.

Weikart, D. P. Preliminary results from a longitudinal study of disadvantaged preschool children. Paper read at the 45th Annual Council for Exceptional Children Convention, St. Louis, 1967. (a)

Weikart, D. P. *Preschool intervention: A preliminary report of the Perry Preschool Project.* Ann Arbor, Mich.: Campus Publishers, 1967. (b)

Weikart, D. P. Preschool programs: Preliminary findings. *Journal of Special Education,* 1967, **1**, 163-181. (c)

Weikart, D. P., Kamii, C. K., & Radin, N. L. Perry Preschool Project Progress Report, 1964, Ypsilanti Public Schools, Ypsilanti, Michigan. (Mimeographed)

Willey, N. A study of social stereotype and mentally retarded children. Unpublished doctoral dissertation, Indiana University, 1966.

Wrightstone, J. W., Forlano, G., Lepkowski, J. R., Sontag, M., & Edelstein, J. D. A comparison of educational outcomes under single-track and two-track plans for educable mentally retarded children. Cooperative Research Project No. 144, 1959, Board of Education, Brooklyn, New York.

Author Index

Numbers in italics refer to the pages on which the complete references are listed.

Subject Index

285